LEGENDS AND LIPSTICK
My Scandalous Stories
of Hollywood's Golden Era

by

NANCY BACON

Edited by

STACI LAYNE WILSON

Published by Excessive Nuance in paperback
ISBN-13: 978-0-9675185-5-8

Also available via Kindle

contents
LEGENDS AND LIPSTICK

- - - - - - - - - - - - - -

beforehand

I have had a fantastic life. I've been lucky. I've been rich. I've lived among the famous. I've known beautiful people and I've been made to feel beautiful through them and by them. I have loved and have been loved, and, to hear my friends tell it, I am still loved.

I know it would be more politically-correct for me to confess and express a lot of guilt about the way I handled my life, but I honestly cannot do that. I take full responsibility for what I did with my life and I do not regret very much of it—not enough to bother with at this late date. I guess the reason I feel this way is because I did all the things I did with pleasure and with the joy of being alive. And at the time I was doing them I never intended to hurt anyone. I'm sure that there is going to be a little fuss over what I have written about some of the people I have known, but everyone can be damn sure that while it was all happening and as long as it lasted, everyone enjoyed!

Inevitably, as the subject of my book became known to friends and relatives, I was asked why I was doing it. And, for the life of me, I can't really say, except that I happen to feel that I have had a pretty unique life. I wanted to put it all down and thereby put it all behind me. (It's called an urge to purge, I believe.) I think writing the book is like closure, to use the gestalt psychologist's term, to one part of this entity known as Nancy Bacon. It has been enlightening, and though I hesitate to use the word therapeutic, it has been that as well.

I learned a lot about that younger Nancy that I was never fully aware of until I sat down and relived her life. She was some dynamite gal, and, quite frankly, I'm glad she did what she did! I know she was all right.

Then, too, I wrote the book because I feel it was a life worth telling about. Not every young girl sees her fantasies become realities—her dreams come true. It happened just the way I wrote it; however, it may be a little fuzzy here and there, among the details, a little difficult to recall that precise moment when the stars burst in my head and I was swimming in the golden cloud of love.

And then, there's the inevitable fall—what goes up, must come down. After you read all about the stunning highs, you'll know the searing lows. When I was thirty-one years old, I was diagnosed with an aggressive form of cancer. I underwent a series of surgeries, which took both my breasts and nearly took my life. I fell into a deep pit of despair that led me directly to the bottom of the bottle. But somehow, I found my way out… I've always been a survivor.

I've been pretty lucky—lucky to have known all the flamboyant, beautiful, rich, and outrageous people with whom I spent my formative years. I have soared on drugs, booze, fright, love, excitement, on the edges of dangerous rides—and unlike so many of them, I am still here. I have done everything I set out to do and much, much more.

If there is any message in all of this, it is simply that I have never soared so high as when I have been in love— cold sober, perfectly straight, and clear of eye. To be in love with life and in love with someone is the ultimate. Someone once asked me, 'Nancy, what was the worst lay you ever had?' 'Terrific,' said I—and I meant it.

I fully believe that life is a very simple matter when you approach it with honesty. All you really need is enough to share, to know the good feeling that comes with giving, to experience all the wondrous gifts of life—that's really *living*!

Nancy Bacon, 2017

Post-Script: Many of the photos herein are being published for the first time, but I can't fit them all... see even more via *Instagram/HollywoodTales*

Also: There's an excerpt from my daughter Staci Layne Wilson's memoir, *So L.A.*, at the end of this book.

initials bb

I was a freckle-faced farm girl, fresh off the bus and wide-eyed with awe at the splendor of the big city: Hollywood.

I was the youngest of nine children, and grew up on a farm in bleak, cold, nowhere Ellensburg, Washington. My earliest memory, I can't even put an age on it, was dreaming of escaping. As soon as I could formulate a clear thought it was to get away, to just run and never look back. I ran away when I was still in a training bra.

I ran out of money in Wickenburg, Arizona, and took a job in Gene's Chili Bowl, slinging hash and chili to truckers, saving every dime until I had enough for bus fare to the City of Angels.

Once I got there, I took a job as an usher in a Glendale movie theater and, just like in the cinema, a suave, elegantly attired gentleman approached me one evening, presented his card and said, 'If you'd ever like to do any modeling or be in the movies, give me a call.' I almost fainted and couldn't find my voice until he was almost out of the door, but then I went rushing after him, yelling, 'I do! I do!' *Goll-ee*, I thought, *imagine that? My dream is coming true just like I knew it would. Hollywood really is a magic place!* I was to be 'discovered' at least a dozen times more during my stint in Tinseltown… But then, I believed everything I heard and trusted everyone I met.

He took me to The Brown Derby for coffee. (The Brown Derby? Omigod! According to the movie magazines I devoured like so many M&M's, every star in Tinseltown went to the Brown Derby.) His name was Jim Byron and he was a personal manager. (Harold Robbins wrote a book loosely based on Jim's life called *The Dream Merchants* about a Hollywood agent who plucked pretty young things from obscurity and turned them into superstars.) The fact that he thought I was pretty enough for this special attention was baffling. All my life, Mom had told me I was ugly, plain, worthless, just another kid taking up space in her already overcrowded life. So, this was a revelation.

Jim told me there was a beauty contest corning up and he wanted to enter me. First prize was a six-month contract with Universal International Studio, home to such stars as Rock Hudson, Doris Day, Sandra Dee, and dozens of huge box-office icons in the fifties.

Much to my amazement, I won! At that time, the French sex kitten, Bridgette Bardot, reigned supreme as the most nubile nymphet ever to grace the silver screen and was known to the world simply as BB. Jim thought America should have its own BB and so he promptly changed my first name to Buni.

The next two months were a whirlwind of photo shoot. I appeared in so many magazines I couldn't count them, but Jim had his eye on the big prize: Playboy. What better place for his little Buni to strut her stuff than the Bunny Hutch itself?

As a warmup, I went to my very first exclusive Beverly Hills pool party with Jim. I was stuck dumb by the opulence, the lush, tropical gardens, the tables laden with exotic dishes, the gorgeous and scantily-clad women, and of course, the open bar where every type of booze imaginable was available. It was surreal.

After a few drinks downed too quickly in the blazing California sun, I was sufficiently relaxed enough to slip out of my clothes and into my bikini and then into the pool. Amid much laughing, groping and horseplay, someone pulled off my top and swung it in the air. I was mortified and quickly covered myself, cringing in the corner of the pool. Without a word, Jim took off his elegant silk shirt, strode down the wide steps of the pool and draped it over my shoulders.

To give you an accurate picture, Jim was tall, aristocratic, his manner and carriage royally intimidating. The waters parted (as it were!) and he led me up the steps to dry land where a waiter immediately wrapped me in the fluffiest towel I'd ever seen. We left the party, as everyone stared in awe.

swept away

Jim introduced me to Bob Darin, an agent of questionable reputation with a small, cluttered office above a shirt shop on Sunset Boulevard. When I arrived the next day, I found a half dozen girls lounging about on sofas and chairs, some touching up their makeup, others reading, others still, napping—but all of them were obviously bored.

Darin appeared and whisked me into his private office and preceded to explain. 'I get jobs for pretty girls,' he said, 'any job, anywhere. The more you work, the more you make. Sometimes the shots calls for semi-nudity, nothin' dirty, mind you, just some bare boobs – and some cheesecake stuff. What do you say, kid? Wanna get yourself in the movin' pitchers? You're a little beauty. I can peddle your ass all over town—figuratively speakin', ya understand.'

I realize now that he had a Brooklyn accent but to my untrained ear he sounded like James Cagney in *White Heat*. I was entranced. He went on to say that everyone was doing pinup shots these days, citing Monroe's infamous nude calendar as an example, and assuring me that producers and directors looked through 'the girlie mags' every month, just in the hopes of discovering another Lana Turner or Susan Hayward.

I bought it, of course, and eagerly signed the contract he shoved across his desk. Within a month, I, too, was languishing outside in the outer office, bored, waiting for a photographer to call and ask for a girl. But Darin kept his word, soon he was 'peddling my ass all over town'—I cut countless ribbons at super market openings, pitched appliances, live, on local TV shows, modeled everything from mascara to mink coats, jumped out of cakes at silver wedding anniversaries and graduation parties, did a thousand 'walk-ons' in a thousand television shows and 'movin' pitchers,' did beach layouts for fan magazines (in those days almost every issue of the very popular fan mags like Silver Screen and Motion Picture ran a series of photos showing starlets cavorting on the beach with the current hunk of the day, such as Troy Donahue, Fabian, Frankie Avalon).

What innocent sounding words those are now—pinup and cheesecake—but in the middle fifties it was scandalous to show a bare breast. Most of the modeling consisted of skimpy outfits, wispy scarfs and lots of innuendo with cleavage down to there but not a nipple in sight. That changed within a year or so, but pubic hair was not shown in Playboy until January 1971 when Liv Lindeland showed hers. (By the way, I never was featured in Playboy, as Jim had hoped—I did make it into a 'college-girls' pictorial in 1960, and was in several fashion ads that appeared in the magazine… the one I did for Van Heusen men's shirts was so sexy it might as well have been a centerfold.)

In the summer of 1955 I was doing a shoot with photographer Harry Maxwell, whom I had worked with a dozen times before. He loved nature and the outdoors and always shot me out in the country somewhere. There was still a lot of country left in those days and we always had plenty of beautiful locations to discover. This day we had gone to Burbank, in the hills surrounding Warner Bros. Studio, and set up our paraphernalia, lights, cameras, costumes, make up, etc. While Harry took light readings, I wandered down along the stream, occasionally wading in the ankle- deep, icy cold little brook, until I came to a small hill overlooking the meadow below.

The Wyatt Earp television series was being shot and the movie company had set up in a clump of trees near the stream. There were several buses, trailers and automobiles parked in the shade of the huge pepper trees and crew members and actors milled about in the sultry heat, wiping their foreheads and downing cans of cold beer or soda.

I saw the star of the series, Hugh O'Brian, saunter across the set and disappear into his trailer dressing room and I caught my breath in awe. He was the very first movie star I'd ever seen up close (close enough to swoon over his rugged good looks and sexy body) and I was a card-carrying fan along with millions of other females of all ages across the country. I wouldn't have dreamed of missing a Tuesday night in front of my television set, watching the dashingly handsome Wyatt Earp mow down a dozen bad guys with his trusty ivory-handled six- shooter while holding a lissome widow in his free arm. His skintight western trousers were always immaculate and they hugged his sexy, well-formed body like a second skin. His dark, curly hair fell just so over his furrowed brow and his smile was slow and crooked. One lazy arch of his eyebrow sent females of all ages into a tizzy of fantasy and I was certainly no exception. I had had a mad schoolgirl crush on Hugh O'Brian ever since his series had debuted a few months before. Now here he was! Not more than fifty feet away from me!

I don't know how I got through the morning, but somehow, I performed to Harry's satisfaction and when we broke for lunch I asked if he'd go with me to watch them shoot. We approached cautiously and asked the director if it would all right to watch for a while and he said, 'Sure, no problem. Just don't move around or talk to anyone.' We watched a scene with a group of outlaws gathered around their camp fire, discussing their next job of robbing the bank or some such thing. I wasn't paying that much attention as I was furtively glancing around to see if I could spot Hugh O'Brian.

At the completion of the scene, everyone started milling about again, setting up for a new shot, moving cameras and cables and checking their scripts. I wandered through the set, frankly thrilled to death to actually be on a real movie location, and several wolf whistles came from the cast and crew, causing me to blush and almost trip over a huge, black cable. I was wearing a short silk shift that stopped at my thighs and was scooped low both in front and back. My hair was almost waist length, dark auburn, tumbling in a mass of wild curls from the wind that swept down through the meadow. I knew I was causing a sensation and I hoped that Hugh was watching. The wind snatched handful of dirt and sent dozens of tiny tornados skittering across the dusty set as I casually meandered toward the trailer I'd see him entering earlier that day.

'Hey, come on in and I'll buy you a drink,' (Psst, little girl, want a chocolate bar?) I heard a voice say just above me and turned to see Wyatt Earp himself smiling down at me from his dressing room window. I hesitated about one second then stepped inside the door that he was holding open for me. 'Help yourself, honey,' he said. 'Beer's in the fridge.' He motioned toward a small refrigerator in the corner and I helped myself, even though I really didn't care that much for beer.

As I stooped over to get a can, I heard Hugh murmur, 'Jesus Christ!' Then his hands were on my hips and he was pulling me down on the sofa with him. He kissed me, all but taking my breath away, and I clung to him, dizzy with surprise and a sudden raging desire. I don't know how he got his trousers unbuttoned so fast, but a moment later I was confronted with what romance novelists call 'his rigid manhood' and before I even had a chance to say, 'How do you do?', I was doing it!

'I'm sorry,' he said, when it was over, but the sexy glint in his gorgeous brown eyes and the amused curl of his lips belied his words. 'Here—drink your beer. Now you *really* look hot.' He laughed and kissed me and I was struck mute on the spot. I couldn't have uttered a word if my life had depended on it. I sat in a state of shock, perched on the edge of the sofa, my hair and clothes in wild disarray, dazed and dazzled. Needless to say, nothing like this had ever happened to me before!

I drank my beer without tasting it, my eyes wide with awe as I gazed into Hugh O'Brian's famous, handsome face as he explained in his sexy, husky voice that he'd just lost his head—and most probably his heart. He'd been on location all week, he said, and he was tired and cranky and horny and when he saw me, in all my nubile sensuality, he simply couldn't help himself. He laughed and tweaked my nose and ran a hand through his crisp black curls, then leaned over and kissed me again, his lips lingering ever so sweetly on mine and I thought I had surely died and gone to heaven.

'Let me make it up to you,' he murmured against my lips. 'How about dinner tonight?'

I nodded mutely and stumbled backwards out of the trailer, my cheeks flaming and my legs so weak I could barely walk. The window above me slid open and Hugh called, 'Hey, beautiful, what's your phone number?' He gave me his cocky, charming grin, adding, 'And your name?'

Too stupid to be offended (and also thrilled beyond words), I told him and ran like hell to Harry's car.

When Hugh called that evening, I had been ready and waiting for an hour, dressed in my very first strapless gown ever. It was black satin and hugged every curve from bodice to knees—in fact, I could hardly move without wiggling my derriere like Marilyn Monroe, but to my young eyes I looked gorgeous! My shoes were also black satin with stiletto heels and toes as pointed and sharp-looking as a dagger. I couldn't wait to sweep into some Beverly Hills eatery on the arm of Hugh O'Brian and knock everybody dead.

But when Hugh casually suggested that I drive over to his place and he'd cook dinner for us, my balloon deflated a bit. It was my first encounter with the typically selfish, egotistical movie star who expected, and got, doorstep delivery. In the fifties, young ladies did not go to a man's house nor did they meet him at a restaurant; they expected their dates to pick them up at their place and present them with a dozen roses, or at least a small mixed bouquet, to show their appreciation for the pleasure of being with you. I was not exactly a virgin angel, but there was still protocol in those days. I hesitated, but I didn't have time to think about it and passion ruled. This was a brand new exciting world to me and I was eager to fit in.

I borrowed my roommate's car and made it to the intersection of Mulholland Drive and Benedict Canyon in record time. Hugh's sprawling bachelor pad set back at the end of winding private road, bordered in all around by towering trees and thick scrubs and hedges. Before I could open the door, two snarling, huge German Shepherds came charging toward the car, leaping against the door and holding me prisoner inside. I was just ready to honk the horn when I saw the porch light go on and Hugh came walking toward me. He called off the dogs, opened my door and helped me out and directly into his arms. He was so much taller than me, he lifted me right off the ground and his mouth was hot and hard against mine.

'Hi, Beautiful,' he said, holding me at arm's length as his lazy brown gaze traveled the length of my body and back again. 'God, you're a pretty little thing.' He took my hand and pulled me inside, through long sliding glass doors and into the kind of living room I'd only seen in Doris Day movies. The low lighting was Hollywood perfect, the furnishings movie star plush, the curved mahogany bar sophisticated and well stocked. He mixed us a cocktail then plopped down on the sofa, a sun-browned hand trailing teasingly along my bare shoulders.

We talked about his series and my aspirations of becoming an actress and every so often he would excuse himself and saunter sexily into the kitchen to check on dinner—and even this insignificant act set my pulses racing. I was being 'catered to' by a desirable screen star that many thousands of women had wet dreams about nightly, fantasizing, I'm sure, that Hugh would kick down their bedroom doors and carry them off on his studio-rented white steed into some painted sunset, compliments of Warner Bros.

Hugh was an excellent cook and after dinner he gently took my hand, gathered me into his arms, lifting me completely off the floor, and kissed me long and deep. I wondered if I should tell him I was underage but I didn't. It's a good thing he carried me into his bedroom for I'm sure I could not have walked!

He put me down and begin to casually undress as I stared around me in awe. I'd never seen a king-size bed before and his huge expanse of masculine velvet seemed to dominate the entire room. I couldn't speak, but I felt I should object or at least protest weakly, but it all seemed so natural. With Hugh's mouth on mine and his gentle hands stripping me of my clothes, I surrendered completely. The velvet voice of Johnny Mathis carried us to cloud nine.

When we had finally calmed ourselves and lay side by side, our breathing labored and our limbs heavy with satisfaction, he grinned down at me and tousled my hair much like a fond uncle would his favorite niece. His naked body glistened with sweat and his dark hair was damp and curly on his forehead. 'Whew,' he sighed, 'what have I found here? You're dynamite, baby—you should go a long, long way in Hollywood!' I accepted it as a compliment and put it down to beginner's luck.

Hugh and I dated quite a lot after that. He even called for me on occasion, and when we were cornered by a photographer or gossip columnist, he was always accurate in the spelling of my name. In fact, my name appeared in print for the first time linked with Hugh's and when I saw that black, boldfaced type spelling out for the world the fact that Hugh and I had been seen at a famous nightery, I was in second heaven.

What is it about seeing your plain, everyday old name in print? I don't know, but something happens. Especially if you have a need to be known, as most people who emigrate to Hollywood do. I was certainly no exception. I bought several copies of the newspaper and sent them to family and friends. To hear me tell it, you'd think I had Hollywood by the short hairs-and this after only a few dates with a notorious swinger. I had a lot to learn. But I pasted that tiny item in my scrapbook, the first of many to follow. It was true, I used movie stars to get attention, and they used me for my face and body, as well as the wit and intellect I was rapidly acquiring. I figured it balanced out.

Now, decades later, I browse through those old scrapbooks and see my life yellowing on the dog-eared pages and I feel no remorse. Rather, I feel delighted that I have lived so fully and am still alive to appreciate my past. Not only has a lot of water passed under my bridge, but raging floods have threatened my foundation and have chipped off splinters and whole planks of wood here and there. This has not weakened the bridge, however, it has merely given to it a richer patina and a stronger character.

For every prick I ever met, there were ten or twenty truly wonderful human beings who gave me a hell of a lot more than I gave them. In my lifetime, I have had an extraordinary range of experiences of the world; met people who would one day win awards for their genius; saw, first hand, history in the making; cried for and laughed with some pretty important personages.

Glenway Wescott, writing of Somerset Maugham, summed it up rather well. He said, 'Maugham had never gone anywhere or cared to have any new person introduced to him, or pursued a particular acquaintance with anyone, unless he had some idea of a function or utility for his literary art in so doing; some study of the narratable world up to date; or a search for types of humanity, in the way of a painter needing models to pose for him; or a glimpse into strange ways of living; or an experimental discussion of ideas important to him with reference to work coming up.'

I was not thinking of future works when I hobnobbed with the illustrious. However, I was filled with a peculiar hunger that only these chosen souls could satiate. There is just something different about movie stars, kings, writers, presidents, senators, and millionaires that the commoners could not possess at any price. I suppose that is why t. are who they are.

My life is certainly richer for having known them. And sadder as well. They're all gone now.

griff the bear

Thanks to Hugh, I had gotten a couple of bit parts in movies and it had gone straight to my head. I was sure this was it—I would be the next Elizabeth Taylor. My poor little country head had been turned at a 180-degree angle and I thought I was pretty hot stuff. It seemed I could do no wrong. Everyone exclaimed over my looks and assured me that I would become a big, big star. Of course, I believed them. (In retrospect, that's really odd because I never set out to be an actress. I had gone to Hollywood to become an artist and work for Walt Disney Studios!)

I joined an acting class and devoted myself completely to losing my farm girl accent, to learning how to dress and walk and apply makeup. Gossip columnists had linked Hugh and I romantically and our names often appeared in newspapers as having been seen at this or that fabulous party or nightclub—and fan magazines ran stories on us, suggesting that we were secretly married or about to be. I loved it! Something happens to you when you see your name in print, it makes you feel set apart, special, chosen, even. I soon became the 'star' of the agency with photographers clamoring for my services and the other models deferring to me with something akin to awe. They were dazzled by my connection with the Hollywood set and by mere association, some of the glitter had rubbed off on me.

Early in the year of 1956, I was sixteen and living the dream. I was sitting in the outer office of the agency, waiting to get my shooting schedule for the next day. It was cold and rainy and I was anxious to get home to a warm dinner and a hot bath. The door opened and I glanced up idly, smiling when the handsome young man shook himself like a dog after a bath. 'Jesus, it's cold out there,' he said. 'Is there any coffee left?' He went to the table in the corner where the models had set up a coffee urn and helped himself. 'Hi', he said, 'my name's Griff.'

'Buni Bacon,' I said, offering my hand.

'I'll call you Rabbit.'

There were four or five other models in the room and they all knew him. They were rushing forward to hug and kiss him and complain that he hadn't called and where had he been, etcetera. I watched him kiss, hug and pat all the girls, pacifying them with his quick, charming smile and sparkling blue eyes. There was no doubt that he was Irish. His hair was crisp, curly black, hugging his well-shaped head and waving in damp ringlets on his neck. His eyes were pure blue, filled with life, mischief, excitement and could only be described as 'dancing.' He had a terrific body, broad shoulders and narrow hips and a certain magnetism radiated from him that kept all the girls clustered around him. Putting his arms around two of the closest ones, he asked, 'Okay, who's going to take me to dinner?' His eyes met mine above a blonde curly head and he winked, wriggling his eyebrows like Groucho Marx.

'Where's your dice, Griff?' one of the girls said. 'We'll shoot craps for you—like the thieves gambling over Jesus' robe!' *Good God*, I thought, *who the hell this guy?* He was certainly handsome enough to be an actor but I was sure I hadn't seen him in anything; his were the kind of looks you didn't forget.

'Come on, Buni,' the curly blonde, Layne, said to me. 'Get in the game—believe me, he's worth it!' She rolled her eyes in exaggerated bliss and the other girls laughed and nodded in agreement. They called him 'the bear.'

We formed a semi-circle on the floor and rolled the dice against the wall, giggling and getting crazy, and Layne filled me in on Griff. He was indeed a struggling actor, fresh off the bus from Cleveland, Ohio with a head full of dreams and pockets full of lint. Extra and bit parts were few and far between and Griff was broke more often than not. But he was never without charm and soon had set up a 'food route,' 'shower route' and 'telephone route' whereas he would 'visit' a friend on Monday, take a shower, 'visit' another friend on Tuesday for his shower and on through the week, never having worn his welcome out at any of his stops. Later in the day on Monday, he would visit another friend, have a snack and some meaningful conversation then move on to his next stop where he would ask to use the telephone to call his agent and answer a few calls— local, of course, if not, he'd offer to pay for it.

He didn't have a car and could be seen striding briskly up and down Sunset and Hollywood Boulevards any day of the week, his warm, quick smile ready for anyone he met along the way. He was a bit eccentric and definitely marched to the tune of a different drummer, particularly in the staid Eisenhower Era. He was a pioneer teenybopper and the first authentic hippie a decade before Flower Power surfaced in Haight Ashbury.

Born Myron Peter Griffin, of upper class parents, he migrated to Hollywood, burning to set the screen on fire. The star system was still in effect then and it was hard for an unknown to get a contract with one of the major studios, and harder still to get an agent of any consequence, so most discouraged kids wound up calling home (collect) to ask for a bus ticket out of the land of broken dreams. But not Griff. He was ingenious as hell and had a knack for surviving that

I've never seen in anyone else. When he was earning, he lived in decent little bachelor apartments and conducted himself in a normal fashion, but when work was hard to find and his bank account was low, he resorted to the most brilliant means of finding shelter.

When I met him, he was living in the pantry of an old mansion in Laurel Canyon. The house was at least sixty years old with huge rooms and thick, solid walls. An old couple lived there alone, and probably had for the past thirty years, with four long haired cats that looked as aged as their owners. I believe it was the so-called Houdini Mansion (though the magician never actually lived there). Griff had taken shelter from a rain storm there one night, not knowing at the time that the house was occupied. It was one of those torrential downpours that assault Los Angeles every spring and fall and it lasted for a good two weeks, trapping Griff in the pantry of the old house and forcing him to forage for food at night when the couple was asleep. This wasn't difficult as the walls were thick and the rooms large, with their bedroom situated on the other side of the house from the kitchen. So, Griff settled in to wait out the storm and when it was over he decided to stay on awhile, just until spring when movies and television began casting for the fall shows. He liked the accommodations and the rent was certainly fair, his surroundings couldn't have been more pleasant. The walls of the large pantry were lined with shelves filled with canned fruits and vegetables and the odor of cinnamon and cloves filled the room. It was warm and cozy, being right off the kitchen, and well lighted which allowed him to read his acting books, make notes in his journal and nap when he wanted to.

That pantry was only the first of a long line of 'free rentals' that Griff would occupy over the years. The list is too numerous to mention here, but a few of his more bizarre residences deserve attention. He once lived for an entire summer on the old Universal-International Studio lot, on the set of Doris Day movie that was a big hit that year. I was doing a C-movie on the same lot, an Albert Zugsmith film starring Mamie Van Doren and Mickey Rooney, and as I didn't have a car—and Griff did for once—he would drive me to the studio each morning then wander around the vast backlot while I toiled before the cameras. Several movies, as well as several television series, were always in production and the lot was always humming with activity. Sometimes Griff would pick up a couple days' work as an extra and earn a few bucks as well as playing my chauffeur. He knew almost everyone in Hollywood so no matter what set he wandered onto, he'd see a friendly face. When he visited the set, he couldn't wait to pick me up after work and show it to me. It was magnificent, as only a Doris Day set could be. A two-story mansion had been erected with a splendid spiral staircase, a booklined study with a real wood burning fireplace, an elegant living room tastefully furnished with real antiques and authentic pieces of art. Upstairs the lavish bedroom held a king-size bed covered in black satin sheets and a puffy velvet spread. Griff could go no further. He fell wildly in love with that bed, fantasizing aloud how it would feel to sleep a whole night through snuggled between those black satin sheets and velvet comforter, the huge sound stage utterly quiet and peaceful. He talked about it until he had convinced himself he just had to try it. What did he have to lose? If a guard spotted him all he could do was kick him off the lot.

The next night I took Griff's car and drove myself home and he stayed behind , hiding out until the huge, bustling lot finally quieted down for the night and the studio guards had settled into their usual posts, then he sneaked onto the set, made his way upstairs, lit a small, discreet lamp by the bed and slid blissfully between the cool black satin sheet propped up by oversize black satin pillows as he read the current issue of The Hollywood Reporter. Once again, he loved the accommodations, he couldn't argue with the price, so he decided to make it his home for the duration of the film. Besides, it was hot in the city, Hollywood was suffering another heat wave, and it was cool and pleasant in the enormous, dark sound stage. He stayed until the wrap party, even managing to integrate himself into the group of cast and crew, eagerly joining them at the sumptuous buffet table and bar that had been set up. He was as sad to see the movie end as anyone else at the party.

Another time he set up living quarters in the empty space above an elevator. He was riding alone in the car one day and his curious Aquarius mind was racing, as usual, and he glanced up and saw that a small handle was attached to the roof. He had to see where it led so he opened it and discovered a cozy little room, the size of the elevator and easily six feet tall or more. The walls were a pleasant natural wood and there was enough space for a cot, a lamp and possibly a small table. It was located in an office building on the Sunset Strip, close to all his regular hangouts and assorted 'routes', most of his friends lived in West Hollywood—it was the place to live if you wanted to feel like you were in show business; every square foot was filled to over flowing with aspiring actors, writers, singers, comedians—you name it, if it was show biz somebody wanted to be in it!

Griff made the move late one night when the office building was empty and found to his delight that the elevator attic was large enough for all his belongings. He had acquired a goldfish somewhere along the way and he placed it on his orange crate night stand next to his army surplus cot. A battery run lamp completed the picture of domestic bliss and Griff lived there until his wanderlust took him to other places.

In the early sixties, when Jayne Mansfield was the hottest thing going, Griff was working for her as a sort of assistant/gofer, helping her out with her line of bar bells and exercise equipment. Her husband, the former Mr. Universe, Mickey Hargitay, had a daily television show on health and fitness where he demonstrated his and Jayne's new line of gadgets and it was Griff's job to drive Jayne and Mickey wherever they had to go, as well as helping them load and unload the heavy bar bells. At the end of each day, after spending almost ten hours with the most fabulous sex symbol of the decade, dining on catered delicacies and sipping imported wine, cruising around Hollywood in a gleaming pink Cadillac, Griff would turn over the wheel to Mickey and wave them off on Sunset Boulevard in front of Schwab's Drugstore, insisting his apartment was within walking distance.

As soon as the Caddy's taillights had disappeared, he would walk quickly across the street to the lot in front of Pandora's Box nightclub and duck into a side door of the long, narrow tool shed that set beneath a huge neon sign that advertised The Tropicana in Las Vegas. Construction workers stored their tools there but there was still plenty of vacant space left—and Griff had partitioned off at least a third of it, turning one end of the shed into a cozy little nest. He had room for his cot, table and lamp and now he had a radio as well and a new electric lamp. He tampered with the wiring on the neon sign above, somehow feeding it into the shed below so he was able to plug in his lamp and radio. It was a bit disconcerting at first, he admitted, because every time the neon sign blinked off and on, his lamp and radio followed suit! It was a reasonable enough adjustment to make for such a good neighborhood and he figured he could get a night job working as a bouncer for Pandora's Box. He wouldn't be able to get any sleep until the young, rambunctious crowd left anyway.

So he settled in, making excuses every time Jayne dropped him off in front of Schwab's because she always asked where his apartment was; this part of the Strip was all businesses. Also, being the big tease that she was, she often suggested coming in with him for a nightcap. Griff had his hands full of the Blonde Bombshell of the 60's that summer—and so did Mickey! Jayne was completely outrageous and I adored her.

By the time the game was over I was completely fascinated by Griff's outrageous exploits and was delighted that I had won the honor of taking him out to dinner. I wanted to know more about him and he complied, keeping me in stitches all the way to Ben Franks and throughout dinner. By the time we arrived back at my apartment, we both felt as if we'd known one another always. It was the beginning of a friendship that endured decades. (We did try, once, to see if there could be something more—but neither of us could stop laughing!)

lust

As Griff was temporarily between moves, I put him up on my sofa for the next few days and together we made the rounds of the studios, looking for work. Griff heard of a beauty contest and told me I should enter; the first prize was six weeks' work in a feature movie. We went together, Griff for moral support, and I found myself parading around and around in a big circle on the dusty backlot in 115 degree heat while producer Albert Zugsmith sat in a tall director's chair, shaded by a large umbrella, chewing on a disgusting, fat stogie and ogling the girls. The gimmick was that the press would be the judges and decide which girl was the fairest of them all and she would be given the role of Lust, the devil's playmate in Zugsmith's *The Private Lives of Adam And Eve.*

Hollywood columnist James Bacon (no relation, although as we became pals over the years; he used to boast to people that I was his illegitimate daughter) picked me at once and marked his ballot in my favor, and by the time the circle had dwindled down to a precious few, I found myself cast as Lust in the worst bomb I was ever to witness!

Martin Milner and Mamie Van Doren starred as Adam and Eve, frolicking in a papier-mâché Garden of Eden on Universal's sweltering backlot. Mickey Rooney was the Devil, stalking about in red long johns (with an actual drop-seat in the back) and black rubber horns and pitchfork, his galley of slaves made up of a dozen scantily clad starlets. The first time I saw him, I was shocked by his diminutive stature and remember thinking, *Jeez, he's so short he must have stood on a chair to reach puberty!* But he was a real, honest-to-God movie star and I was duly impressed.

The plot of the film was confused and the dialogue was corny, consisting of dirty jokes told in leeringly bad taste. It was also one of the first movie roles for Tuesday Weld and Paul Anka (way before his nose job) although their parts were almost walk-ons; they were involved in a bus accident in the first ten minutes, went into a coma and never made it into Paradise, but surfaced again at the end of the picture mumbling something about having had a nightmare. I think everyone on the picture felt as if the 'd been in the same nightmare by the end of the shooting on that turkey.

Back then, of course, I was floating ten feet off the ground. This was it. My big break. I just knew a talent scout from MGM or Warner Bros. would see me and immediately sign me to a seven-year contract and make me a STAR! I showed up for work every morning at the ungodly hour of four-thirty in the morning to be in makeup (they tried to get in as much early morning shooting as possible before the temperature climbed to 100 degrees or more in the San Fernando Valley).

Adding to the heat was the fact that as Lust I spent all my time in Hell, a semi-circle of papier-mâché cliffs painted red to look like flames, or sometimes in the top of a tree, trying to balance myself on a rather shaky wooden platform while the Devil and I peered down on Adam and Eve in the Garden of Eden. We were supposed to give the illusion of hovering in space, the Devil being magical and all, but it ended up being one of the funniest scenes in the movie. Half the time the audience could see the wooden platform sticking out between the sparse bits of foliage the set decorator had glued on it, or the microphone would dip down too low and be in the shot—it was really hilarious.

Albert Zugsmith, not known for his good taste, was one of those producers who turned out a dozen quickie movies a year, the kind they used to show as the second feature in a drive-in movie. He stocked them with gorgeous, stacked, young girls, dressing them in sexy, scanty attire and parading them through almost every scene for no apparent reason. He always had a stable of beautiful, eager young women, willing to do almost anything to become a star. After my stint as Lust, I became one of Zugsmith's girls with miraculous ease and was cast in the next dozen or so films with such speed my head spun. I shouldn't have been surprised—after all, I had all the requirements—I was beautiful, star-struck and ignorant as a rock.

Being in Zugsmith's movies also meant being at his parties, of which there were plenty. He loved to entertain and had a lovely, palatial mansion high above the valley, huge and sprawling with manicured lawns and fabulous gardens and an enormous pool which he encouraged all the starlets to use... *please*. I almost fainted when I saw Zsa Zsa Gabor and other big stars waiting in line with me as we helped ourselves to Ann Zugsmith's sumptuous buffet and I was positive, now, that this was it. I had arrived. Wasn't I rubbing elbows with this glittering collection of Hollywood jewels? And wasn't I just as glittering in my hot red, skin tight, plunging-necked gown (trying to give Mamie a little competition!) and my spike-heeled, backless shoes? I was definitely the next sex pot of the silver screen. Well, sort of. My next role was in a goofy romp called *Sex Kittens Go To College.*

swashbuckler

I miss the heroes of old, the swashbucklers and gallant young men who overcame every obstacle in their path (and there were always outrageous adversities) to reach an inspired goal. They were filled with valor and always chivalrous to the end, dapper and poised even in a sword duel.

I fell in love with Errol Flynn when I was a mere slip of a girl back home on the farm and sneaking off to the movies whenever I could. I would sit in that darkened theater, gazing up at the screen where Errol Flynn flashed his pearly smile and leaped nimbly twenty feet to the deck of a pirate's ship (or the ballroom of a decaying Southern mansion or the stone stairway of a French palace or the foggy moors of a gloomy castle somewhere in England, it made no difference; I was enthralled). Needless to say, never in those adolescent early fifties did I think I would one day be held passionately by those same arms or kissed by those sexy and mocking lips.

When I was under contract to Universal-International and would occasionally see Errol strolling along one of the wide streets. When we passed one another, he would give me a lingering glance that turned my knees to butter. I discovered he could be found almost nightly at The Garden of Allah (a famous nightclub-hotel) and talked Griff into escorting me there one evening.

We sat at a small table near the glass doors that led outside to the swimming pool, sipping cocktails and watching all the beautiful people. The dance floor was crowded, the atmosphere romantically Polynesian. Griff and I got up to dance and in the dimly lit room I saw Errol Flynn swaying slowly not two feet away. My heart started beating faster and I hissed, 'Griff! It's Errol Flynn! Do something!'

'Like what—trip him?' growled the Bear, glancing idly in Errol's direction.

'I've got to meet him,' I whispered into Griff's ear. 'Think of something.'

'All you have to do,' replied the Bear, barely concealing his boredom, 'is wait until the dance floor is empty, then get up and walk across the room to the john.'

I knew what he meant. I was wearing a new red strapless gown, skintight, that showed off every ample curve. All Errol had to do was get one look and he'd want to be in like Flynn! As if on cue the music ended and everyone went back to their tables. I waited a couple of beats, stood up, wet my lips, smoothed my red gown over my hips and slowly and sexily undulated across the empty dance floor and into the ladies' room.

When I stepped out a few moments later, Errol was leaning casually against the bar, drink in hand, that devilish smile upon his mouth as he watched my entrance. As I came abreast of him he bowed low, presented me with a tall, crimson drink, and murmured, 'Would you care for a Singapore Sling, m'lady?'

It was just like in the movies and I felt like Lady Wellington. However, my ability to speak chose that moment to abandon me and I just stared, blushing furiously. My affliction seemed only to amuse (and enchant) him and he chuckled softly and took my arm, drawing me close. 'Here, little one,' he said. 'Drink this—it'll make you feel better, and it matches your smashing red gown.' He placed the frosty glass in my hand and gently guided it to my mouth. 'Have you ever had a Singapore Sling before?' he inquired politely as I swallowed and tried to shake my head at the same time. I downed half the drink at once and tears sprang to my eyes. 'Not so fast, pretty, not so fast. These things have the kick of a mule.'

'Thanks,' I finally stammered and wiped the tears from my eyes. He leaned in close and gazed down into my face and I felt like I was flying. It felt like invisible arms had lifted me and now held me aloft, somewhere in limbo, enabling me to witness the scene below.

The moon was a perfect globe, as yellow as daffodils, with just the right amount of stars scattered about. The bar was lighted with muted red clusters of grapes, the Polynesian decor so warmly romantic that I imagined myself to be on a Tahiti beach. And there beside me, holding my hand tenderly and smiling down at me as he charmed me with his cultured tones, was Don Juan, Captain Blood, the Earl of Essex, Don Quixote, Sir Walter Raleigh, Robin Hood—all rolled into one. Is it any wonder that I had difficulty breathing?

I forgot completely about Griff, so I was startled when he tapped me on the shoulder and said, 'You seem to be in good hands so I think I'll split.'

'This is my brother, Griff,' I said quickly, not wanting Errol to think I had a date. I saw the amusement in his eyes and felt like a real dummy, but he played along and offered to buy Griff a drink. I was kicking Griff in the shin and prodding him in the back until he got the message and declined. (Some years later Griff and Errol became close friends and Griff nicknamed him 'Doc.')

The rest of that evening has gone down in my memory book as one of the most romantic nights of my life. Errol and I sat at a small, round table, holding hands, gazing into one another's eyes, our knees pressed close together, the passion building like a head of steam in a pressure cooker. The music was soft, painfully lovely, sounding of yearning and desire but with an undercurrent of raw native sexuality. I didn't need any more Singapore Slings to know that I was a goner. He traced a finger across the tops of my breasts (which were heaving above the low-cut gown) and said teasingly, 'You seem to have trouble breathing, princess, shall we get out of this smoky bar and into some fresh air?'

'Yes, it's awfully warm,' I panted, shoving away from the table and taking his hand. He led me outside and we stood looking at the moon for a moment. Then his arms went around me, pulling me so close I gasped and my toes barely touched the sidewalk as he crushed his lips down hard on mine. I thought I would drown before he stopped kissing me and led me to a cottage in the back. He made drinks and we sat on the sofa together. Before I had even tasted my drink his arms went tight around me and he was kissing me again in that breathless way he had. His hands were at the top of my gown and before I knew it, my breasts were in his hands and my dress was crumpled about my waist.

'God, what delightful tits you have,' he murmured and proceeded to bury his face in their softness. I could feel my nipples grow hard and hot from his touch and my face was flaming and my hair grew sticky and damp on my forehead. With one hand, he tore my gown away. I heard the fabric rip but it was a faraway sound and then his naked body was on me and his burned and sang against mine. He whispered the most outrageous things to me as his hands moved urgently across my body, grasping my buttocks and holding me up to meet his swift thrust. I know I cried out, but his mouth soon cut off any more sound except the soft moans that now emitted from my parched throat.

It was over in five minutes, but I felt like I had been glued to him for two days. I lay back against the cushions, eyes closed, too embarrassed to look at him, and he leaned over me and gently kissed my eyelids. 'You are a rare gem, little one,' he whispered. 'A real find...' I felt the couch give with his weight as he got to his feet and I lay there wondering if I should get dressed and sneak out before he got back.

Quite frankly, I was a bit of a novice at this love game and did not know what was expected of me.

'Come to Papa,' Errol said softly and I opened my eyes to see him sitting next to me, a wet washcloth in his hands. He tenderly washed my breasts and belly and thighs complimenting me on each one as he did so. Then he tossed the cloth onto the floor and handed me my drink, settling in close and putting an arm about my shoulders. 'Look at that moon,' he said, taking a drink and then gesturing with his glass. 'Reminds me of the moon in Jamaica.' He laughed softly, huskily. 'But then, I suppose it is the same moon, heh, little one?'

I shook my head 'yes' and took a long pull of my drink. I felt completely dehydrated, drained. He placed a cigarette against my lips and I took a drag, then I sighed and let my head fall against his shoulder. His voice was so wonderful as he spun stories of his flamboyant and often hilarious life. I was completely captivated by his earthy good humor and his lust for living. He had lived it to the hilt, to be sure. Many people thought that Errol had become a tragic figure in his later years, but this was not exactly true. He had merely become tired. He had had all the fun he could stand. He had done everything he had always wanted to do and then some; he had paid his dues, therefore, whatever way he chose to live out his remaining years was his choice alone. I admire him for that. He answered to no one.

He spoke softly and kissed me even softer, his lips barely brushing my skin as he grazed my eyelids, mouth, breasts, thighs. He took my drink from my hand and pressed me back against the cushions, whispering, 'Now that I've had a taste of you I will show you the true joy of lovemaking.' He seemed unhurried, floating, fully enjoying each moan of ecstasy that I emitted. His lips lingered on mine, driving me into a fine fit of insanity until I clung to him and begged him to make love to me.

'Not so fast, little one,' he chuckled. 'Good love takes time." And he held my breasts in his hands, kissing them before he moved down between my thighs. His tongue was magic. I writhed against him, not completely understanding why this new form of sex should feel so damn good. I mean, I had heard all my life that it was 'dirty' and 'perverted' to let someone kiss you there. But Errol made it seem like a special favor.

By the time we finally lay side by side, almost an hour and a half later, my body was soaked with perspiration and I was completely exhausted from the multitude of orgasms. If this was what it was all about then I certainly intended to do a lot more of it! That was the first time in my young life that I knew the difference between making love and just fucking. Errol taught me well about romance, love, atmosphere, the beauty of the act itself. He was a superb master. I, a most willing pupil.

I awoke at dawn with the first hangover I'd ever experienced. I thought I would die. I'd always enjoyed perfect health so this incredible pain was shocking. It felt like someone was pounding me over the head with a sledge hammer and I couldn't stop barfing—even after the last red vestige of Singapore Slings had swirled away down the toilet, I was still racked with dry heaves. I crawled into bed and huddled under the covers, shaking and sweating, ignoring the telephone when it rang and rang. I made a pact with God: *If you let me live, I'll never drink Singapore Slings again.* I should have said booze of any kind but I was young and thought I had the soldier of fortune.

I remember one very funny scene that happened a couple of months after Errol and I met. We were in bed, making love, when suddenly we smelled smoke. Rolling over we discovered that a carelessly discarded cigarette was burning a hole in the pillow. With one leg still wrapped around his waist, keeping him in place, I picked up a glass of champagne and casually poured it over the smoldering pillow. 'Now,' I murmured, 'where were we?'

'By Jove, I think you've got it!' Errol crowed like Professor Higgins in My Fair Lady and laughed out loud. 'That's the perfect attitude, my little beauty, never let anything come before romance. There's so little love in the world we must give what we can...' Then he proceeded to prove his point.

I miss Errol. I miss all the old friends and lovers who taught me so much about life and living. It wasn't all sex with Errol; he was a very wise man in many ways. He had traveled extensively, knew many languages, had had firsthand experiences with the natives of many countries-as well as with the ladies of many countries—and people from all walks of life. It is said of Errol that he was the most-fucked man in the world. Everywhere he went, movie actresses, waitresses, princesses, wealthy widows, teenyboppers, airline stewardesses, wives of powerful men threw themselves at him like bitch cats in heat. They were his for the taking, all of them, and, being the courtly gentleman that he was, he rarely had the bad manners to say, 'No, thank you.'

In his early life, before Hollywood beckoned, he had had numerous experiences abroad; a true soldier of fortune and one of the real expatriates of our time. He was born in Tasmania so he came by it naturally, I suppose. His pals were King Farouk, Prince Ranier, Orson Welles, Rita Hayworth, Ali Khan. He fought in small wars, like New Guinea, and had a bankful of experience to draw upon that would captivate and enthrall any listener.

Being something of a reporter of Americans overseas, he had firsthand information about the expatriates that overflowed the European countries. It wasn't all glamour and taxes that kept many Americans abroad, he told me. There were uglier reasons that our citizens lived overseas. One of them was that exiles liked to kill people. They called themselves mercenaries, or soldiers of fortune, and they lived in Madrid or Brussels, and from there they liked to fly to the wars, usually in Africa, and killed for the joy of it and, of course, the salaries that ran as high as a thousand dollars a month as long as the war lasts.

Errol loved Europe and the islands, Tahiti, Haiti, Jamaica. He once said of Jamaica: 'My dream of happiness: A quiet spot by the Jamaica seashore, looking out at the activity of the ocean, hearing the wind sob with the beauty and the tragedy of everything. Looking out over nine miles of ocean, hearing some happy laughter nearby; sitting under an almond tree, with the leaf spread over me like an umbrella, that is my dream of happiness.

'Unfortunately, an hour later, I might not be happy with that.'

Errol was one of the true livers. He believed in living every pulsating moment to the hilt. That's what life is all about, really, the living of it; I mean, after all, a plane could fall on your head tomorrow and there you'd be with all those unfulfilled dreams—still unfulfilled. I completely agree with Errol and perhaps he was the first man in my life that taught me to live fully and completely. It is my contention that the reward of a life well spent is a death that is easy on your relatives. Errol said, in his biography *My Wicked, Wicked Ways*, 'I love all the simple things of life; breathing, eating, drinking, frolicking, fishing, all the f's. I love fundamental excitement. A baked fruit-bread can be as exciting to me as a visit to see a Rembrandt My favorite occupation: a prolonged bout in the bedroom. The greatest calamity: castration. What would I like to be at seventy? At seventy I confidentially hope I will have had at least eight more wives, have grown a stomach that I can regard with respect, and can still walk upstairs to the bedroom without groaning or aching.'

Unfortunately, my darling Errol did not live to see seventy—or anything close to it. He died, still a young man, still feeling, still living it to the hilt in a big stone house on the north side of Jamaica overlooking the Caribbean.

paging doctor casey

Over the next couple of years, I had dozens of bit parts in as many forgettable movies and television shows and my ardor for fame and fortune had begun to wane a little. I didn't really enjoy acting that much and I thoroughly hated getting up before dawn and making that long drive to the studio in the dark, while sane people were still asleep in their warm beds. However, the pay was good so I continued to take whatever job came my way.

But I didn't want to be just another pretty face. All my life, I'd craved knowledge, hungered for substance. From the time I could put two words together, I'd become a voracious reader, devouring the written word like a vampire at a blood bank. Don't get me wrong; I wanted recognition, but I realized I didn't want to see my face on the silver screen. I wanted to see the words 'Screenplay by Nancy Bacon' or 'Based on the Novel by Nancy Bacon.'

My roommate, Jody Holmes, and I were living in a very nice, new apartment on Franklin Avenue and I had a decent car for once and modeling jobs were more plentiful than ever. I was raking in big bucks when I was suddenly struck with appendicitis and was rushed to a Burbank hospital for an emergency appendectomy. When I came to the next morning, still a little groggy and in a great deal of pain, I glanced across the room and saw the most beautiful woman I'd ever seen in my life.

Even without makeup, Kathy Smith was a naturally exquisite creature with piles of rich chestnut hair tumbling about her sun-kissed, peachy skin and framing her perfect oval face like a painting. She was a model, of course, and told me she'd just signed a three-year contract to be spokeswoman for Vic Tanny's Health Clubs. She was as friendly and kind as she was beautiful, therefore it didn't surprise me in the least that she had a steady stream of good looking men visiting her every day and night.

One of those gorgeous hunks was a big, burly, sultry Italian dude from Brooklyn, New York, Vincent Edward Zoine. He had dropped the 'Zoine' and added an 's' to Edward and went on to become the fabulously successful television doctor, Ben Casey. But the day he walked into my hospital room to visit his friend Kathy, he was just another out of work actor—albeit one with an incredible Adonis physique and melting velvet brown Latin eyes. Even before he became TV's surly surgeon, Vince was already experimenting with the possible cures for mattress fatigue and other common Hollywood ailments. He spent most of his time hanging around Santa Monica Beach, lifting weights, flexing his bulging biceps for the beach cuties and working on keeping his tan permanent while he dreamed of getting a movie contract or getting laid—and in those lean years it was usually the latter.

I was preparing for my first trip to the bathroom since my surgery and I was still awfully shaky and couldn't seem to straighten up all the way. As I was making my way across the room, crablike, suddenly I was scooped up in a pair of strong, hairy

arms and carried into the bathroom and deposited upon the throne.

'Take it easy,' Vince smiled warmly. 'I'll wait outside the door if you need me.'

A moment later I rapped rather weakly upon the door and Vince opened it, flashed me his sexy smile, gathered me up from my undignified seat and carried me gently back to my bed. Kathy introduced us and I learned they were just good friends, with no romantic entanglements to speak of. Vince shook my hand, fixing me with one of those sober, dark-eyed stares that was soon to become his trademark as Dr. Ben Casey and I was hooked.

Kathy left the hospital the next day but Vince kept coming back to see me and when I was released, he drove me home. After that he would drop by the apartment every day to see how I was getting along, often bringing Chinese food or deli sandwiches to keep us busy. He often teased that if I had not just undergone major surgery he would be devouring *me* rather than an egg roll! I learned everything about his background during those long, lazy afternoons when we lolled in front of the television set and talked for hours. He had been a college swimming champion as well as a contender for Mr. Universe and he still worked to keep his large frame in top notch condition. He was sleek and trim as a jungle cat without an extra ounce of fat any place on his body and his face was as perfect as the rest of him.

When my doctor pronounced me completely recovered, Vince took me out to Don the Beachcombers to celebrate and from there to his Hollywood hills bachelor pad. Sunset and Hollywood Boulevards glittered below his window like so many sparkling jewels spread out on a jeweler's black velvet cloth and the sweet, soft summer breeze pushed gently through his drapes. He put on a stack of Ray Charles and Frank Sinatra albums, took me tenderly in his arms and began dancing me slowly around his big, luxurious living room.

I was so young and he was so handsome and the music was so romantic, the night so jewel-like, that I fell in love with a thud that could have been heard all the way to the San Fernando Valley. He kissed me then, taking my breath away, then scooped me up and carried me into his bedroom and lay me carefully upon the silken folds of his mammoth king-size bed where he proceeded to administer postoperative care.

We were both perfect physical specimens in those young years and it seemed only natural that we should get together every so often to admire our beautiful physiques and feel each other's muscles. We had a lot in common. We were both health food nuts and loved to work out at the gym and go for long, brisk walks. When we were together, we'd sweep into a restaurant somewhere, our heads held high, our carriages proud and erect, and every head in the room would swivel to watch us pass. We were like a pair of gorgeous young animals and we gloried in it. never tiring of being stared at—or of staring at ourselves in his full-length mirror.

After we had made love, Vince would leap out of bed, pulling me with him, and we'd pose and preen before the big mirror on his closet door, loving our reflections almost as much as we loved one another. Vince had a surprisingly good voice, a deep, sexy baritone, and he would throw back his head and belt out a verse or two of the currently popular songs. Vince was so joyous in bed that his partner could not help but be infected as well. He would gaze down into my face, his dark eyes shining like brown diamonds, and he would laugh with the sheer pleasure of how good we felt together.

'Open your eyes,' he would demand, 'look at me when I'm loving you.' He would keep his drapes and doors open in his bedroom which afforded us a panorama sweep of the bright city below and he would stare rapturously out across the broad expanse of twinkling lights. 'I feel like we're making love on them,' he would whisper huskily. 'They look close enough to touch.' His hot, smoldering gaze would devour my face. 'If I could, I'd reach out and scoop up a handful and give them to you.' (He once gave me a handful of peanuts, his dark eyes somber and his voice deep with emotion when he said, 'I wish they were diamonds.')

Vince had been dating Joan Collins when I met him but he stopped seeing her when our romance burst into flame. I remember the night he asked me to be 'his girl' and how cute and gentle and shy he was about it. He had come from the school of hard knocks and was leery of most people, suspicious and distrustful of their motives, but I guess he must have trusted me because we were soon inseparable.

It was only after months of dating that I began to notice a serious flaw in my hero. He loved the ponies and couldn't seem to stay away from the track. Of course, his gambling is legendary now, but in those days, it was something of a shock to see someone so hooked on horseracing. During racing season I was often left alone while Vince spent his time at Hollywood Park, Santa Anita or Del Mar. When he won, he was delightful, taking me out to the best restaurant in town and buying me any crazy gift that caught his fancy, but when he lost (which was often) he would sulk in black, surly moods of anguish and then our lovemaking would be violent, deep, dark and frightening. He would demand that I tell him I loved only him and make me promise to never leave him.

And I didn't think I ever would, but when Jim suggested a stint in Las Vegas, dancing in the chorus line at The Sands Hotel, I jumped at the chance. So, it was off to Vegas, like Dorothy skipping down the yellow brick road toward an unknown and slightly frightening Oz. (Gamblers and gangsters and hookers—oh my...)

vegas, baby

Back in the day, The Mob owned most of Sin City and it was rumored that the desert was littered with the bodies of those foolish enough to try and cross the big guys. I settled into a little bungalow just down the Strip a ways from The Sands and put on my dancing shoes: four inch stilettoes. I wasn't eighteen yet but I pasted on a double pair of thick false eyelashes, plastered on another layer of Max Factor Pan-Cake Makeup, shimmied into a G-string the size of dental floss and made my debut. With my wholesome baby-face I didn't look anywhere close to being twenty-one, but little things like birth certificates didn't mean much in Sin City.

The Rat Pack (Frank Sinatra, Dean Martin, Peter Lawford, Joey Bishop, Sammy Davis Jr.) was appearing at the same club nightly and shooting the movie *Ocean's Eleven* during the day. I had had a huge crush on Dean

Martin for as long as I could remember. Those dreamy, melting brown eyes. That soft sensuous mouth. The thick, tousled, black curls. The ultra-cool, laid back persona. Damn! I wanted that man!

Between every show, I raced to the curtained-off area backstage and waited breathlessly for Dean to pass by. He would pause, gaze appreciatively at my pert, heaving bosoms, sigh deeply, and move on past. One night, he stopped, took my hand in his and pressed a dime into my quivering palm, murmuring, 'Call me when you're twenty-one.'

After about a month of constant, adoring surveillance, I was finally invited back into the inner-sanctum where the Rat Pack drank, partied, and made love until dawn. But none of the boys dared lay a glove on me. Word had come down from The Chairman of the Board, Frank Sinatra, that I was underage and could only be ogled from afar. So honed my drinking skills and picked up intel no young lady should ever hear!

My cozy little bungalow was nestled among some trees behind the famous and notorious El Rancho, a hot spot for Mafia, molls and seething vendettas. One night, it was torched and burned to the ground: a clear sign it was time for me to get out of Dodge.

satyr

Jim Henaghan. Just his name brings a smile to my lips and a chill to my heart. He was both brilliant and mad, fair and deceitful, tender and dangerous, and I fell wildly in love with him.

He was a writer by profession and a world traveler by choice, having spent much of him time living abroad and visiting countries almost at random. He was fond of the bottle and would often begin drinking in Paris and wake up with a hangover in Italy or Spain, not remembering how he got there. 'I saw a hell of a lot of great countries that way,' he laughingly told me. He had been a script writer back in the 40s, penning classics for Alan Ladd, Gloria Swanson, Ingrid Bergman, Humphrey Bogart and other stars of their ilk, but when I met him he was working (sort of) for Batjac Productions, John Wayne's movie company.

Jim and Wayne were buddies from way back, with a sort of Butch Cassidy / Sundance Kid type of relationship and I loved being around them when they were reminiscing about some of the pranks they'd pulled. We were having dinner one night at Au Petit Jean's in Beverly Hills, when Jim turned to Duke and asked him, 'When you were Marion Morrison growing up on the farm, did you ever imagine in your wildest dreams that you'd someday be a world-famous movie star?'

To which Duke honestly replied, 'No—I thought I'd be president of the United States.'

Duke was great fun and hanging out with him was like spending time with my father or older brothers. He was so easygoing and natural I often had to remind myself that he was the biggest star in world (at that time), a living legend, bigger than life. But all I saw was a good man, a little wary now and tired, but still willing to embrace new ideas. He was in the process of putting together the epic film, *The Alamo*, which he would co-write, star in and direct—his directorial debut, as a matter of fact, so he was understandably nervous.

A huge and magnificent set had been built in Brackettville, Texas, where the movie was to be shot and Jim had decided that we should fly down and see how his old pal was doing. Laurence Harvey arrived the same day we did for his role in the film. He was in a petulant mood, sulking about the 'bloody Texas dust' and pouting because he couldn't get a decent drink in the local pub. 'These bloody heathens serve nothing but that dreadful bourbon,' he sniffed. 'I'd rather drink gasoline!'

Jim was in one of his mischievous moods and immediately called the nearest big city and had one hundred cases of wine delivered to Larry's dressing room. He instructed the deliverymen to stack the cases in front of the doors, as high as they could reach, until the small trailer was completed obscured by wooden cases of wine, then we hid in the foliage and waited for Larry to return. He came dragging in after the day's shooting, tired and dusty, a frown creasing his forehead—and stopped short, staring up at the mound of wine higher than his head. He threw back his head and exploded with laughter. 'Where the hell are you, Henaghan?' he shouted. for this!' Only my mad Irishman, a living satyr if ever there was one, could be responsible.

The next day Larry was in a charming mood and sat under an umbrella, daintily sipping his wine as he waited for his call. He had a habit of yawning hugely before going into a scene, claiming it relaxed him and cleared his head, but Duke didn't know this. He called for Larry to take his position for the next scene and Larry complied, slowly sauntering onto the set and yawning mightily. Duke jerked off his hat and threw it on the ground, cursing and yelling at Jim, 'Now look what you've done with your damn imported wine—my actor is falling asleep!'

Duke never did know quite what to make of Larry. They got along well enough, but Larry's scandalous antics and candid homosexuality was a bit much for the conservative Duke. Later in the week they had a big scene coming up where Davy Crockett (Wayne) and Jim Bowie (Larry) and the others at the fort realize that they are completely surrounded by hundreds of Mexican soldiers.

It was a very impressive scene which required hundreds of extras and a great deal of time in setting up. The stone walls enclosing Fort Alamo were literally covered with 'soldiers'—ammunition belts strapped across their chests, knives resting on their hips, as they stood or crouched above the small circle of men in the center of the dusty fort, their rifles at the ready. Duke yelled, 'Action!' and Larry came swishing into the fort with an exaggerated sway to his hips, one limp wrist practically flapping in the breeze as he minced toward the rugged group of men dressed in dusty buck- skins and holding rifles. He jutted one slender hip out, placed his hand upon it and lisped sweetly, 'I say my good fellow -- where in bloody hell did all those fucking Mexicans come from?'

Cast and crew alike broke up with laughter and Duke jerked his hat off and threw it to the ground, literally stomping on it with his high-heeled boots. 'Goddamn it, Larry,' he exploded. 'Will you stop kidding around? We've got a movie to make!'

Larry smiled gently, kissed Duke on the ear and murmured, 'But, Duke, dear, I'm not kidding.'

It was great fun being on location with Jim. He was the most brilliant man I'd ever met and I could sit for hours, dutifully curled up at his feet while he regaled me with scandalous stories of his past. He was the definitive raconteur and I never grew tired of listening to him. When we were sitting with Duke and he and Jim got into a drinking story-telling mood, I wouldn't open my mouth all night, I'd just listen and try to imagine the splendor and excitement of it all. I was dying to travel and see the world, to taste and experience everything life had to offer, so just listening to these two world weary men fascinated me no end. Usually they got along really great (they'd been close friends for over twenty years), but sometimes they disagreed and this inevitably led to battle.

One night we were all sitting around in a small bar and grill and Duke and Jim were putting away shots of bourbon hand over fist. There always was a sort of competition between them and Jim would taunt Duke about his intelligence, sneeringly referring to him as 'Movie Star' and saying that it didn't take a brain to be an actor, any dumb animal could be taught to do tricks in front of a camera. Usually their arguments were good natured and they would weave their way back to their bungalows, arm-in-arm, buddies to the end. But this particular night the bantering insults were not funny and before anyone knew what had happened, they both jumped up, knocking over the table, and Jim punched Duke right in the nose. Duke grabbed his nose and bellowed like a wounded bear and made a lunge for Jim.

The fight was on. As everyone knows, Duke was six-foot-four-inches, but Henaghan was a mere five-foot-eight and weighed about one hundred fifty pounds. It was like a pussycat going up against a lion, but Jim hung in there, getting in as many punches as Duke until everyone in the bar threw themselves into the fray. Seven or eight guys threw themselves on top of Henaghan to pull him away from Duke, but not one person tried to stop Duke from maiming Henaghan!

Suddenly Larry Harvey leaped across the room and landed on Duke's back, got him around the neck and tried to pull him off Jim, but it didn't faze him in the least. He reached one huge paw over his shoulder, grabbed Larry by the shirt collar and flung him over his head, sending him crashing through a plate glass window. As Larry flew gracefully through the air toward the window, Duke saw who it was. 'Oh, my God, it's my actor!' he cried, and reached out as if he could pluck him back. Too late. The glass shattered and Larry disappeared from sight.

Everyone rushed outside and there sat Larry in the dusty, narrow street, broken glass in his hair and clothes, unhurt but haughty. He flicked a couple of particles of glass and dirt off his sleeve and said tartly, 'Quite frankly, Mr. Wayne, this is one hell of a bloody way to treat a British subject! '

My life revolved completely around Jim Heneghan by this time. He didn't want me to model anymore, so I quit. Just like that. (My agency was furious!) He said if I wanted to be a writer, I needed to learn my craft from the ground up, so I immediately took a job as editor of Knight magazine, one of the conditions being that they would publish one of my short stories every three months. When Jim saw that I seemed to have a natural flair, he declared that we must leave at once for Europe. 'In order to be a good writer, you have to live life to the fullest, 'he said. 'You must visit exotic places you've only read about in books—see sights even your hungry mind could not imagine—smell, hear, taste.'

'But... can you get away for that long?' I asked.

Jim was married to the famous Broadway superstar/dancer, Gwen Verdon, and they had had a son together, Jim, Jr. who was only a few years older than me. They were husband and wife for all intents and purposes, but lived separate lives.

Jim went straight to the bar and poured himself a full glass of St. James scotch. 'You know she'll never give me a divorce. I thought you understood that.' I nodded my head. 'But, hey, it won't be so bad. We'll just be a younger, more hip version of Tracy and Hepburn.' He was referring to Spencer Tracy and Kathrine Hepburn who had a 30-year love affair without marriage because Mrs. Tracy's Catholic beliefs would not allow for divorce. I poured myself a gin and tonic and snuggled against him. · 'Alright, Spence— here's to living in sin.'

He laughed happily, his good mood restored. 'Here's looking at you, kid!'

'Wrong movie,' I quipped.

We were sitting on our patio, having a nightcap. We'd just come home from a small dinner party given by director Richard Quine and Jim was in mellow mood. He pulled me close and kissed the tip of my nose.

'Come away with me, little Nancy,' he whispered. (He refused to call me by the name Buni. 'Jesus, it sounds like a stripper in an X-rated Disney cartoon!') 'I'll show you all my favorite haunts and watering holes, I'll introduce you to kings and presidents and even movie stars if I have to. Come on,' he urged, 'it'll be a hell of an eighteenth birthday gift!'

'Oh, please, 'I mock-groaned. 'The next thing I know you'll be saying 'we'll always have Paris.'

'We will always have Paris, little Nancy. God, I can't wait to show it to you!'

first, london

One month before my eighteenth birthday (and just after Jim's forty-ninth) he decided he had to move back to Europe, for good. He couldn't take the States for too long of time, he said, he missed the madness that was Europe in those days.

He had always loved travel and had been in Paris in the late 20s when a struggling group of American artists, most of them writers, had tripped abroad individually and eventually wound up together where Gertrude Stein (herself an expatriate) dubbed them 'The Lost Generation.' Among these runaways there were some who were to become giants in international letters, including Ernest Hemingway, F. Scott Fitzgerald, Ezra Pound, T.S. Eliot, John Dos Passos, Archibald MacLeish and many others less well known. The tag 'expatriate' had had a rather unsavory definition until then, but now it became respectable and even envied. Soon other Americans were taking to the ships to make a reputation abroad before trying their craft at home.

Robert Cummings, then a young actor, was having trouble getting good parts in Hollywood, so he went to London and stayed just long enough to rent a theater marquee and put his name up in lights. He took pictures of it, returned to Hollywood with the prints testifying to his stardom abroad and crashed those gilded gates of success with ease.

Orson Welles was another impatient young actor, even younger than Cummings when he hit Hollywood. He worked for a few years but was frustrated by the slow grind of old time Hollywood and, while still in his teens, went to Ireland and served an apprenticeship with the Abbey Players in Dublin. He was 'discovered' and brought back to the states to begin a show business career that can only be called brilliant.

Jim and I arrived in New York in late summer and checked into the Hampshire House, an elegant and exclusive hotel on a tree-shaded block just across the street from Central Park. Everybody, it seemed, walked in New York and Jim ran my legs off showing me the city. We saw *The Miracle Worker* on Broadway with Anne Bancroft and Patty Duke and later met with Anne and her husband, Mel Brooks, for drinks. Jim knew everyone, it seemed, and I met more stars in the week I spent in New York, then I had in all the years I'd been in Hollywood.

Jim dazzled me with fabulous dinners at 21, The Top Hat, Sardi's and other famous eateries, seemingly delighted that he could spoil me rotten. He bought me a complete new wardrobe, my Southern California beach girl look would be unacceptable in Europe, including my first mink stole. (He was to buy me three more minks during our stormy relationship because every time he got really angry at me, he'd destroy my mink!) We went for romantic moonlit rides in a Hansom cab, snuggled together beneath a cozy lap robe, necking like teenagers and taking small nips of brandy from his silver flask. We walked for blocks every day, taking in the sights and smells of that remarkable, fast-paced city as Jim pointed out famous buildings and landmarks.

One day we were strolling along and came upon a construction crew working on a new subway, so we stopped to watch for a minute. Jim was silent for several minutes, watching the men dig, then tapped one of them on the shoulder and asked, 'How long before it's finished?'

'Oh, about three years,' replied the man.

'Hmm,' said Jim, glancing at his watch, 'guess we'd better take a taxi then.' He whistled for a cab and escorted me inside, leaving the astonished workers staring after us.

Jim was so much fun to be with when he was sober, or even just drinking a little bit, but when he was on a binge he behaved like an evil little tyrant. He had wanted to pick up a few extra bucks before heading for Europe by writing some articles for the fan magazines and had sent off a proposal to one of the leading publishers at that time. Unfortunately, the publisher had dealt with Jim before and had vowed never again! No matter that he was a brilliant writer, his alcoholic rages were becoming legendary and many publishers wouldn't deal with him.

We left for London the following day, 'just a pecker length ahead of the law,' Jim laughed as we boarded a Flying Tigers airplane, compliments of Jim's old pal, Bob Prescott, president of the airlines.

There was just the two of us and the crew making the flight to London and it was like a fairy tale for the entire ten hours. It seems incredible now that it took that long to fly from New York to England but it did and I enjoyed every fantastic moment of it. Jim could charm anyone in the world in ten seconds flat if he wanted to—and he turned it on full voltage for the pretty stewardesses (as flight attendants were called then), sending them scurrying here and there for more pillows, a certain brand of scotch, a few sandwiches to tide us over until dinner was served, and they were thrilled to accommodate him. He had that effect on most people. They loved to please him.

We dined on Maine lobster and chilled champagne, compliments of our host, finishing the meal off with flakey Napoleons, hot coffee and warm brandy. Jim put the backs down on six of the seats, making one large bed, then completely covered them with pillows and a blanket. 'Madam,' he grinned, 'your berth awaits.'

We jumped in together, covering ourselves up to our chins and giggling and necking at the same time. The necking won out and somewhere over Shannon, Ireland, I joined The Mile-High Club as we made slow, dreamy love amid the clouds in a star-filled night.

We arrived in London early the next morning and took a taxi to the Savoy Hotel. I was pretty shocked to find that the taxi cabs had no doors at all—the driver careened around corners so fast I was afraid that both Jim and I would wind up on the sidewalk! I was wearing a pantsuit when we entered the lobby of the Savoy and started toward the registration desk, and we found our way blocked by a tall, courtly gentleman in a in- striped suit, sporting a red carnation in his lapel buttonhole.

He whispered something discreetly into Jim's ear and Jim, known far and wide for his impromptu outrages, leaned away and bellowed, 'You've got to be kidding! For eighty bucks a day my dame will wear pants or go stark naked if I tell her to!'

In those days, it was considered unseemly for a woman to wear trousers in the swank and elegant Savoy, but Jim was determined to change that stuffy rule. He demanded to see the manager, whom he had known for years, and when the poor man arrived, looking flustered and anxious when he saw who was causing all the commotion, Jim came right to the point.

'What the fuck is this?' he demanded. 'I've been staying here for years—hell, I've probably sent more business your way than anyone else who stays in this dump!'

The manager tried to quiet him but Jim wasn't buying. 'I want a room—now!' he said. 'And if I don't get it, I'll set up housekeeping right here in the fucking lobby!'

Needless to say, a room was found at once and we were escorted quickly upstairs. I rushed to the window to look down at the Thames River as it rolled silently between the trees that edged it. It was smooth and dark, its black waters looking cold and uninviting, but to me it was fascinating. I'd read so much about the famed Thames River and I had to admit it didn't look like any other river I'd ever seen.

Jim was already working on a bottle of scotch and grumbling about the shabby treatment we'd received upon our arrival. 'Let's blow this joint,' he said, waving an arm about the room.

'Let's leave. It's nothing like it used to be. It's old and shabby and rundown a faded memory. Who needs it?' He called for room service and had breakfast sent up for me (he was drinking his) and after I'd showered and changed my clothes, he informed me were checking out. I couldn't believe it, after all the trouble he'd gone to get the room but I was getting used to Henaghan's wild mood swings. I dutifully packed and followed him outside where he hailed a cab and instructed the driver to take us to The Mayflower Hotel across town.

'This is more like it,' he said as we were shown into a huge, luxurious suite complete with sitting room. He had a magnum of Mumms champagne sent up, along with three tins of caviar and a platter of tiny watercress and tomato sandwiches. We sipped icy champagne, nibbled on caviar, made love, slept a couple of hours, then dressed for our first night on the town.

The streets were shrouded in mist as we stepped outside and began walking toward Siegi's, a small but famous restaurant just behind the Mayflower Hotel. Judy Garland and Sid Luft were there (old friends of Jim's) and we joined them for cocktails while we waited for our table. Judy was there for her appearance at the London Palladium and she invited Jim and I to be her guests on opening night. I was totally in awe of her, hanging on her every word, never dreaming for one second that one day we would be close friends and share many evenings together, discussing men and the meaning of life.

But this night I was just another fan and as Jim and I settled into our seats at the Palladium, I craned my neck to ogle the glittering audience. I was sure they were all earls, dukes and princes and my heartbeat accelerated just being in the same room with them. Judy was late coming on and it was obvious she was nervous. She wore a short, tight black skirt, spike-heeled pumps and a brightly-sequined blazer that seemed aflame beneath the lights. She took her famous stance, legs spread wide apart and solidly braced on the stage, one arm raised, her pelvic and hips jutted arrogantly forward. The audience started applauding and cheering when she hit the first note and did not stop until the song was finished. They loved her and she knew it.

She relaxed as she ran a hand through her short, dark hair and threw a crooked grin to the crowd. Then something seemed to take over. I could actually see it. She stood straighter and her voice was strong and perfect, like a golden bell, her movements were smoother, the earlier jerky, nervousness now gone. She prowled the stage like a panther, growling, purring, seducing the audience into near frenzy and one could actually feel the love flowing thick and swift between her and her fans. It was overwhelming and even a little frightening. She seemed too frail to handle this onslaught of raw emotion that she herself was conjuring up. It was like a mass love affair between all those strangers and the tiny, wren-thin figure on stage.

For the next two hours Judy completely captivated the audience, holding them firmly in her little palm as she belted out hit after hit for their roaring approval. When the curtain came down, she was wringing wet, her hair plastered to her head and her lipstick worn off, but no one cared. Like a tidal wave, the audience heaved to its feet and gave her a five-minute standing ovation. I was no exception. I applauded until my hands hurt.

the lush life

According to Webster's Dictionary, to rove means to wander, to ramble, to roam—in any direction, in any manner, walking, riding, flying, or otherwise. And the definition of a rover is one who rambles about, a wanderer, a fickle or inconstant person, sometimes a freebooter, a pirate, or an adventurer. I find none of these definitions unkind. Rather, I think, the lot fits me loosely, like a borrowed bathrobe, and I accept the total as a sort of minute biography of myself.

I was pleased to discover that Mr. Webster did not see fit to include the word aimless in his definition, because I am of the opinion that wandering, rambling or whatever without proper preparation is a deprivation of some of the joy, and joy is what travel is all about.

I admit that I am a bit weird about traveling. I experience rapture just touching the door knobs of travel agencies at night, long after they are closed. And the sight of one of these enchanted establishments actually open, with pilgrims crowding the counters and fondling travel folders, air-travel cards at the ready in sweaty hands, sends me reeling to banks and pawnshops looking for the bread to join them. If I see a bird fly by I want to go with him. Of course, times have changed in the decades since I was a rover... I pity anyone who never got to experience the freedom and joy travel once held. Dreaming, in any of its forms, thinking about it, talking it over while not yet committed, mulling on it, wishing it could happen. And then one day, when passion is almost overpowering and you faint in a strange travel office, you do it. Your dream becomes a reality, a thing of beauty, something it would never have become without the preliminaries in your head.

I was a dreamer long before I ever bought a ticket. While other little girls were out playing hopscotch and jacks, I would lock myself in the bathroom and journey to faraway places with some assurance that no intruder would barge in on me in the middle of one of my trips. I would sit on that cool plastic and wish I had a hundred and twelve dollars so that I could visit beautiful Omaha. And later on, when my wishing got a little more sophisticated, I would rent rooms in cheap hotels and lock myself in and trip off to the more exotic areas. It was a tricky business. Now and then I would chatter out loud in alternate soprano and alto voices so I wouldn't appear to the management like some fruitcake who checked into hotels alone. And in the mornings I would emerge, pale and haggard, looking as though I had spent the dark hours in the company of Joe Namath and Jim Brown. Dreaming can be hard on a person, but it's worth it.

There were a few dreams that were better than all the others. In the first, I ran breathlessly down the Champs Elysees to a secret tryst beneath the Arc de Triomphe where Clark Gable awaited me, his uniform stained with blood. In one, sponsored by Somerset Maugham, I walked into the Raffles Hotel in Singapore, strode to the bar, and ordered a Strega. In another, I sat huddled in a small cafe off the Via Veneto while bombs exploded in war-torn Italy and Humphry Bogart kissed me and promised he'd be back for me. In still another, I stood on a beach at Bali and stared out to sea, looking for monsoons.

Well, dreams they were, and they didn't come true exactly as I had dreamed them, but they were close enough. I sat one day in La Coupole restaurant in the Boulevard Montpamasse in Paris and sipped Campari with Ernest Hemingway, fascinated as he spun stories of his life. I bought that Strega at the Raffles one day and slept in the Mandarin suite that night as well. And I sat in a small cafe on the Via Veneto in Rome with Orson Welles, a true mercenary and soldier of fortune, tossing down Cinzano on the rocks and watching the promenade from Doney's. I stood on that Bali beach, a little ludicrous in my native sarong perhaps, and ignored the monsoons while I gave my full attention to my dark-skinned companion.

Getting there is a joy indeed. But dreaming about it is where it's at. And then, of course, the ultimate: The remembering.

When Jim and I were in London, we ran into Sammy Davis, Jr. He had been invited to 'The Big Smoke' by Her Majesty, Queen Elizabeth, to appear at the Royal Command Performance at Victoria Palace and he had arrived in town a few days earlier. He would also do a two-week engagement at the Pigalle. Jim, being a member of the press, had been invited to opening night, and I was in a fever of excitement at the prospect of my first English nightclub. We stepped out of the taxi and Jim held my arm as he guided me down the flight of stairs that led to the Pigalle. The place was packed. I saw Judy Garland and Sid Luft as we made our way to our table and Jim grinned at them and said, 'Are you two following us?'

Everybody who was anybody was there that evening and Sammy gave one of the best performances of his life. He was onstage for over two hours, almost three hours, actually, and still the audience would not leave. They screamed and whistled and pounded on the tables and chanted 'Encore!' and 'More!' He sang until he was hoarse, his tuxedo as limp as a wet rag, then finally he begged to be allowed to go home, saying he would love to stay all night but he had to meet someone very special at the airport the next day. The audience laughed and applauded and yelled, 'Way to go, Sammy-baby'—they knew he meant his steady companion of the last few weeks, May Britt.

I have never seen such a reception for a performer as Sammy received that evening—with the possible exception of Judy Garland's Carnegie Hall appearance. The English newsmen seemed to dig Sammy as much as he dug

London. Jim and I would be taking a walk and see Sammy and May, hand in hand, strolling along like a couple of tourists, with a covey of fans and reporters following at a respectable distance. We covered a lot of ground, Jim and I, during the next couple of weeks. My neck was permanently cricked from staring up at street signs: Fleet, Regent and Bond Streets, White Hall, Pall Mall, Piccadilly, the Strand, etc. And I was slightly dizzy from trying to see everything at once as we cocktailed at the American Bar at Grosvenor House or the Dorchester Hotel or The Top Hat, or lunched at Les Ambassadeurs. There were so many American actors silting around I sometimes had trouble remembering I was in a foreign country.

We saw Robert Mitchum across the lobby of the hotel one day and Jim, who had known him for years, invited him to dine with us that evening. I was in ecstasy as I had wanted to meet him for the longest time. He was one of my favorite sex symbols during that era. I began at once to anoint myself for the big evening, I had my hair done and was in the process of trying on and rejecting every gown in my wardrobe when Jim lurched through the door, roaring drunk. He leaned against the bureau and stared at me with bloodshot, half-closed eyes, a sneer on his face. My heart sank. As mentioned earlier, Jim had had a running bout with the bottle for a couple of decades. Sometimes he won, sometimes the bottle did. It looked like the bottle had the edge this night.

Jim may have been brilliant in other areas, but he was a typical alcoholic; that is, one was never quite sure what he would do next. He might try to bash my brains out with a Scotch bottle or weep uncontrollably and beg me to forgive him and stay with him forever. After a little over a year with the unconventional writer, I was of the opinion that he would more than likely try to bash my brains out with a

Scotch bottle. Violence had thus far outweighed remorse. I had grown up in a place and an era where domestic violence was the norm… it was the devil I knew.

I hurried to him and put a hand on his arm and tried to get him to sit down. He pulled away and unbuckled his pants and stepped out of them then flopped upon the bed, still wearing his jacket, shirt, tie, and shoes. 'Come over here and suck my cock,' he slurred, his rheumy eyes glittering from between the saggy folds of flesh. (Jim used to say that he had been born with more wrinkles than John Houston had acquired in a lifetime.) He fondled himself and stared at me, that hated and evil grin upon his mouth. I knew that if I refused he would beat me up and probably toss me out of the window as well.

'Oh, Jim,' I groaned, suddenly tired to death of playing his alcoholic games and wanting so much for this trip to go right. 'Why did you have to get drunk—tonight of all nights!'

'Didn't have to—wanted to,' he mumbled. 'Ran into John Ireland downstairs and we bought a few rounds.'

'But what about tonight?' I asked. 'Did you forget that you invited Robert Mitchum to have dinner with us?'

His pale little eyes suddenly lit up with a demonic glint and he sprang to his feet and stood glaring at me. 'So that's it!' He advanced toward me and I had to stifle a giggle at the sight he made—proper gray tweed suit jacket, neat tie, knee-length black socks, shiny black shoes, and no trousers. 'So that's what all this frenzied preparation is all about.' He snatched the gown I was holding and flung it across the room. 'You're getting yourself all prettied up for Mitchum, huh? You want to fuck him, don't you?'

'Jim, that's crazy, I don't even know him,' I protested, knowing it would do little good when he was in this kind of mood. Whenever Jim got drunk he accused me of every black sin known to man and insisted that I wanted to ball every guy we ran into during the course of the evening. Argument was out of the question. In fact, he hoped that I would start an argument because it gave him an excuse for a real knock-down-drag-out battle royal, a diversion he was highly fond of. 'Really, darling, you know that's silly—I love you and only you.' I smiled sweetly and put my arms around him and kissed him, pressing my body close-anything to get him out of the mood he was in, and his mind off Bob Mitchum.

'You sly little cunt,' he giggled and grabbed a handful of my hair, twisting my head back, then shoved his face in close.

He smelled of strong whiskey and I gagged slightly and tried to turn away, but he held me fast. He stared into my face for such a long time that I was beginning to get frightened. I wondered what new sadistic plan he had in mind for me. Then abruptly he released me and began gathering up all my gowns, shoes, slacks, coats, etc. I watched in amazement as he stuffed them into the closet and locked the door then pocketed the key. He stepped into his trousers, buckled them, smoothed his coat into place and walked jauntily toward the door. 'Well, gotta run—I don't want to keep Mitch waiting.' He opened the door, gave me a broad grin, and added, 'I'd take you along, but obviously you haven't a thing to wear!' He slammed the door just as the ashtray I had flung bounced off and shattered on the floor.

Needless to say, I was furious. Not so much because he had dared to lock me in like a child, but because I would not get to meet Robert Mitchum. I had made my mistake by letting Jim know how important it was to me. I fumed for a few minutes then called the desk and told them I had misplaced the key to the closet, would someone be kind enough to bring up a pass key and open it for me? I slipped into Jim's bathrobe and let the man in to unlock the closet.

I got dressed, then paced the floor, not knowing what to do next. I should be gone when he returns, I thought. But then I remembered that this wasn't Hollywood, where any number of friends would have come to my rescue (and had, on many occasions since I had met Jim) and taken me safely home. I paced some more, ordered dinner from room service, along with a fifth of vodka, fumed, drank, watched the clock. It was after two in the morning and Jim had not returned. I was very angry by this time (and a bit looped from all that vodka) so I decided I would leave him. I began packing, wondering who I knew in Europe this time of year who would be kind enough to put me up until I could get plane fare back to the States.

Then I remembered that an old girlfriend of Jim's, Elana Da Vinci, was 'doing' Europe this year. She had given Jim her Paris address when the three of us had been together in New York the month before. I found her address and quickly copied it down, then called a cab. I was gone without so much as a hairpin left behind to remind Jim that I had been there.

Elana whirled me about Paris for the next few weeks, but I don't remember seeing anything. I kept thinking how much more fun it would be if Jim were there to explain it all to me and tell me the legends and history of each building and work of art. He was a walking encyclopedia and could spin a yarn that would charm a cobra. Finally I couldn't stand it any longer. I loved that arrogant, brilliant bum. I went back to London.

our paris

It was honeymoon time. There's no other way to spend a summer in London, I decided then and there. Jim wanted to go on to Paris before the cold weather set in, so we made plans to leave our little love nest in the Mayfair. Our last day in London we walked all over town, revisiting the spots that had held magic for me—and memories that would always be a part of me. A fine gray mist hung in the air and the branches of the trees had traded in their leaves for a blanket of frost. A chilly drizzle had started by the time we arrived at Les Ambassadeurs for a farewell lunch. As we entered I noticed a sparkling group sitting off to one side. At closer inspection I saw that it was Elizabeth Taylor, Eddie Fisher, and a well-dressed and beautiful group of friends. They seemed to send off sparks they were so beautiful.

Jim, who had known Elizabeth since childhood (hers), stopped by the table and chatted for a moment. He introduced me and Eddie said, 'We know Nancy. We met in Hollywood last year at P.J.'s —remember?' How could I forget. It had been one of the highlights of my young life to meet the fabulously tragic and gorgeous Miss Taylor. Eddie had dubbed me 'Little Liz,' and that had been the most lavish compliment that I had been paid to date.

Actually, Elizabeth and her entourage had been expected for several days. Lavish preparations had been underway for some time at London's largest studios for the epic *Cleopatra* which would star the queen of Hollywood; the most beautiful woman in the world. Jim had taken me to see the spectacular sets and I was completely flabbergasted to see the mighty river Nile flowing serenely and placidly through the back lot of Pinewood Studio. The ancient cities of Cairo and Alexandria towered above me in all their splendor. It was so unreal and fantasy-like to be standing in a London movie studio in 1960 and see the lifelike reconstruction of the very cities and river that the queen of Egypt had left her mark upon. Hollywood, I decided, was better at make-believe than any of the gods or goddesses who romped through the pages of Bulfinch's Mythology.

I wanted to stay another few days and see some of the shooting but Jim convinced me that all of France awaited my charms—besides, London in the fall is cold, damp, and ugly.

We left the next morning, via the boat-train (so named because it transported you part of the way by train, part by boat) and curled leisurely through the rugged mountains and chugged slowly past the lovely white cliffs of Dover. Jim pointed out that the Strait of Dover separated England from France and also connected the English Channel to the North Sea. The mystery of the snow white cliffs is simply that they are made of chalk. This passageway was once referred to as the 'key to England,' and my imagination allowed me a glimpse of kings and queens and their royal court going about the business of being royal at Dover Castle. I wished that we had been able to see the Castle up close.

We arrived in Paris at dusk and took a taxi to a small hotel that John Ireland had told us about in London, the Hotel de Mont Blanc on the Rue Lariston. The narrow, cobble-stoned street ran parallel with and lay one block behind the Champs Elysees. We checked in, then went in search of nourishment.

The lights had begun to go on along the streets and a kind of transparent mist surrounded each one., giving the avenues and buildings a soft, pastel, mystic look. I could now see why Paris had been dubbed 'The City of Lights,' and why so many Americans had fallen in love with it and stayed on. We walked hand and hand down the Champs

Elysees toward Fouquet's (one of the more famous sidewalk cafes) and I saw the Arc de Triomphe towering in the far distance. I remembered all the wild stories Jim had told me about Paris and the outrageous and famous folks he had met there; his kind of people. Staying in a posh hotel and dining with other American tourists was not Jim's idea of visiting a foreign country. He got acquainted with the natives and let them show him where the action was. I sincerely believe that Jim Henaghan was the first expatriate and soldier of fortune. And I also believed he lied about his age: He must be close to two hundred years old to have been and done as much as he had.

We dined on delicately roasted partridge that evening and then Jim suggested that we go to the Algerian section and watch a belly-dancing act. It was awfully dark as we got out of the taxi, the only source of light coming from a few puny poles that stood on the street corners. Jim took my hand and led me down a dark, narrow, cobble-stoned alley that was much darker than the streets had been. Every few feet there was a doorway set back from the alley, a tiny yellow bulb glowing faintly and softly and eerily illuminating the robed figure of an Arab. They slouched in the doorway and watched silently as we passed by; rich Americans slumming in the Algerian section... I could almost feel their hatred. We may not have been French, but we were white and, to these swarthy-skinned chaps, that alone qualified us for their hostilities and old grudges.

Once inside the tiny nightclub, as several belly-dancers jiggled just inches from our noses, Jim filled me in on the history of the Algerians. (Remember, folks, I had but an eighth-grade education and Jim was my Professor Higgins in almost all things. I have long-since graduated and now am a card-carrying Road's Scholar.) Anyway, at that time, everything interested me. I was fascinated with the history and legends surrounding things I had heard only vaguely about.

According to Jim, France had won complete control over Algeria (except for that area that bordered the Sahara Desert) way back in the 1800s and for years the Algerians seethed and plotted to free themselves. They got their chance during the aftermath of World War II and the Algerian Independence Movement was born. They took another giant step in 1954 and broke out in open rebellion. However, France waged war against the straggling troops of Arabs in 1955 and gained control once more. Even though DeGaulie offered them autonomy (the right of self-government and independence) the Algerians were still pissed, and waiting for another crack at the government. (This was in 1960; in 1962 Algeria finally became independent.)

I was a little nervous and glanced about the dimly-lit room. A sea of stern, immobile faces stared back at me. I shivered and told Jim I wanted to get out of there.

'Just a minute, little Nancy,' he said, digging into his pockets for some coins. He pulled out two American half-dollars and placed them on the edge of the table. 'First we must tip the charming young lady for her lovely dance.' He grinned—and I knew from the twinkle in his eye that it wasn't going to be the usual tip.

The dancer swayed and bumped to our table, flung back the transparent panel of silk that hung between her thighs, held her arms over her head, squatted over the coins, gave a jerk of her belly muscles and stood up. The coins were gone! As I was still gaping, she reached between her legs, crouched slightly, and I heard the tinkle of the coins as they fell out of her vagina and into her waiting palm. She got a big hand for that one and we left.

Perhaps it was a throwback to his newspaper days, but Jim has an uncanny knack of smelling out important people. The fact that he was thousands of miles from the Hollywood beat did not dim this gift. He was on the telephone most of the morning while I tried to bathe and wash my hair in the tiny water closet that was all the way down at the other end of the hall. (Even in some of the more posh hotels, it was almost unheard of to have a private bathroom in the room. There was, however, a bidet in even the shabbiest of establishments. This stubby little porcelain bowl has been the butt of many an American joke, but I found it utterly delightful—and I did not wash my stockings in it!)

We went to the dining room for a continental breakfast that consisted of flakey, warm-from-the-oven croissant rolls, thick porridge, and strong, black coffee expresso, compliments of the management. A lovely green garden sprawled between the rooms and the lobby. There were several small white tables, each with its own private white telephone. (The French had a lot of telephones, it's just that they usually didn't work!) Jim ran into a writer friend of his, Johnny Melson, who had been living in Paris for several years (another expatriate) and had been writing for American television, mostly for the *Gunsmoke* series. I remember someone at the table being quite amazed at this and asking him how in the world he could write westerns while living in Paris, France. Said Johnny, 'What difference does it make where one lives? All the western stories I've ever heard of happened over a hundred years ago anyway.'

We left John, breathlessly awaiting the arrival of his Polish mistress, and took a cab to the George V Hotel. The lobby and bar were packed with the pretty people set and the decor was magnificently done in antique veined mirrors, ankle-deep carpet, and Louis the Fourteenth chairs. We took a table in the bar and ordered drinks and a few minutes later I glanced up to see Glenn Ford coming toward us, a smile of greeting on his face. He and Jim shook hands, hugged, and pounded one another on the back, and then I was introduced.

I was terribly impressed with Mr. Ford. He was darling in person. Sexy, a bit shy, handsome as hell, and so charming I was constantly blushing at his compliments. He and Jim exchanged old memories then he told us he was in Paris for the filming of his latest movie, *The Four Horsemen of the Apocalypse*, and Jim asked if he would make arrangements for us to visit the set sometime that week as he'd like to do an article for the fans.

'Gotta keep making those bucks,' Jim grinned by way of explanation. He was a little embarrassed that a writer of his talent and brilliance had to write for the fan mags. 'Man, it's expensive keeping a child mistress, let me tell you,' Jim laughed and looked fondly in my direction. 'This one keeps me broke just buying candy and bubblegum!'

Glenn laughed, then assured Jim that if I became too much of a burden he could probably handle a couple months' supply of bubblegum.

We did Paris up royally and I met so many famous and beautiful and exciting people that space does not allow description.

The Frank Sinatra of Paris, Eddie Constantine, was one of Jim's old and close friends (Henaghan knew everyone, everywhere!) and we spent quite a lot of time with him. Eddie was an expatriate and also one of the most celebrated movie stars in the world, and yet, ninety-nine percent of his fellow Americans have never heard of him. He was a young Jewish boy in Los Angeles in 1949 and he thought he could sing. He wasn't terribly attractive (his face was craggy and pock-marked) so he had some trouble getting jobs.

He decided to try Europe. The way he tells it, he was performing as a way-down-the-bill singer in a Paris show that starred the sad little sparrow, Edith Piaf, and as he walked by her dressing room one night she reached out and pulled him inside. 'She kept me there for eight months,' he said wryly. And in gratitude for his heroic effort to keep her content, she got him a bit part, playing an American detective in a French movie. He was so cute in the part, and his accent so fetching, that French audiences demanded to see more of him. In just two years he had become the biggest box-office star in French movies. His fans were all over Europe and the Middle East. He made millions. His fame was so great at one time that a theater in Dusseldorf, Germany, played his films twenty-four hours a day, fifty-two weeks a year! He out-grossed Bardot, Gabin, the best of them everywhere he played. Monstrous, bigger than life posters of Eddie with the title of his latest flick were everywhere. They were pasted on walls, alleys, fences, buildings; literally everywhere you looked there was Eddie towering above you. What an ego trip it must have been for him to saunter down a Paris boulevard and see himself each step of the way.

Europe has always been the playground of the rich and famous, and they pretty much had it to themselves until the late thirties when a handful of ballsy (but broke) actors started trekking over to grab their piece of the rainbow. Actors who couldn't make it big in Hollywood descended on Paris, Madrid, and Rome like locusts, some of them never to be heard of again; others got rich beyond their greediest dreams. For the ones who found the going tough at first, dubbing foreign films is a way to earn the rent. Back then, all European producers tried to get their wares into English-speaking markets, so they needed genuine accents, and they paid about ten dollars a day for them. Once in a while the actors are all busy acting, and saw film producers button-holing strangers in tourist hotel lobbies and hiring them to dub movies into an English version. I worked in a couple of those flicks myself during my stay abroad.

It was fall in Paris, lovely, crisp, cold. Jim had found an apartment and we had set up housekeeping together. He was still drinking steadily, but his violent fits came less often and he was able to do some writing so that we had food on the table. We were listening to the radio one evening and heard the announcement that Elizabeth Taylor was dying in a London hospital. Jim put through a call immediately, spoke at length to whoever was on the other end, quickly scribbling down notes as he spoke.

He replaced the receiver, gave me a wink and a 'Ah-ha— we're in business, little Nancy!' and placed another call, this time to New York. He spoke to the publisher of *Motion Picture* magazine and told him that he had the inside scoop on Taylor's illness, that he had, in fact, interviewed her personally and was willing to peddle his 'secret information' for five thousand dollars. There was a moment's silence— then Jim's face split into a wide grin and he slammed the receiver down, whirled me about the room and laughed like a kid.

'We did it,' he chortled gleefully. 'I got that prick Podell to go for five grand!' Nothing would do but we had to go out on the town and celebrate the money we didn't have yet.

Well, the celebration lasted for the better part of the week, with Jim getting more bombed (if that's possible) with each day. Suddenly he had a mere three days to get his piece in on Elizabeth Taylor—but he was still drunk and sick and surly. 'You'll have to do it for me, little Nancy,' he moaned piteously from beneath a silken quilt. He had the shakes and insisted that only another shot of booze would help. He poured a water glass full of the amber liquid, and trembling as though he had palsy, he downed it in one gulp. 'I'll help you,' he said when he was able to speak again. 'I'll tell you what to write and you type it up for me, okay?'

'Okay,' I agreed reluctantly. I had been typing Jim's gossip columns for several months, so I knew a little about his style. However, as he had taught me how to type and as he only uses two fingers to type with, that's the way I learned.

It took me all day to write that story on Elizabeth Taylor. Jim crashed and slept through the whole thing. When he awoke I was finished with the article and was editing it. He was amazed and delighted as he read it over and promptly stuffed it into an envelope for mailing.

That was the beginning of my writing career. It was also the beginning of the time I would spend as Jim's alter ego. In the months that followed, whenever Jim was too drunk or too hungover to write his column and articles, I would do it. He was very careful, however, to make sure that each article contained his byline. At first, this didn't bother me. After all, I was learning my craft from the master.

Then it did start to bother me.

Whenever Jim would receive a fan letter praising his writing, or a movie star or someone else of importance would write a note saying how much they enjoyed his last column, I would feel a little twinge of resentment. After all, those were my words that he was taking credit for. However, it just tickled Jim. He thought it was a real giggle to be fooling all those publishers and editors who were paying fifty cents a word (unheard of in those days) for knowledge, talent, and the Jim Henaghan by-line. I had learned my craft well, he said; no one could tell the difference in our writing style. In fact, my style was his style.

For the next several years, I was to earn a very good living as a writer. I owe it all to Jim Henaghan.

reeling through rome and yonder

Petty criminals by the hundreds populate the big cities of Europe, hiding out in places from which they cannot be extradited, living from hand to mouth rather than face justice on counts ranging from stealing library books to tapping the boss's till for enough bread to get by on until pay day. They proudly wear the label expatriate and collar tourists in airports and train depots, offering to exchange their American dollars for the currency of that particular country. Anyone naive enough to fall for this oldest of scams says goodbye to his American dollars—as well as that friendly little chap who offered to help.

There was no accurate figure on the number of expatriate Americans residing permanently in foreign lands back in the sixties, but experts who were willing to guess put the figure at well above a hundred thousand. Add to these the itinerants who go away for personal reasons, vowing never to return, and stay a few years, and the number rose to close to a quarter of a million—I met my share of them while abroad and, in some cases, found myself envying their flamboyant way of life.

Perhaps my favorite expatriate (and certainly the most colorful) is Orson Welles. I will never forget the first time I saw him.

Jim and I had flown to Rome as he was trying to get some screenwriting assignments and knew several producers who lived there. We checked into a marvelous old hotel at the top of The Spanish Stairs, about a block behind the Via Veneto. Roberto (Jim's producer friend) had sent over a gleaming black limousine and chauffeur which would be at our disposal twenty-four hours a day during our stay in Rome. We stepped inside and were whisked toward the outskirts of the town where Jim had an appointment at Cinecittà Studio.

The Tartars, a sword and sandal epic starring Victor Mature and Orson Welles, was shooting there. Jim disappeared someplace and I sat down to watch the action. All of a sudden, this apparition appeared striding briskly down the dusty path. It was Orson Welles, a plush velvet cape swirling about his rotund figure, black sunglasses hiding his eyes, a foot-long cigar clenched between his teeth, and a harried cluster of secretaries, valets, flunkies, groupies and go-fers scurrying frantically about him as they tried to stay apace. He looked neither right nor left, but strode purposefully forward, His Majesty, the King, dictating orders in a clipped tone. A couple of secretaries ran gallantly alongside, trying to take it all down as their papers fluttered and scattered in the breeze. Ashes fell from the end of his cigar, a couple of flakes adhering to the lush velvet of his cape. Orson, without breaking stride, pointed a finger at the offending ash and immediately a valet sprang forward with a whisk broom and flicked the ash into oblivion.

It was the most ludicrous sight I had ever seen and I burst out laughing. Orson stopped in midstride, pointed a bejeweled finger in my direction, and boomed, 'Who is that person?' Immediately, his entourage began dashing here and there, asking crew members who I was.

'I'm sorry,' I said, still laughing as I walked over to him. 'I really am sorry, Mr. Welles, but the whole scene just hit me funny.' I stifled a giggle and held out my hand. 'I'm Nancy Bacon.'

He took my hand gingerly, a thoughtful set to his mouth, went 'uhmmm' then said, 'So you found my entrance a bit too pompous, eh?'

'Yes, just a bit,' I laughed and to my delight, he threw back his head and boomed with laughter as well. He gave me a pat on the head, snapped his fingers at his gaping entourage and continued striding toward his destination, picking up the dictation where he had left off.

Jim returned soon after that and we got into our waiting chariot and drove back to Rome. We went to The Excelsior Hotel, and just as we stepped inside this big, burly dude came charging through the door, almost knocking us down.

'Watch where you're going, movie star,' Jim growled and grabbed the guy's arm, wheeling him around to face us. It was, I saw, Victor Mature. He looked blank for a second, then scooped Jim up into his massive arms and gave him a big bear hug.

'Henaghan, you old son-of-a-bitch! What in hell are you doing in Rome?' He set Jim back upon his feet and stood smiling fondly down at him. They exchanged information and Vic glanced at his watch and cursed. 'Christ! I'm late. Should've been on the set twenty minutes ago. Listen, how about dinner tonight? Meet me in my suite—I'm staying here—about eight or so?' He gave Jim a slap on the back that almost finished him off, and went barreling through the door, bellowing at a couple of fellows to follow him.

'Great guy, Vic,' Jim said, taking my elbow and steering me toward the dining room. 'It'll be fun to talk over old times with him.' We sat down and accepted menus from a waiter and Jim ordered cocktails. A moment later the waiter appeared with our cocktails, bowed low, and murmured in a thick Italian accent, 'Your drinks, Senior Prick.' My mouth fell open and Jim half-rose from his chair, stared, then laughed boisterously. 'Charlie! How the hell are you? I was going to call you later on today.'

The 'waiter' set down the drinks and hugged Jim, and they got into a lot of fond curses as they pounded one another on the back. This was getting to be a habit, I thought, wondering who this new member of Jim's European family would turn out to be. Possibly a fallen prince or an exiled king. One could never be sure with Henaghan. He was, it turned out, the legendary Charlie Fawcett. Legendary because of his outrageous behavior and way of life.

Charlie had left his wealthy, social Virginia family before World War II to join the French Foreign Legion. He served admirably in the legion during the war, then went to live in Rome where he became, next to the Pope, the most respected citizen of that city. Charlie Fawcett lived just for the good he can do, and he had absolutely no regard for money. He was married once to the Baroness Von Thyssen, a billionaire German lady, and when she committed suicide, he walked away without a penny because that is the way he wanted it. Whenever there was a catastrophe in Europe (an earthquake, a disastrous flood, a political upheaval involving refugees) Charlie Fawcett would go there to be of what help he could. Consequently, he had as personal friends the heads of state of many nations. If you were going to Iran, Charlie would give you a note to the Shah. If it was Morocco, Charlie would slip you a message to hand to his pal the King. And if you were short of money, Charlie would give you what he has in his pocket. According to his multitude of friends, Charlie Fawcett was without a doubt the best unofficial ambassador America ever had abroad.

It was a delightful luncheon, listening to Jim and Charlie reminisce about the good old days in Europe before the tourists ruined it.

'Remember Jerry?' Charlie asked Jim over coffee and brandy. 'He's doing pretty good now—ever since King Farouk bailed him out of that jam he was in. He just opened a new restaurant right around the corner. The Luau, he calls it—you'll have to take your charming companion there for dinner one evening.'

They were referring to Jerry, proprietor of Jerry's Bar, a little place off the Via Veneto, down one flight of steps and across the hall from the famous Bricktop's bar. Jerry was another expatriate who had been created along with hundreds of others at the end of the war. The kind who fell in love with a foreign country and elected to remain there. Jerry was an Italian from New Jersey and had decided that he would stay on and open a restaurant. It was a tiny little place, hardly any larger than your average American hamburger joint, and it had an American jukebox and a big, friendly kitchen that welcomed anyone who wished to come back and have a hand in the preparation of their dinner. It was almost always filled to overflowing with American actors, most of them broke—or between pictures—who knew that Jerry would let them sign the tab until their ship came in. Well, as with most ships, they don't always arrive when expected and one day Jerry had to face the awful truth. Not only was he broke, but he owed an astronomical two hundred thousand dollars! He sadly gave a farewell party at his little cafe and said a tearful goodbye to his freeloading friends.

Suddenly the door burst open and the portly king of Egypt, Farouk, strode purposefully toward the kitchen. He kicked everyone out and conversed privately with Jerry for several minutes. When they emerged, those closest to them overheard King Farouk saying, 'Now, let's have those hamburgers, my good friend—I'm ravenous!' (Farouk never ate just one of anything!) The next morning all of Rome (it's an incredibly small town) heard what had happened. King Farouk had paid off Jerry's debts so that the little New Jersey guy could stay in business. Seems Farouk had become hooked on American hamburgers and Elvis Presley songs—and there was nowhere else to get them!

I met the good king several times during my visits to Rome and found him a fascinating person. He was quite obese, weighing close to three hundred pounds, and his main passion was, of course, food. After he had polished off a huge dinner, downed a couple of bottles of wine and a tot of brandy or three, he would burp, cast aside his napkin, and prepare himself for his second passion women.

In our chauffeured limousine, Jim and I went sight-seeing in style. Rome, the Eternal City, was everything I had imagined it would be and more. (It's still my favorite city in Europe.) The great monuments of the past are still there in all their glory to be investigated and appreciated: The Forum, Colosseum, Lateran, St. Peter's Church. We stood in the cobble-stoned courtyard of the Vatican and looked up at the balcony, where once a day the Pope would appear and bless the peasants who had gathered below to cheer him. Jim told me that during the war a tunnel had been dug that ran from one end of town down under the city and came out in the Vatican. They had used it to smuggle soldiers to safety, in or out of the city. Now, he said, with his satyr's smile, they used it to smuggle in hookers for the 'celibates' who resided there! I found this information a bit shocking and hard to believe but Jim assured me that it was not only quite true but also a well-known secret among the citizens of Rome. I guessed even Cardinals and Bishops get the hornies every so often.

We visited Jerry's new restaurant, the Luau, a couple of days later. It was done in Polynesian decor and the floor of the bar area was a wall-to-wall aquarium. It really felt strange to walk across the floor, glance down, and see whole schools of goldfish, tropical fish, turtles, etc. swimming lazily beneath your feet! It was lighted from the inside and slim slips pf seaweed swayed hypnotically with the motion of the water as brightly-colored fish darted through them. Down a couple of steps was the dining room, which was done in rather a woodsy Polynesian and held a huge, ceiling-to-floor cage at one end. This was the permanent home of Jerry's pet falcon and many an inebriated customer claimed that the damn bird could actually speak—in Italian!

Van Heflin was seated at a table with Guy Madison and a couple of other people. When he saw Jim they got into that hugging, back-slapping routine and then he invited us to join them. I think Guy Madison was still carrying a torch for his ex-wife Gail Russell (she died the following year from a failed liver due to alcoholism) because he looked very sad and forlorn and hardly joined in the conversation at all—which consisted exclusively of speculation about whether or not John Kennedy would be elected.

The next day everyone knew the outcome, of course, and all of Rome went on a binge that lasted a week. I've never seen so many delighted and delightful folks. They literally danced in the streets, stopping traffic and pulling people out of cars and cabs to join them in the dancing and cheering. Tony Steele and his new bride, Anita Ekberg, watched from the safety of the Paris Cafe while Jim and I made our headquarters at Doney's sidewalk cafe for most of the frenzied week. We were joined periodically by John Barrymore, Jr., Guy Madison, and Orson Welles. They would pause for a Cinzano, watch the mob for a moment, then totter on down the Via Veneto toward the next rest station.

It took several days to sober up and restore our heads to some semblance of order, but we managed. We had another glorious week in Rome, then it was back to Paris.

The weather in Rome had been lovely; just enough bite in the air to make one feel alive and adventurous. Paris, however, was rainy, cold, and dreary. Jim's temperament matched the inclemencies, and our fights became loud and frequent. In fact, most of Paris seemed to be in the same lousy mood. John Melson (an expatriate writer) was fighting just as bitterly with his mistress and one night, after an all-day brawl, Jim and I heard screaming, shouting, and running feet coming from the hallway. We rushed outside into the courtyard and there was little Johnny, naked as a jaybird, his wrists and throat slashed, running wildly through the garden. Someone threw a blanket over him and carted him off to the American Hospital.

The next day we found out what had happened. Johnny's mistress had met Anthony Quinn in Italy or Greece (we were never sure of the country) and had run off with him. Johnny got drunk and decided to kill himself. He cut his wrists and throat and sat moodily watching them bleed for a few minutes. When he saw that nothing much was happening he drank some rat poison and, as a final act, took all the sleeping medicine he had in his room. However, in Paris they did not sell sleeping potions in pill form; they were, instead, suppositories. But this hadn't daunted our tragic Romeo—he stuffed twenty-five suppositories up his rump and waited for death to come. Can you believe it? He actually survived all this!

Another of our neighbors got into a bit of a row during that gray, moody period in Paris. She was a Boston school teacher who had been saving all her life for a trip to Paris.

She was thirty-eight and not bad-looking, but she wore proper suits and her shoes had sensible heels. We got to be friends and one day I suggested that if she wore a little makeup, got rid of her glasses, and bought some sexy French clothes she'd be a real knockout. She agreed immediately and we made her over. The result was fantastic! She looked like Ava Gardner and with her new wardrobe and makeup, she acquired a new personality. We would wave her off every evening as she went tripping into a taxi for another night on the town.

About six o'clock one morning, Jim and I heard this terrific crash, followed by rapid, angry French. We peeked outside and saw our Boston schoolteacher standing helplessly by, clad only in a transparent French gown, as the management flung her trunk and suitcases from her upstairs window. Seems she had wandered into the Algerian section, had a few belts of the local grog, picked up six studs, and brought them home with her where they got into an all-night orgy! (Paris does strange things to people.)

You can't blame the management for kicking her and the boys out. Just a few days before, the Algerians had started a riot at a newspaper office on the Champs Elysees. They were tossing furniture out of the windows and trying to do as much damage as possible before the cops arrived. Jim and I were sitting at a sidewalk cafe, watching the action with interest (we were so close that a couple of pieces of broken furniture skidded across the sidewalk and landed at our feet), when the waiter appeared, apologized profusely, and removed our drinks from the table. We could have them back, he promised, when the riot was over. I guess people sometimes get caught up in these things and join in the action. The gendarmerie arrived, swinging their huge, leaded capes, and began flooring everyone within range. It was almost a work of art, the way they used those capes, and as I watched them knocking people to their knees, I was reminded how dangerous they could be. The hems of those flowing, heavy capes have lengths of lead in them, and when the cop swings it the result is like being slugged in the teeth with a blackjack. I saw one old woman go down where she lay in the gutter, shaking her fist at the gendarmerie and spitting broken teeth and insults from her bloodied mouth. They soon cleared the streets and sidewalk and, as promised, our drinks were promptly returned.

Both Jim and I were drinking too much during that period and the constant rain and sunless skies pitched me into dark depression. It was the dreary let-down feeling of what to do now that Christmas and New Year's was over. I was unhappy and homesick. I missed all my friends and the warm, sunny, familiar Hollywood Hills. I wrote my old pal, Griff, and he wired me the money for a ticket home.

Tearfully, Jim and I prepared to part. It was useless, we both knew, to try to remain together. One very important reason was that he was still married and his wife was not overly fond of me. Also, over thirty years separated us in age. But the most important reason was his drinking problem. I was not yet twenty-one years old and I had been lover, friend, mother, pet, punching bag, and confidante for two years. I had traveled in a superfast crowd and had learned firsthand all the uglies of life. Needless to say, I was weary.

My last night in Paris we dined at home, mostly champagne with just a touch of caviar to balance the booze and coat our stomachs. The more of the bubbly we consumed the sadder we became. With our arms wrapped about one another a la *Our Gang*, balancing our champagne glasses and gazing moodily out at the City of Lights, we tearfully remembered every outrageous act we had ever committed as well as every insane stunt we had pulled.

The evening was a comedy-tragedy, ending with us falling drunkenly into bed and attempting to make love. Hot candle wax dripped from the wall sconce that hung above the bed, splattering on our bare skin, and it sent us into waves of weepy laughter. We decided that we could not part; we were meant for each other and besides, who else would have us?

The next afternoon we sailed from Le Havre aboard the S.S. United States, which heaved and rolled for five and a half days to its destination, New York. Jim behaved quite well on the ship; he only threatened to throw me overboard once and was only asked to leave the ship's bar four times in the five-and-a-half days. It was dawn when we pulled into New York harbor—gray, misty, a yellowish haze shrouding the buildings—and I stood at the rail and watched the Statue of Liberty growing larger and larger. What a thrill to see billboards printed in English with familiar brand names and the roar and smell of that city! I had been away too long.

The brevity of our reconciliation was exceeded only by its violence and insanity. Jim cut my wrists one drunken evening (I still have the scars) and left me to die in our posh hotel room while he then attended a dinner party at 21. Fortunately, in a moment of reason, he returned to my rescue and had me sewn up at the emergency hospital, where I quipped that the young intern would have made one hell of a fine tailor. That cute little remark got me a psychiatric examination at Bellevue. That was the most memorable violence.

The most memorable insanity (and there were many) was when Jim had had a query turned down by a local and well-known magazine editor on the grounds that 'he (Jim) was too fucking drunk to write his own obituary.' Jim carefully planned his revenge. He bought a bag of prunes and a fifth of Scotch and sat down, grinning his satyr's grin as he gleefully lapped up both fruit and booze. The next day, when the editor had gone out to lunch, Jim sneaked into his private office and pulled out the top drawer of the sleek, expensive mahogany desk. He climbed upon the desk, perched upon the edge, dropped his trousers, and relieved himself into the drawer. Replacing both the drawer and his trousers, he went whistling out of the building, his vengeance complete.

I found Jim's pranks hilarious and brilliant when they involved other people, but too often his barbs were aimed at me. I decided (for the hundredth time) that I had had it. I packed my bags and called TWA, vowing never to see him again.

home again

I had only been back in the states a couple of weeks when I ran into Vince Edwards at a local Beverly Hills gin mill. He tossed me boisterously into the air, kissing me on the way down, and we left immediately for his hilltop home.

Vince had changed in those two years that had passed. He was cagey, wary of strangers, and anybody with a pencil and piece of paper sent the hair up on the back of his neck. His success, even though over ten years coming, was just as difficult to handle as the rock idol who makes it in less than a month. He was suddenly named as the latest lover of this aspiring starlet or that aging actress, and guys who needed a publicity break told national fan magazines that they had grown up with Vince in the Brooklyn streets. People who had not given him so much as a nod last year were suddenly inviting him to their most intimate dinner parties, and everywhere he went fifty thousand screaming teenyboppers ripped his clothes and gurgled for his blood. He was mobbed everywhere he went and the most outrageous stories were written about him in the current crop of trash publications.

His gambling became the most talked-about item of gossip among underground Hollywood since Errol Flynn's statutory rape charges and Bob Mitchum's marijuana bust. He hadn't a free moment. He did not know who were friends, enemies, or just parasites. He became as surly off-screen as on, and many a miffed lady journalist went smarting to her typewriter to tell tire world that sexy, virile Vince was really just a rude, crude street kid who had let fame go to his head. This wasn't true, of course. He spent agonizing hours with his analyst trying to find out who and why he was. He tried to grow and all he asked was to be allowed free space to grow in. He shook off the Hollywood bloodsuckers with a snarl and the back of his hairy paw, and everyone knew that you didn't fuck with Vince Edwards unless you knew his mother's maiden name.

Therefore, he was delighted to see a familiar face and a friend who had loved him when he was nothing more than a trying-to-get-there actor. We talked for days about my European travels and the crazy Irishman I had gotten strung out on. Vince gave me some advice on what to do with my life and I, in turn, tried to understand what he was doing with his. After several dates where we were seen at Don the Beachcombers or the Cock and Bull, Vince grinned wryly at me and said, 'You realize, of course, they'll (the press) will have us secretly married and sneaking off to Tijuana for an abortion because my career comes before a family!'

'Just tell them I loved you before you grew all that chest hair,' I replied, and we laughed all the way to the bedroom.

Vince and I remained close friends through the years, even though we didn't see each other often. When he flipped for the sexy Kathy Kersh, I was the first to know that he planned to marry her. And when the marriage ended in divorce a year later, it was my shoulder he cried on. Every afternoon for almost two weeks he stopped by my house and talked about Kathy. She had hurt him badly. His ego was in pretty sorry shape. When she walked out on him for Burt Ward, the 'Robin' of the old Batman series, Vince was furious and bewildered.

'It's not the greatest compliment in the world,' Vince told me, 'knowing that my old lady prefers that puny punk to me. But what really hurts is knowing that a couple of kids will be raising my daughter.' (He and Kathy had had a baby whom Vince simply adored.)

In the end, my old buddy took the divorce in style and consoled himself with tribes of eager starlets and panting groupies who visited his bachelor adobe nightly. He still played the ponies regularly, just like in the old days, but instead of placing five-dollar bets and maybe losing twenty bucks a day, he now laid down a staggering fifty or sixty thousand dollars in just one afternoon! But he could afford it. He had been wise enough to get a piece of the *Ben Casey* action rather than just an actor's salary.

As everyone knows, once you've been out of the Hollywood scene for more than ten minutes, your name is totally forgotten and no one will admit to remembering your face. I had been away for some time, so it was a lucky break for me to be reintroduced on the hairy arm of the currently reigning sex symbol. One evening Vince and I attended a sneak preview at The Academy Theater and ran into Hugh O'Brian, with the ever-present gorgeous lady draped upon his arm. It had been four years since I'd last seen him.

a handkerchief for liz

Elizabeth Taylor. What can one say about Elizabeth that hasn't already been said? That she was as kind as she was extravagant; as soft-hearted as she was infamous? Volumes have been written about her. Her every move has been dutifully recorded by her adoring fans and turned into screaming headlines, from the harsh accusations, 'Home-wrecker!' to the tear-jerking proclamation, 'Courageous Liz Faces Death!' Her every thought and feeling has been blown up into gigantic proportions, almost dwarfing the woman herself. She was the target of the most outlandish accusations and predictions of anyone in show business back then.

I talked to Richard Hanley (Elizabeth's long-lime secretary) one day about his famous boss and what she was really like. I had, of course, talked with her on many occasions myself over the years, but I wanted a really intimate viewpoint: the viewpoint of someone who had lived closely with her and knew her when she was frightened and unhappy. I was doing an article on Elizabeth and asked Dick a few questions about life with Liz.

'I'll never forget the first time I ever saw Elizabeth,' Richard Hanley smiled fondly. 'It was back in '43 or '44—somewhere around that time. I was working at MGM at the time, for Louis Mayer.' Dick shook his head and smiled as he recalled that day so long ago. He had been sitting at his desk, occupying himself with letters and memos, when he heard loud noises coming from behind the elaborate door leading to the most inner sanctum of MGM. He was, to put it mildly, used to the racket. On the other side of the door, Louis B. Mayer, the greatest mogul Hollywood has ever known, was 'straightening out' an actress—something he was celebrated for.

In this straightening out process he used many devices. He had been known to fall to his knees and weep before a stubborn actor who did not fear him, to make a point. He often roared in rage and threatened to destroy them in the business. And there are reports that he did exactly that, in collusion with other film tycoons, on more than one occasion. He was known to have physically assaulted others, for he was a burly, powerful man and had floored actors and agents when it seemed the thing to do, or when his verbal intimidation technique wasn't working.

On this day, however, there were two females on the carpet. A grown woman (known as a stage mother in the trade) and a child actress, age twelve, terrified and not understanding, named Elizabeth Taylor.

Because there were only the three of them in the office and the harangue was filtered through the heavy door, no real record of the substance of the tirade exists. But the secretary, Richard Hanley, knew it well.

Mayer, florid, sweaty, his mouth filled with street language, was jumping up and down in a more or less feigned anger (they say he could rush the blood to his face, simulating apoplexy at will) and shouting at the woman and child that they would damn well do the picture he wanted them to do, when he wanted them to do it, or the child would never work again. And it is in that office that she may have acquired such an ambition. Mayer pushed his face in close, within inches, of Mrs. Taylor's, and spouted one or two expletives and clenched his fists as though he intended to floor her. With a scream of fear, the child, Elizabeth, turned and ran to the door, snatching at the weighty knob and tugging, wanting to get out of there. She was gorgeous even then and tears streamed down her cheeks, sobs almost strangling her as she got the door open and raced into the outer office, leaving her mother alone with the big bad man.

As Elizabeth charged from the room, Hanley looked up from his work. As she raced by him, he reached out and took her in his arms.

The little girl was frightened for a moment, then Hanley smiled at her. His eyes were kind. 'Don't be frightened,' he said. 'All this business is really just nonsense. It isn't real life. He won't hurt your mother.'

Then he picked the sobbing child up and sat her on his lap. He took out his handkerchief and dried her eyes, then handed the hanky to her. 'Blow,' he said. Elizabeth did. She smiled at him. 'That's better,' Hanley said and as she started to give the handkerchief back to him, he said, 'Keep it. You may not be through crying yet.' And without realizing it, he had made a prophecy.

When she was settled, the hanky now a ball in her tiny fist, Hanley kissed her on the cheek. 'Whenever anyone gives you any trouble or frightens you on this lot,' he said, 'you come and see me. I'll look after you.'

Years passed. Many years, as Hollywood standards are, and the frightened child had become one of the most important stars in filmdom. Stature was the name of the game and she had it. At the box office, in the newspapers and magazines, even in the fickle hearts of movie-goers—some of them because of her extraordinary beauty, many of them because she had become a superb actress.

But things had taken a turn for the worse with Hanley. The tycoon, Mayer, had been deposed of his seat of power and one day Hanley, who had been with him for some twenty-odd years, was suddenly handed his walking papers. He was stunned, hurt, and worried about the future. Mayer didn't have many friends and his close employees were not particularly liked either. Richard Hanley found himself facing an uncertain future.

Then he got a telephone call. It was Elizabeth Taylor, asking him to drop around to her house at his convenience, as she would like to talk to him.

He did.

Richard sat across from Elizabeth in her splendid living room feeling almost as though he should have a hat in his hands in the presence of such eminence. But she was warm and even a little shy. 'Dick,' she said, 'I heard about what happened. I don't know what your plans are, but I want to make you an offer. Come to work for me, as my secretary. I will pay you more than Mayer did—what you are really worth—and you will have a job with me as long as you want to work.' The violet eyes sparkled and she added, 'And I won't abandon you.'

Hanley was stunned. From despair, he was facing heaven. He managed to stutter one word. 'Why?'

Elizabeth smiled and got to her feet and left the room, returning a moment later with something in her hand. She sat reside him on the sofa and put the object in his hand. He stared at it. It was a handkerchief. He admitted to being choked-up at what was happening. 'It's the one you gave me quite a few years ago,' she said. 'I've always kept it.' Hanley picked up the handkerchief, not knowing what to say. Elizabeth smiled. 'Blow,' she said.

Richard Hanley was Elizabeth's secretary for the rest of his life. When he started getting on in years and was ill much of the time, Elizabeth flatly refused to replace him. Instead, she supplied him with two secretaries to help carry the load so that he might function as she knew he wanted to.

Perhaps few people know about the Richard Hanley incident, but those who know Elizabeth well wouldn't be surprised. I knew Elizabeth casually for several years and have seen her in many roles. I know (because she told me) that Michael Wilding was the weak point of her life. She was looking for a father and she found him. For Wilding was much like her father, whom she adored even though he was considered henpecked. Her mother was the dominating force in the Taylor household, the strong one who told everyone else what was good for them. Elizabeth always swore she would never be that way when she grew up, and yet her first two marriages proved to be carbon-copies of the very things she despised.

Records are filled to overflowing with the causes of the demise of the Hilton and Wilding marriages, so no mention need be made here. And, of course, everyone knew that Mike Todd was the love of her life and the tragedy. But perhaps few people know that her marriage to Eddie Fisher was not the big sex thing that it was touted as being. There was very little sex in her life with Eddie. She looked on him as a big brother, someone to lean on, someone who had loved Mike as much as she had. And Eddie, even though he loved Elizabeth desperately, could not help but feel great guilt. For he had truly loved Mike Todd and looked upon him as a father. And Elizabeth Taylor Todd had been a kind of glamorous and unreal stepmother. One doesn't marry one's stepmother and live happily ever after. So the guilt that drew them together drove them apart. And left Elizabeth still searching.

I was around them on occasion during their marriage and I saw, firsthand, how they lived. Eddie was always grinning, always clowning, trying to make Elizabeth laugh. They clung together that first year and a half of the marriage simply because they had no one else. The world was against them. Even Hollywood and longtime acquaintances turned their backs on them. They dined out constantly and drank too much champagne and said 'I love you' too often and too loudly. It was really all over by the time they flew to Rome to do *Cleopatra*.

When Elizabeth fell in love with Richard Burton she didn't even blink as she told Eddie to take a hike. She was used to having what she wanted—and she wanted Burton.

Cleopatra was not even halfway through filming before she began making comments about retiring. Her major interest in life never was a career. She stated dozens of times that she just wanted to be a wife and mother. Perhaps it all started that day long ago in Mayer's office. MGM was a factory then, turning out movies like so many cans of peas. There was no glamour for the younger stars—just hard work. Too hard for a twelve-year-old kid, and she must have resented it. But if she has any fond memories at all about her early years at MGM, it would have to be the little schoolhouse on the back lot. There she giggled like the child she was and shared secrets, and her best friends were Judy Garland and Mickey Rooney. They understood because they were going through the same thing and they belonged to one another.

Whenever I was around Elizabeth and talk turned to show business, she would screw up her face in a grimace of distaste and make some caustic remark. She went through a period in which her movies did rather badly at the box office and her career seemed to be slipping. Rather than be disappointed (as most actors would) she seemed delighted, saying, 'Well, now maybe I can retire and become just plain Mrs. Burton.' However, even with bad notices and adverse publicity, Elizabeth herself was more popular than ever, somehow remaining the number one actress people wanted to read about and know about.

I believe it was her sense of honesty that drew people to her. She was a woman who never lost her sense of wonder or her curiosity. And her belief in marriage remained unshakable. Each time she took the marriage vows, she announced that this was it—she would retire and have dozens of babies. With Burton, she truly wanted to be a homemaker and wife, but it was denied her. Their very lifestyle made a mockery of her dreams to be 'just plain Mrs. Burton.'

Another reason the American public was so loyal to Elizabeth was her obvious love of children—all children— and her own were not nanny-kept like the offspring of most movie stars. During her stay at the Dorchester Hotel in London when her children were younger, she startled some pretty important people by her concern for her kids. They were playing in Hyde Park, just across the street from Elizabeth's terrace and yet, every five or ten minutes, she would walk out onto the terrace and look across at Hyde Park to see that everything was all right. It mattered not the least hit that her sitting room was filled with important producers and money men who were discussing a possible movie with her.

She did exactly what she wanted to do—which meant doing exactly what Burton wanted her to do. And she loved it. Her one desire was always a dominating male. She thought she had found it in Burton, and with all due respect to Burton, I believe she really did find it for a while. All her husbands and lovers were always been so in awe of her beauty that it blinded them to the woman and her needs. Not so with Burton. From the very beginning he called her 'a pretty little thing.' What? Not beautiful? Not gorgeous? And her stardom only amused him for he considered himself a better actor.

The fact he bought her huge gems didn't hurt: Richard's first jewelry purchase for Elizabeth was the 33.19-carat Asscher-cut Krupp Diamond, in 1968… the first of many.

He used to refer to her in public as 'Miss Elizabeth Taylor'—said in that slightly haughty Welsh accent, but with a glint of mischief in his eyes because they both knew that at home she was just his woman. Elizabeth loved it. She even began referring to herself in the same manner: 'Elizabeth Taylor would like another drink,' she would say to a passing waiter.

When I heard about the first divorce I was really stunned. This was her only marriage that I was convinced would work. I suppose Burton contributed to the break-up with his boozing and womanizing, and, finally, his complete love and dependence upon Elizabeth. ('I love her too much,' he once told newsmen, 'so much that it is beginning to devour me.') When they married and divorced a second time, in the mid-1970s, I was less stunned.

I've thought a lot about Elizabeth as I gathered information for this book and I wondered how I could paint a true picture of the most famous woman in the world. Then I realized how easy it was. Easy because she was so open, honest, warm, and simple. It's merely a matter of listing her likes and dislikes.

She loved: rare champagne, gourmet food, fabulous furs, children, sleek yachts, Mexican beer, laughter, feather boas, huge houses that can be turned into homes, music, sensitivity, chili beans and hot peppers, dominant, protective, strong men, swear words, femininity, orphans, puppies and kittens, emeralds, her villa in Gstaad, orchids, gray hair, power, caraway seeds, honest critics, her Lear jet, chipmunks, her enormous diamond, yesterday, today, and tomorrow.

She hated: death, cheap millionaires, pain, cold weather, sleeping on the same sheets twice, backaches, warm champagne, taxes, uninvolvement, last year's sable, gossip columnists who misquote her, being an actress, users, slow waiters, being alone.

Humor was Elizabeth's secret weapon and she used it well to cover unshed tears and private hurts. Her fans considered her the most fortunate woman in the world. She had everything she could possibly dream for—everything material, that is. She was even dubbed Dame by Queen Elizabeth II in 2000, but I doubt that changed much for her. She'd divorced her final husband four years before, and never married again.

When she became the first big star to champion HIV/AIDS activism in the eighties, it was because her friend and former co-star Rock Hudson announced he was dying of the disease... Liz raised more than $270 million for the cause over the years. Finally, she was more than just an actress—more than a tabloid headline.

From those tears cried into a handkerchief some sixty years before, a true salt-of-the earth woman emerged and left an indelible impression on the world.

beach bumming with marilyn monroe

It's harder than hell to be a superstar and have all your loves and hates, triumphs and tragedies, marriages and divorces spread out for all the world to see. When they really wanted to curse or cry, they couldn't, because there was always that glare of flashbulbs popping and reporters shoving microphones into their faces and fans screaming for a piece of them and cops holding back mobs that would crush and destroy their idols if they could just get to them.

It's strange; we make them stars and then we give them no time, privacy, or peace to enjoy that stardom. Whenever I think of superstars who have been hounded unmercifully and have been public pawns most of their movie career,

Marilyn Monroe is the first to come to mind. Poor little Marilyn, she was dubbed tragedy's child by the media and the title was most apt.

She was a twentieth century Cinderella but, unlike her fairytale counterpart, she did not live happily ever after. Her search for a strong, handsome prince was much more desperate and pathetic than Elizabeth Taylor's search. Elizabeth had had a rich, comfortable, secure childhood; Marilyn was an orphan, raised in several foster homes and hiding the shame of a neurotic mother who drifted in and out of her life whenever she was released from her latest mental institution. Elizabeth had famous movie stars sending her roses by the dozens and proposing marriage when she was still in her teens; Marilyn was ducking the pawing hands of foster-fathers and being frightened half out of her wits by boys who had something a lot more basic than roses on their minds. Elizabeth married handsome young millionaire, Nicky Hilton, and went on a honeymoon cruise around the world, while Marilyn was stuck in a little cracker-box flat with an uneducated laborer she had married simply because she 'wanted something alive around the house.' When Elizabeth married her second husband, the suave, English gentleman, Michael Wilding, Marilyn was beating the sidewalks of Hollywood in search of work and posing in the nude because she was hungry and could not pay the rent.

Even when Marilyn made it big in pictures, she was still a frightened, insecure little girl. She was so unsophisticated and trusting and sincere—and she was used badly by just about everyone she came in contact with. There are some people who have an aura about them that's almost as blatant as a sign reading KICK ME and that's how it was with Marilyn. She loved people and wanted them to love her in return but too often they exploited their friendship with her for their own personal gain—whether career-wise or intimately. By the time Marilyn was a firmly established superstar she became so neurotic and had developed an inferiority complex so terrifying that she was frightened to leave her home. She was habitually late for appointments, but it wasn't that she was inconsiderate, just terrified of seeing people. And being the unsophisticated girl that she was, whenever tragedy struck, she simply could not handle it. Most glamorous stars move like queens through the throngs of reporters as they leave the courtroom after their latest divorce, but Marilyn couldn't do that. I remember the ugly scene of her split from Joe DiMaggio. She was wrapped up in beige mink, her eyes swollen from crying, her fluffy-duckling blond hair in wild disarray about her tear-streaked face as she tried to ward off the jabbing microphones that insensitive reporters stuck into her face every step of the way out of the courtroom.

And again, this time when she had suffered a miscarriage while married to Arthur Miller, they would not let her suffer in privacy but insisted on shouting stupid questions at her. 'Marilyn! Marilyn, is it true that you'll never be able to have babies?' Or—'Marilyn, does this mean that you will devote your time to your career?' And perhaps the most insulting of all, 'Marilyn, what are your measurements now?'

'Why can't they just leave me alone?' was her pathetic plea. 'What do they want from me? I don't understand.' And she did not understand. She was so innocent for all her ugly past and painful childhood. She believed anyone who took the time to talk with her. She always felt surprised and grateful that important people wanted to be in her company. She was even in awe of her own success and like many beautiful women, she did not think she was beautiful. 'Look at me—all pale and plain I'm not even pretty,' she said to me one day as we sat at her beach house. 'I wish I had Ava Gardner's coloring. To me, she's a real beauty.'

And I looked at her and saw such an adorable face—her skin was almost translucent in its pale perfection; her hair was like cotton candy spun by angels, with the same substance and texture; her figure was flawless and much smaller and vulnerable-looking in person. I shook my head, wondering if she was really that naive not to know how beautiful she was. She truly was unaware of her beauty but, for all her modesty, she had an innate vanity that came to the fore when needed—almost subconsciously, it seemed.

One afternoon we were at the beach, just kind of doing nothing, walking along the shore and looking for shells, talking about life. I had just driven out that morning and was dressed in a smashing new pants outfit that had cost a fortune and had matching everything. Marilyn was dressed in a pair of faded Levi's and a terrycloth halter that was worn and stretched. She was barefoot and totally without makeup while I had just come from the beauty salon and was coiffed and painted up like a Picasso.

A young man approached us and asked if he could take a picture. (He recognized Marilyn even in her undressed state.) She agreed, but only if I was in the picture with her. We stood side by side with the ocean behind us and the young man snapped his Polaroid. One instant before his finger released the shutter, Marilyn kind of shrugged her shoulders, straightening them. Her hip went up slightly and out, rounding sensually as her legs seemed to grow longer and slimmer before my eyes. She pulled herself up in that brief instant, throwing her head back so the blond tendrils were falling sexily across her forehead and curling around her face as her expression changed into one of warm seduction.

When the young man took the finished photograph from the Polaroid and showed it to us, I couldn't believe my eyes. There we stood, Marilyn in her faded blue jeans and sagging halter, looking every inch the glamorous and beautiful movie queen—and me, in all my finery, looking like the stepsister. It was a hell of a shot, one which I wish I had today. After the young man had thanked her profusely and rushed away with his prize, we continued to walk and Marilyn went back to being the artless girl. She didn't comment on it and I didn't know her well enough at that time to make any statement, but I've never forgotten it. That was either the best acting I'd ever seen or she had some built-in device that turned her into the public Marilyn Monroe whenever it was needed.

I visited with Marilyn quite a few times. I really liked her as a human being. I felt so sorry for her and knew what extreme pain she was suffering. She was so honest she couldn't have hidden her troubles even if she had tried. She was the most childlike creature I've ever met. A pure innocent. For all the ugliness of her past and all her unhappy love affairs and marriages, she seemed never to be hard and hitter. Rather, she seemed to become more insecure and childlike, always waiting for the butterfly to come out of the cocoon.

I remember one evening when she was staying at the Beverly Hills Hotel in one of the little cottages in the back. I was having cocktails with Jim Henaghan and two Texas millionaire oilmen in the Polo Lounge of the hotel and talk turned to Marilyn and the fact that she was staying there.

'Wanna meet her?' Jim asked the two cowboy millionaires. 'I know her intimately—she'll do anything I tell her.'

He wasn't exactly bragging. Marilyn and he had been buddies for many years and she was prone to do anything

Jim asked her. Of course, the boys couldn't say yes fast enough and soon we were walking through the gardens to Marilyn's cottage. It was quite late and we had obviously gotten her out of bed because she answered the door in her pajamas and rubbing sleep from her eyes. She looked like a small tow-headed child that had been roused from a deep slumber as she stood there in her large, baggy pajamas with her hair curling softly about her face and clinging to her neck in sweat-dampened tendrils.

'Hi, Jim,' she said softly and opened the door for all of us to come inside. Henaghan was quite drunk (as usual) and he wasted no time.

'These guys are buddies of mine from Texas,' he said. 'I want you to show them your appendectomy scar.'

Nodding sleepily, Marilyn pulled down her pajama bottoms, swaying slightly and yawning as the two men ogled her beige pubic hair and the tiny white scar that ran parallel with it.

Then, just as casually, she pulled her pajamas into place and climbed back into bed, asking Jim if he would tuck her in and give her a good-night kiss. The cowboys from Texas could not believe what they were witnessing.

It may seem rather cruel what Jim had done at Marilyn's expense that evening, but actually they were very close friends and enjoyed a relationship that was both beautiful and honest.

Jim was a brilliant man and had great insight into people and their problems. He pegged Marilyn the first time he saw her (at a press conference party) and took her aside and said, 'Don't let these creeps get to you, honey. They have to pull down their pants to take a shit, same as you and me!'

Marilyn cracked up giggling and clung to Jim throughout the rest of the party. When she won the Photoplay Award for Most Promising Newcomer, she sent it to Jim with a note saying that it really belonged to him because he had taught her how to handle 'the creeps.' Jim, not one to be bested, sent her a BB gun with a note saying, 'What else can a little boy give a little girl he likes a lot except his most prized possession—his BB gun.' Marilyn spent about seventy-five dollars to have that little toy rifle mounted above her bed. She had a rich mahogany plaque made with ornately carved brass arms to hold the little rifle, and she proudly showed it to friends.

But even the silly games of a little boy grown old and a frightened woman who could only play at childhood, could not save her from her destiny. She was almost violently unhappy, constantly seeking relief and escape from her very existence. She drank vodka and champagne, sometimes at the same sitting, and gulped sleeping-pills and tranquillizers by the dozens just to take the edge off and allow her to get through the night. Her days were little better. She had friends who worried about her and loved her and tried to help. But the nights—those long, agonizing nights with no one to talk to or hold close or even to eat dinner with.

I remember one evening with Marilyn that was pretty typical of her when she was feeling good. We were at a restaurant in Malibu, sitting at the bar as we waited for our table. The bartender kept staring at Marilyn and finally he walked over and said, 'Aren't you Marilyn Monroe?'

Marilyn's eyes grew round and she shook her head from side to side. I was afraid that she was going to have one of her stammering attacks where she would be so frightened of someone that she was literally unable to speak. But she surprised me. She began giggling and reached out and grasped the bartender's hand, laughing out loud now, and said, 'Oh, wow! Thank you! Hey, Nancy, did you hear what this guy said? He thinks I look like a movie star. Isn't that a scream?'

'She putting me on?' the bartender asked. 'She's Marilyn Monroe, ain't she?'

'People usually tell me that I look like Mamie Van Doren or Marie MacDonald,' Marilyn said, giving me a wink.

'Well,' he said coolly, miffed that he had been wrong. 'You could pass for that Monroe dame and that's the truth.' He gave her a closer look and added, 'I think she's got a few pounds on you, though.'

Marilyn and I laughed all through dinner at that one. It was to happen several more times when I was out with her. She was at her best when pretending not to be Marilyn Monroe.

However, when we were sitting together alone and having a vodka or three, she was painfully and acutely the tragic Marilyn Monroe that she had invented as an escape from being the lonely Norma Jean Baker. She found that no matter what name she called herself, the scars of a malnourished and loveless childhood was to plague her to the bitter end.

I talked with her two and a half weeks before she died and I knew that she was having terrible problems. It had nothing to do with her career (which was going well) or her physical well-being (she was the slimmest and prettiest and healthiest I had ever seen her) or men (there was no one man that she was in love with)—it had to do with the inner Marilyn or Norma Jean. There were life-long battles taking place inside her skull and heart that only an analyst could have known how to handle.

I was shocked at how nervous she had become. Her hands were constantly moving, plucking at a thread on the sofa, smoothing her skirt, fiddling with her hair, and she stammered more often and her voice was a weak whisper as if she were frightened to speak out loud for fear I would reprimand her. She seemed vague and fuzzy as if she had lost her equilibrium, and her life during that period was like an out-of-focus picture.

Poor little Marilyn, she was an innocent victim of her parents' neurosis. Born illegitimate, she never saw her father, and her mother's guilt and inability to cope with or really love the child drove her to search for the ever-elusive perfect love. Hers was an endless quest toward a mystical goal.

Maybe she sensed the end was near, but she did not kill herself. I fully believe that, because she was too frightened of life to end it. She was not strong enough or brave enough to commit suicide. I can almost see what took place that night she died as clearly as if I had been in the bedroom with her. She was alone (again), drinking (still), worried about the future, wanting more than anything a husband, a strong man in her life to protect her and listen to her dreams, and she couldn't find one. She saw all her woman friends and other actresses with their strong, handsome, successful husbands and their beautiful children, and she felt worthless and soiled and didn't think she deserved anything good because she was no good. The men she wanted always belonged to someone else; they would never belong to her because she wasn't worthy. She was too kind and sweet to be jealous of the wives of the men she coveted. She envied them and thought they deserved those wonderful men that she couldn't have. I had seen her in such moods, had heard her speak similar words, and that's the way it must have been that sultry August evening when there was no one there to hear her cry for help.

She was afraid of being alone, weary of problems, and sleep wouldn't come with her brain so full of her unhappiness. She would take a couple of sleeping pills, just to relax her and allow her to drift off to sleep. But sometimes the little red devils turn on a person and instead of giving them the oblivion they seek, they wire them and keep the thoughts churning, but on a more lethargic depressed level. Nothing to do but take a couple more, after all, they're strong and the doctor said they would give her relief. And, while waiting for the pills to take effect she had to have something to occupy her mind. A drink. Fixing a drink would keep her busy for awhile and sitting down to drink it would take up even more time—time for the pills to work and blessed sleep to come.

Sleep did come—but not the dawn.

no rainbow for judy

In Hedda Hopper's book, *The Whole Truth and Nothing But*, she stated: 'Our town worships success, the bitch goddess whose smile hides a taste for blood. She has a habit, before she destroys her worshippers, of turning them into a spitting image of herself. She has an army of beauties in attendance at her shrine.

'Not many survive the encounter with success. Wreathed in smiles, she kills them in cars, like Jimmy Dean; or with torment, like Marilyn Monroe; or with illness, like Jean Harlow. She turns them into drunkards, liars, or cheats who are as dishonest in business as in love.'

How astute is Miss Hopper's observation. I, too, have seen the bitch goddess, success, turn nice people into sick, ravaged, tormented souls who end up enjoying nothing of what they gave so dearly to obtain. Judy Garland was one such person. Her burning ambition for success finally consumed her. She was one of those child stars on the MGM lot back in the days of Louis B. Mayer. She was not cute, even as a child. She was chubby, short, stocky, with enormous round eyes under straight, dark brows. Mayer never liked Judy (whom he referred to as 'that fat kid, Garland') because he didn't think she was pretty enough to be a star.

His taste ran to the Shirley Temple look and he had under contract one of the most successful young girls of that era, Deanna Durbin. However, someone at MGM made the mistake of letting Deanna's contract lapse and she was whisked away by Universal Studios where she became an even bigger star and was given the honor of leaving her footprint in the cement at Graumann's Chinese Theater. This burned Judy up almost as much as it did Mayer. Judy moaned that she had been in show business longer than Deanna and still hadn't had a starring role; Mayer swore to get even with Universal by making Judy a bigger star than Deanna.

That's where it all started.

The shrewd mogul gave orders to the MGM commissary not to serve Judy anything but 'cottage cheese and chicken soup—no matter what she orders!' And soon the diet pills started. Not believing that the American public could fall in love with a chubby little girl, he set out to make her a skinny little girl. In fact, Judy was not even the first choice for her most popular movie role as Dorothy in *The Wizard of Oz*. They had wanted Shirley Temple hut her studio (20th Century Fox) would not release her. Grudgingly, the role was given to Judy, and she has been a superstar ever since.

She was still a child when the vicious cycle of Seconal and Benzedrine started. Determined to keep her name up in lights, she worked herself into near collapse and gulped diet pills for energy and to curb her appetite. At night, too exhausted to sleep, she would pop a Seconal and fall into bed and let unconsciousness take over. It was a pattern that was to follow her throughout her life.

She made one musical after another at MGM in those early days, working long, hard hours, driving herself into a frenzy of perfection, sometimes so dead tired she would faint at the end of the day's shooting. By the time she had reached her twenties, she was so thin and haggard-looking she appeared much older than her years. She was, by this time, addicted to Benzedrine and took them simply because she could not do without them. Friends tried to encourage her to eat but she would not—or could not.

Hers was a constant battle to be number one. Even when she had obtained 'living legend' status, she was not content. She relentlessly drove herself to be better—and then never believed that she was any good at all. She wanted desperately to be beautiful and she just simply was not. Her early life at MGM, under the heavy-handed rule of Mayer, ruined her forever. What an evil man he must have been. I can think of at least twenty stars that he destroyed with his cruelty and stupidity. Thank God the era of the all-powerful movie mogul is dead and gone.

I met Judy in London when I was there with Jim Henaghan and I found her a most enchanting and delightful person. That time Jim took me to see Judy's performance at the Palladium, as I watched (and wept) with everyone else in that huge theater, I found myself feeling great empathy for the slight, nervous figure up there behind the footlights. She seemed too frail to handle this onslaught of raw emotion that she was conjuring up as surely and deftly as if she were a sorceress.

There was something of the sorceress about Judy. She had the amazing ability to make hundreds of thousands of people from all over the world love her wholly and without reservation and to forgive her every indiscretion; but she could not keep the love of just one good man. She was so famous that the name Judy was all that was needed to sell a million records or fill the Hollywood Bowl to overflowing. In fact, the evening she appeared at the Hollywood Bowl it was cold and dreary and the rain poured down, but not one person seemed to notice or to care. They sat spellbound while their little star, the rainbow girl who believed in magic, spun tales of hope and love for them. I think she made people really believe in bluebirds and miracles and dreams that came true.

It's sad that she did not believe hard enough herself. She never thought she was any good and strove toward a perfection that was unattainable because she had already attained her perfection without quite realizing it. Her fans realized it. They knew they were witnessing greatness whenever she stepped onstage and threw back her head and played that tiny silver microphone like a solid gold trumpet.

Her personal life was as tragic as Marilyn Monroe's had been. She had terrible hang-ups about her mother that haunted her all her adult life. She was so hooked on pills and booze by the time she was thirty that it would have taken a much stronger person than herself to kick the habit of a lifetime.

I saw her several times after that first meeting in London. One time she would be reed slim, hands shaking, eyes blinking, nervous as hell, unhappy—the next time she would be fat, dumpy, the pounds settling on her small frame like so much unkneaded dough, her eyes almost disappearing into the bloated folds of flesh, still unhappy but not giving a damn. I felt so sorry for her.

Her problem was no different from Marilyn's or Elizabeth's. She wanted to be in love with a man that was in love with her. Sounds simple enough, doesn't it? And yet, every superstar sex symbol I have ever known couldn't find it. Out of all of them, Elizabeth was the only strong one, the only survivor. Judy's father had died when she was twelve; she started seeing a psychiatrist at eighteen; and she was married five times. Poor little Judy, who was used to seeing everything she wanted going to somebody else, could not convince herself (or her husbands) that she was worthy of love. So she continued her search for the perfect match, marrying and discarding one man after another until even her own children sneered at her attempts. When she was marrying for the fourth time, she allegedly called her daughter, Liza Minnelli, and invited her to the wedding. Said Liza, 'Gee, Mom, I'm sorry I can't make it. But I promise you I'll come to your next wedding!'

The actor Andre Phillippe, an old friend of mine (and Judy's) brought her to my house several times during the last years of her life. She looked terrible. She was depressed and shaky and slightly off-center. She drank quite a lot and excused herself frequently to go to the ladies' room where, I'm sure, she was popping another pill to help her get through the party. (She hid pills in cigarette packs.) I often wondered why she even bothered to go out if it was an effort to maintain just those few hours. She once locked herself in my guest bedroom and stayed there for the duration of the party, coming out only after all the guests and even the caterers had gone home. And yet, she seemed to enjoy herself at my house, I have always loved parties and used to give rather lavish ones that were the talk of the town.

How very sad that our little Judy, the miracle girl who sold hope and magic to millions, didn't have any left over for herself. She attempted suicide more than once, and finally died in 1969 at the age of forty-seven of an accidental overdose.

vera jane palmer mansfield hargitay cimber

An accurate accounting of Hollywood's tragic stars would not be complete without Jayne Mansfield's story. Hers was the most shocking, shameful, and wretched of all. I knew Jayne quite well for several years, and shared both good and bad times with her. She wanted to be a movie star from the time she was a very small girl named Vera Jayne Palmer, growing up in Dallas, Texas, and she used everything within her power to attain that dream.

Jayne hit Hollywood in 1954. She was just twenty-one years old, mother of an infant daughter, Jayne Marie, freshly separated from her young husband, Paul Mansfield, and thoroughly convinced that Hollywood was waiting for her alone. She lost no time. She snared the talents of Jim Byron and told him, 'I want to be a movie star and I know I'll need you. Shall we sign a contract?' Jim knew a good thing when he saw it and immediately put Jayne to work modeling bikinis and posing for every magazine he could think of.

Her first publicity gimmick paid off in spades. It was during the Christmas holidays and Jim came up with a rather unique idea of introducing Jayne to the press. Dressed in an extremely tight, sexy, low-cut gown, she visited the newspaper offices in Los Angeles. Slipping seductively into the columnist's or editor's office, she would present him with a bottle of booze, kiss him lingeringly upon the mouth, and wish him a Merry Christmas as she slipped out of the door and into the next office.

The scheme worked—better than even Byron had hoped—and the next day newspapers were filled with photos and descriptions of 'Hollywood's latest aspirant.' That was the beginning of a love affair between Jayne and those hard-nosed types that was to endure a lifetime. Jayne was shrewd enough to realize that she would need these boys in her corner if she was going to crash Hollywood's golden gates overnight and they knew that they would always get a good, sexy quote and a sexier photograph of the bustiest gal to hit town in a long time. They both got what they wanted.

Jayne had done a few small parts in movies and had had reams of publicity but her big break did not come until she had starred in the Broadway play *Will Success Spoil Rock Hunter?* When she returned to Hollywood, 20th Century Fox was waiting with a seven-year contract—and the rest, as they say, is history. She took off like a comet with the release of the screen version of *Will Success Spoil Rock Hunter?* followed closely by *The Girl Can't Help It.* Whatever Jayne wanted, Jayne got. She wanted a handsome Hungarian muscleman, Mickey Hargitay, and the fact that he was married did not stop her. It merely slowed her down. They had to wait for the divorce, but they waited it out together—mostly in bed.

By the late fifties, Jayne was the movie star she had always dreamed of being. Movie stars had to have the proper setting so she purchased a large, rambling, three-acre estate in Beverly Hills, painted it pink, and put Mickey to work refurbishing it in a style befitting a celluloid queen. I visited Jayne and Mickey's pink palace many times and was always a little in awe of it. It was certainly most grand, if a bit nouveau riche, with ankle-deep white carpets, velvet furnishings, crystal chandeliers dripping icily from every room in the house. Her bathroom was done in mirrored gold tile and held a sunken, heart-shaped bathtub; the floors and walls were carpeted with thick, pink plush and the faucets were twenty-four carat gold. Her bedroom was pink and white with a gigantic, specially made, heart-shaped bed, and a small alcove off to the side (which she called her 'balling room') that had a wall-to-wall mattress, and the whole affair, bed, walls, and ceiling were covered in thick, lush pink carpet.

It overlooked the huge, heart-shaped swimming pool which Mickey had built (lovingly) with his own two hands and had even signed in gold tiles 'I Love You, Jaynie' at the bottom near the steps. (Years after her death, when other tenants bought or rented the pink palace and tried to paint over the tiles, they would mysteriously reappear, refusing to stay covered and out of sight; much like Jayne Mansfield herself.) A large cabana-bar was built alongside the pool with a ceiling-to-floor aquarium built in behind the dark oak bar. The grounds were lush, plush, a garden of Eden, and I think that Jayne sometimes believed that she was the first woman, Eve. She thoroughly enjoyed her success and all that money, saying to me at one time, 'If you've got it, honey, why not flaunt it?'

Downstairs was a huge playroom with the entire walls and stairway covered with literally thousands or photographs and magazine covers of Jayne Mansfield, sex symbol. She had indeed arrived. She should have been happy, but she was not. She was restless, bored with Mickey and her two handsome sons, Mickey Jr. and Zoltan. She fumed and fretted to Jim that her career was not moving ahead fast enough. I can well imagine Jim's bewilderment. She had taken off like a rocket just a few short years before and was the most photographed and talked about star in the world —even more so than Elizabeth Taylor during that era. In fact, she became angry with her agent, Bill Shiffrin, one day and demanded of her assistant (and my good friend to this day), Raymond (Rusty) Strait, 'Get me the name of Elizabeth Taylor's agent!'

She was never satisfied, even as she cooed to the press that she was 'fabulously happy and very much in love with my husband,' and went on to prove it by practically raping poor Mickey whenever they were in public. One amusing tale is told of a plane trip they took to New York. They both disappeared into the same bathroom and it wasn't very long before even the squarest passenger knew what they were doing in there. One flight attendant was to say, 'The door on the bathroom was actually moving in and out as they bumped against it and I could hear Jayne's moans of passion.' They emerged, Jayne radiant as she always was after having sex, and returned to their seats. There they snuggled and cooed until they reached their destination.

Mickey was crazy in love with 'his Jaynie' and would do anything to please her. More than once I walked into their bedroom to find Mickey on his knees by the side of the bed, painting Jayne's toenails as she lolled back against pink cushions, sipping a bourbon and reading a script. Even though Jayne knew that Mickey worshipped her, it soon became a drag—and not nearly enough for the seething sex symbol of the fifties—she needed more, much more, adulation to feel truly loved.

While playing a gig in Las Vegas, she found a new turn-on—two men at once telling her how wonderful and beautiful she was. The gossip was hushed-up, but Jayne admitted it to Rusty; Mickey had walked in and caught her in bed with an agent and a young chorus boy. Things were never the same after that and I, personally, feel that was the beginning of Jayne's tragic plunge downhill.

It wasn't long after that incident that I began to notice the nervousness and restlessness with which Jayne moved through her days. She was taking diet pills, she told me, to help keep her weight down. This did not shock or surprise me. In the fifties and sixties (before all the reports were in on drugs) just about every star, starlet, housewife, teenager, and me, were popping pills as a means to keep our wafer-thin figures. Jayne, however, wanted results yesterday and she took to popping three or four spansules (timed-release) a day—washed down with a tall glass of bourbon. It was a lethal combination. Mickey objected vehemently to the pills and booze, and Jayne, trying to keep peace in the family, took to hiding her supply of pills and to sneaking drinks when he wasn't around.

They began fighting daily and did not stop even when friends or business associates dropped by. Jayne began to openly flaunt her sexual encounters with other men and then to jeer at Mickey for being so spineless as to just accept her promiscuity and not do a damn thing about it. She wanted him to beat her up, curse her, or, better still, leave her. She did not believe that he was a 'man' if he would calmly accept the fact that his wife was a tramp. Mickey saw it differently. He felt that his love was strong enough to pull Jayne through this defiant period she was going through.

'Why would I leave her?' he said miserably. 'I love her so much—would you leave someone you loved just because they are sick?' What a wonderful, sweet guy Mickey was and how badly Jayne mistreated him.

By this time the vicious cycle of booze, uppers, downers, and tantrums had flourished into an everyday nightmare. She took so many pills to keep her up that she could not come down to sleep without as many more downers, followed by a whole fifth (sometimes more) of bourbon. Sometimes even this deadly combination would not work and sleep still evaded her. That's when she would pace the floor of her elegant pink palace and conjure up some wild scheme to get more publicity or a different, more exciting man.

She found him in Italy while doing a picture there. His name was Bomba and she enjoyed a tempestuous love affair with him, even going so far as to invite him to visit her in

Hollywood where she was still married to Mickey. God knows what would have happened to this sick triangle had not a much larger tragedy struck.

In August of 1962, Marilyn Monroe died and sent Jayne reeling into shock. She took the news like her own death sentence and mourned Marilyn for weeks. It was a period of heavier doses of booze and pills, self-pity, recriminations, hopelessness. The short, quick trip down the road of no return had officially begun.

Her career was going to pot along with everything else in her life. All of Jim Byron's carefully laid plans for her had been personally screwed up by Jayne herself. Her wild, distasteful antics and her public display of bad manners and blatant sexuality made a mockery of the sweet girl from Texas who Jim saw as an intellectual, though sexy, movie star. It was the final blow when she fired him.

From the superstar of *Will Success Spoil Rock Hunter?* both on Broadway and in the movie version just a few short years ago, Jayne had slipped way down the ladder to appear in a nudie-cutie flick called *Promises, Promises*—a ninety-minute dirty joke produced by Tommy Noonan. She was so stoned on pills and booze when she did her nude scenes that fellow workers feared she'd drown in her bubble bath. How Mickey managed to stick it out with her I'll never know, but he continued to follow her everywhere she went, trying, I suppose, to keep a little stability in her life.

While on tour with her nightclub act, she fell in love again. This time with a singer and performer named Nelson Sardelli, and immediately sent Mickey home so she could have an uninterrupted affair with Nelson. She had wanted his baby from the moment she laid eyes on him and, as mentioned earlier, whatever Jaynie wanted, Jaynie got. She became pregnant and was radiant with love. Mickey, finally defeated, signed the divorce papers.

If her love life flourished with the thrice daily administerings of Nelson Sardelli, her career did not. Her performances were in gross bad taste and could not even be completed without the daily consumption of a fifth of bourbon and a handful of pills. Audiences that once had whistled, cheered, and stamped on the floor for Jayne Mansfield, now booed her and left before the show was over. Very soon there was not even an audience to leave because, on more than one occasion, there was no audience at all.

Her attacks of manic-depression (that's what bipolar disorder was called in back then) and her fits of rage were increasing at a terrifying and shockingly steady rate. On more than one occasion she threatened to kill her lover with a broken whiskey bottle, and cursed and raved at even her closest friends and relatives. It was now obvious to everyone that Jayne needed the care of a psychiatrist—to no one did a damn thing about it! Said Jayne, 'They wouldn't dare have me committed. Who would pay all the bills around here?'

Her affair with Nelson came to a screeching halt and she returned to Mickey where, in January of 1964, she gave birth to the little baby she had always wanted, a girl named Mariska. Mickey's strong arms and broad shoulders sheltered both mother and child as he took them home to the pink palace. What other guy would do that for a woman who had embarrassed, hurt, and misused him?

I remember when Mickey was involved with Joe Louis (the boxer) in some venture he had going at the old nightclub, The Moulin Rouge, where he put on prize fights every Friday and Saturday nights. I went several times with them and sat with Jayne as Mickey clearly did not trust her to be alone. I was shocked at her reaction. Arriving quite bored and in a sour mood, Jayne sat slumped down in her seat until the young boxers jogged onstage and into the ring. At the first blow she sat up a little straighter; at the first sign of blood she was leaning forward in her seat, a fine sheen of sweat on her upper lip, and as the pounding in the ring went on, breaking noses and causing blood to spurt from open gashes, Jayne could barely contain herself. Clenching her fists, her eyes dilated like a junkie, she hissed, 'Kill him! Kill the bastard! Make him bleed! I want to see blood!'

I was horrified the first time I witnessed her obsession with violence and blood and remembered it much, much later (when it was too late)—when she was already destroying herself and her last boyfriend, Sam Brody. But this night I was not aware of how very sick she had become. Mickey asked me to drive her home and as we walked outside to my car I was aware of Jayne's restlessness. She wiggled and squirmed like a cat in heat as we drove down Sunset Boulevard toward her home. The moment we were inside the pink palace she went straight to the telephone and dialed a number, spoke urgently into the receiver, then hung up.

'Nancy, do me a favor, will you?' she asked as she poured a healthy slug of bourbon into a glass and dug into her purse for her pills. 'I've got to get fucked—those boxers turned me on so much, I can't tell you!' She gulped down the booze and pills, rubbed her crotch with her free hand, and continued, 'Will you stand guard for me? You know, stick around awhile and if Mickey comes home before I'm through, try to keep him busy—no matter how you have to do it!' She gave me a wink as she slipped out of her dress and ran lightly up the stairs to her pink bedroom. This sort of thing was quickly becoming the norm in Jayne's life and I was quickly becoming shock-proof concerning the eccentricities of my friend, the sex queen. A moment later a tall, good-looking man arrived, nodded in my direction, and went up to join Jayne. She was lucky that night. Her resident stud had already finished and gone before Mickey got home.

Every time we attended the fights (which was often now that Jayne knew what the sight of beating up another human being did to her sexually) this scene was to repeat itself. Usually she was already undressed by the time we reached her pink palace, as the moment we got into my car she began flinging off her clothes with a kind of frenzy.

One evening a very funny incident happened. We were driving along Sunset Boulevard and Jayne was half-naked, as usual, higher than a kite, drunk, giggling, horny as hell because a sexy, young Mexican kid had been busted up pretty badly in the ring that night, and she was looking to get laid. A car was keeping right alongside us and Jayne had noticed the fact that the driver was a young, handsome guy. She was hanging out of the window, giggling, trying to catch his attention even as I tried to pull her back and tell her to behave herself. Glancing over, I saw that the guy in the other car was my old buddy, Griff the Bear, and I waved and yelled, 'Hello, Bear!'

'Who is it? Do you know him, Nancy?' Jayne asked, peering intently into Griff's car as if she were sizing him up for dinner.

'Sure,' I answered. 'It's Griff you know, my old friend? You've met him—he worked with you and Mickey at The Home Show when you guys were showing your barbells and stuff.'

'Griff?' she fairly shrieked. 'You mean the one with the big cock?' She flung herself half out of the window, the famous Mansfield boobs naked and gleaming in the street lights as she yelled, 'Hey, Griff—wanna fuck?'

Jayne's final miles were quickly approaching by 1964. She was still the most talked about sex symbol in the world, but now people were referring to her as a dirty joke and the photographs of her showed a booze-bloated face painted in a parody of a sex goddess (a la Cleopatra), topped by an uncombed tangle of blond hair and wiglets. Her outfits would have been appropriate on a sixteen-year-old girl (skin-tight miniskirts and white go-go boots), but on a big, busty woman of thirty they merely looked ludicrous.

Her movie career was all but washed up and she reluctantly went back to New York and the stage—but not on Broadway as she had begun. This time she was slated for a run at Yonkers Playhouse in one of Marilyn Monroe's old vehicles, *Bus Stop*. The director, Matt Cimber, was a young, ambitious Italian, and, as everyone knew, Jayne loved anything Italian—especially their sausages! It was 'Goodbye, Mickey' again and 'Ciao, Matt' as Jayne proceeded to charm her third and final husband. She promptly moved Matt and his entourage into her suite of hotel rooms where they balled every spare moment that she was not onstage.

As always, Jayne had several dogs with her as she 'couldn't travel without them' and it wasn't long before the hotel carpets were replaced with wall to wall dog-shit. It was a scene that was to become a part of Jayne's remaining days. Wherever she went after that, hotel managers all over the United States had the embarrassing task of telling her that she was not welcome back. Several magazines and newspapers ran articles describing the utter, stinking mess that Jayne and her entourage left behind them when they checked out; broken whiskey bottles, crushed beer cans, dog mess everywhere, urine-stained beds, drapes and carpets and just plain dirt and disregard in every room. As with most junkies and alcoholics, Jayne no longer cared if she was clean or dirty—just as long as she was high.

I remember running into Jayne one evening at Jerry Lewis' old restaurant on the Sunset Strip and how shocked I was at her appearance. She was wearing a lowcut white dress that dipped almost to the navel, a white fox stole with a white satin lining that was more gray than white. It was streaked and stained with old makeup and just plain old-fashioned dirt all over the inside, and had fallen to the floor where one of the guys at the table had unconsciously placed his foot upon it. I picked up the fox stole, folded it to cover the dirty lining, and handed it to Jayne.

'Here, Jaynie,' I said. 'You'd better watch this thing or somebody may walk off with it.'

She merely shrugged, then said, 'You want it—you can have it.'

'No, I don't want it,' I said.

'Okay, then how about a drink?' I sat down and we talked for a few minutes. She really looked like hell. She was wearing several falls in her hair, all different shades of blond, that looked so cheap and obvious. Her eyes were painted in those thick, black lines that now were melted and greasy, looking like slick, oily snakes. Her lipstick was smeared. The small, fine lines around her neck were caked with days-old makeup that settled in the creases. Just then, Vic Damone (who was appearing there that evening) came onstage and began singing. Jayne's eyes gleamed and she squeezed my arm and breathed, 'God! He's gorgeous! I want that man!' I didn't have the heart to tell her that a decent man like Vic Damone would not be caught dead with the woman Jayne Mansfield had become. I left early, so I do not know the outcome of the evening.

Jayne and Matt were still making headlines and ugly stories appeared about 'a kidnapping' (Mickey had taken the baby, Mariska, away from Jayne, as he considered it an unsafe place for an infant) and newspapers ran an almost daily account of the continuing battle. Mickey and Matt actually traded blows for the grinding television cameras and cursed one another for the media. It was a sordid time for a once glamorous movie star.

Matt and Jayne were finally married, in Mexico, and nothing was ever the same again. Jayne did not love Matt and the day after the wedding she took Rusty aside, and whined forlornly, 'Cooz, tell me why I married Matt?' That was her nickname for her friend, and it's stuck to this day.

However, regardless of the fact that Rusty had known Jayne intimately for ten grueling years, he could not answer that question, and so Jayne buried her mistake in a fifth of bourbon. (Rusty wrote a tell-all about the time he spent with his famous and eccentric boss, entitled *The Tragic, Secret Life of Jayne Mansfield*, which I consider to be the best ever written about a public figure.)

Jayne's drinking was so intense by this time that many thought it would kill her if the pills didn't get her first. Her home life was nonexistent. Her two sons by Mickey and her daughter by Nelson Sardelli were kept by this maid and that one, sometimes (more often than not) they were given in the care of Jayne Marie, the teenage daughter who was an innocent victim of this horror movie that was her life.

Jayne's career was also nonexistent. Every major movie studio in town knew of her alcohol and pill addiction and wanted no part of her. The lesser, independent studios offered her parts in the currently popular skin flicks... pornography. But something of the old Jayne still lived within her and she refused to even read the scripts.

Her nightclub engagements were few and far between and the money was almost embarrassing; she now received for the run of the act the same money she had been paid for one night's performance just a few short years before. Her audiences, who had once loved the impish blond bombshell, now left in disgust as she staggered onstage, tripping over light cords and practically falling into the orchestra pit, as she was too stoned to stand up. A few diehards stuck around for the strip number so they could tell their friends that they had seen Jayne Mansfield naked, but that was about all. (Against everyone's wishes and advice, Jayne insisted on stripping in every act; she had a compulsion to show her body to the world.)

She fought Matt like a tiger, trying to claw his eyes out even as he tried to help her to bed and the much-needed sleep that was hard in coming. She had taken so many sleeping pills during her life that they no longer had any effect on her; instead of calming her, they wired her in combination with the booze and uppers. Matt had to resort to shoving suppositories up the famous Mansfield derriere almost nightly so her exhausted body would have at least a few hours of rest to rebuild some of the damage done by the drugs and alcohol.

She cheated on Matt with anyone who took her fancy and dared him to leave her if he didn't like it. She openly rebelled against any advice given her by her family or friends and made life a living hell for anyone unfortunate enough to be trapped in the same room with her for any period of time.

She was a sick, sick woman, and yet not even those who professed great love for her did anything about it. All it took was a signature by a member of the family to have her committed to an institution where, perhaps, something could have been done to arrest her psychotic condition. They were reluctant, I guess, because even in her mentally deteriorated state, Jayne still pulled in enough money to pay everyone's bills. When I think of such a thing my stomach turns, and I wonder who the 'sick' ones really were.

Jayne's final act came when she kicked out Matt and embraced a sadistic attorney, Sam Brody. Brody was the only man who was able to match Jayne drink for drink, rage for rage, mood for mood. In fact, he even taught her a few new quirks in her already twisted mind. He turned her on to that old killer, LSD, and together they flew higher than the highest high. So high that there was no place else to go- but down.

Jayne had had a beautiful baby son, Tony, by Matt Cimber, and when she kicked him out, Matt started proceedings to have his son taken away from Jayne. God knows, he was well-acquainted with her fits of violence, despondency, and drug-induced illnesses, and he feared for his son's safety. It was to be a long, drawn-out court battle, one that was settled only when Jayne was dead.

Jayne, who once had been touted as 'Hollywood's best mother,' began mistreating her children shamelessly. The baby, Tony, seemed to receive the brunt of her rages and she would kick him and slap him and lock him up in a small room off the maid's quarters, a room that was without heat or even within hearing distance of the other part of the house. Rusty told me on many occasions how shocked he had been by Jayne's treatment of her children. Rusty was perhaps the only man in Jayne's life (with the exception of Mickey) who truly loved her and cared enough to be extremely worried with her sickness.

'More and more I began to notice the huge, black bruises and cuts on Jayne whenever I saw her,' Rusty told me once. 'I knew what was happening; Sam was beating her up again—but what could I do? She apparently liked it—even begged him to beat her.' He shook his head sadly. 'I don't know, Nancy—I just don't know...'

The more Jayne got into LSD the more she rejected reality. For a woman who once loved babies so much that she refused to take birth control pills, she now turned on her offspring and seemed to want to kill them.

One passage in Rusty's book stands out in my mind for its horrible sickness. Sam Brody had telephoned Rusty and as they were talking, Rusty asked, 'Is it true that you really beat up Jayne Marie?' (The daughter.)

'Well-yes. I mean, I whipped her with the belt. But I never hit her in the face. Not that Jayne didn't want it. I was whipping her with the belt and Jayne was screaming at me over the intercom, 'Beat her! Kill her! Black her eyes like you do mine! If you love me, make her bleed. I want to see some blood. Make her bleed!' That's when I stopped. She wanted me to beat her daughter up, but she didn't want to watch. I was letting her hysteria motivate me. I was sick. I just dropped the belt and stopped. So help me God, Cooz, I never hit the child in the face!'

The scene turned my stomach and I visualized the terrified teenager, Jayne Marie, running out into the night and walking to the nearest police station where she stammered out her horrible story to the officers on duty. It became a court case, of course, but with the cunning and sadistic Sam Brody as Jayne's attorney, little Jayne Marie didn't stand a chance. She was sent back home to endure as much as she could before fate freed her from her mother's tortured, demented grasp.

Then there's Rusty's recollection of another grim incident: Rusty had gone to Jayne's house at her request to look over some business papers that needed attention. He says:

'I couldn't have been gone more than five minutes when the air was pierced by a blood-chilling scream. *My God*, I thought, *Sam is killing her.* I raced through the house to the red leather office, certain that I would finally have to confront Sam physically. Rushing into the office, I stopped in my tracks. Jayne was climbing the bookshelves, her throat filled with such screeching noises that she sounded more animal than human.

'What's the matter?' I was completely baffled.

'The lizards, the lizards! The fucking lizards!' she screamed. 'Look at them! Oh, my God, look at them!' She clung to the shelf with one hand and poked her finger toward the desk.

'I started to ask what lizards when I heard Sam's voice: 'Do it, Baby, do it. Beautiful. Eat the little pussy, little lizards eat the little pussy.'

'My head jerked to the right—there huddled in the corner was Sam, crouching and masturbating, eyes set and glassy. His tongue kept flicking his lips as he hammered himself toward some incredible satisfaction.

'That was the last time I ever saw Jayne Mansfield, and the memory of that ugly moment haunts like the specter of the photographs of her horrible ending.'

On July 29, 1967, on a dark and deserted stretch of Louisiana highway, Vera Jayne Palmer Mansfield Hargitay Cimber met her death at the age of thirty-three. Also dead was the driver of the automobile and the last lover Jayne would ever have, Sam Brody. They apparently had crashed into the rear-end of a slow-moving truck—and their fast-moving automobile climbed right up inside the truck's entrails, slicing off the top of the sedan as well as the heads of the three occupants in the front seat. The three children, Mickey Jr., Zoltan, and little Mariska, escaped injury when some suitcases fell on top of them, protecting them from the final impact.

Jayne had been a Hollywood movie star and sex symbol for exactly thirteen years. A very short-lived career for a girl who wanted to be the biggest superstar in all the world— but it was thirteen years too long considering the way she used them. Poor little Jaynie would have all the rest she needed now.

My reaction was typical, I suppose. I was shocked—but not too surprised. Rusty called at dawn of that tragic morning, his voice husky with emotion and unshed tears as he tried to piece it all together. He had loved Jayne and had been one of the most important mainstays in her life for ten of her turbulent years. He did not know what to do with himself.

Mickey stopped by my house one afternoon, his eyes reddened with the many tears he had shed even though it was days later. He looked thin and old beyond his years, but there was about him a kind of peace, as if he knew that now his little Jaynie belonged to no one but him. For even as Jayne flaunted her indiscretions, Mickey remained the one man she truly loved throughout her life, and when he claimed her body and laid it to rest, it was almost the same as being back in the safety of Mickey's strong, protective arms.

Jayne Mansfield's life, both privately and professionally, had been a vast stage; the footlights were dimmed forever now and the orchestra pit was empty. The audience had gotten their money's worth and had all gone home.

Her daughters fared better in spite of the odds, thank God. Mariska Hargitay is a famous TV actress, and, after famously following in their mother's footsteps by posing for Playboy—making her the first daughter of a Playmate who appeared in the magazine herself—Jayne Marie bowed out of the scene and is rarely spotted in public.

laurence harvey, r.i.p.

In the late fifties and early sixties, Laurence Harvey was the darling of the jet set. As I said previously, he was

British, handsome, dashing, suave, debonair, outrageous, a social climber and perhaps the first self-professed homosexual in show business. He adored brilliant, outrageous people and surrounded himself with the infamous. He seemed to have a penchant for older women, and his much-publicized love affairs and marriages were always with ladies several years his senior. (His unpublished love affairs were something else again!)

I met him for the first time at Trader Vic's where I was dining with Jim Henaghan. Larry came sailing through the restaurant like a fluttering peacock, kissing a captain here, pinching a waiter's ass there, nodding, beaming, bestowing his radiant smile upon the open-mouthed patrons as he swept toward our table. He had the aura of a swashbuckler about him and I'm still not sure in my memory if he was wearing a full, flowing cape that evening. If he wasn't, he certainly gave the appearance of having worn one. He glided smoothly to a halt, unraveled gracefully into a chair, wrapping one slender ankle snake-like about his other ankle as he took my hand and kissed it firmly, gazing mischievously into my eyes. With a chuckle he dropped my hand, grabbed Jim in a tight hug and kissed him soundly upon the mouth!

'Henaghan!' he shouted joyously, 'how the hell are you?' He held Jim by the shoulders and looked at him with genuine warmth. 'So the mad Irishman returns,' he said fondly.

They exchanged friendly obscenities for a few moments and fell easily into recounting old times they had known together. I sat spell-bound, fascinated with the charming Mr. Harvey, captivated by his flawless speech and fetching accent, his movie-star perfect good looks, his enthusiasm and zest for life. I wonder if he knew he would die young? He seemed so intent upon living life to the hilt. Around every corner was a new adventure, a new pleasure. He was a true hedonist—one of the few I was to meet in my life.

He was doing a film with Elizabeth Taylor, he told us, a little piece of puff called *Butterfield 8* which he detested, but it was made bearable by the presence of Elizabeth. 'I simply adore her,' he gushed, leaning forward to emphasize the point. 'She's something special—she's as bawdy as a waterfront broad, and yet she's so fucking majestic and sort of queenly I sometimes get the urge to drop to one knee when she enters a room!' He laughed gaily, downed his drink in one swallow, and beckoned the waiter for refills all around. 'She's the most honest and open person I've ever met,' he went on, deftly fitting a cigarette into a long, slim black holder. 'I think I shall have to marry her. She has the power to make anyone—husband or lover—a superstar by mere association. And I most definitely wish to be a super, super star!' He leaned back, puffing contentedly from his chic holder, his eyes half-closed in thought. 'Yes, I shall simply have to marry her,' he murmured softly. 'But I suppose I must wait until she tires of that Jewish lad, Eddie—you know, the boy who sings for a living.'

Actually, Eddie Fisher was not doing much singing during that period of his life. His main occupation seemed to be following Elizabeth at a respectable distance of ten feet, struggling with dogs, cats, children, luggage, hairdressers, and go-fers, while she snapped over her shoulder, 'Hurry up, Eddie! Where is that stupid husband of mine now?'

Jim and I attended a party Elizabeth and Eddie threw for the Russian Moiseyev Dancers when they appeared in Los Angeles. They had taken over P.J.'s (a popular night spot of the era) and the place was packed with stars and persons of importance. Larry had been dating Joan Cohen (widow of the hated movie tycoon, Harry Cohen) and we joined them at their table.

Elizabeth looked enchanting. She was the slimmest I have ever seen her, and when her weight is just right, she has a perfect figure; most sexy and bewitching. She wore a simple black sheath, skintight, and her dark hair was completely hidden by a close-fitting, caplike hat made of emerald green and black feathers. Her magnificent purple eyes sparkled with mischief as she watched Larry ogling the taut-assed young male Russian dancers. Joan's eyes, on the other hand, narrowed jealously as she watched.

No one stayed any one place for very long; it was one of those parties where a lot of table-hopping went on. I chanced upon Larry and Elizabeth sitting at the bar on tall stools, deep in animated conversation and I stopped to listen. They were both laughing and I heard Larry say, 'You know why I adore you? You're as big a cunt as I am!' To which Elizabeth replied, 'Nobody's as big a cunt as you are, Larry!'

'Say you'll marry me,' he pleaded urgently, grasping her two hands in his and leaning in close and adoringly. She merely laughed and shook her head-much as a harassed mother will when her child is acting up. She and Larry were good friends and enjoyed the outrageousness of their lives.

The party went on into the wee hours-with everyone getting progressively drunker—with the exception of Joan who was getting progressively angrier as she watched Larry flitting about the room and flirting with everyone in sight. Finally, she asked Jim and me to drive her home. As we wound our way through the undulating mob, there was Larry, three young male dancers in his arms, his hands doing as much exploring as possible and his wine-scented lips seeking out Russian territory. He waved magnanimously before he was literally sucked up into the hugging arms.

Of course, Joan forgave him. No one could stay angry with Larry for long. He was too much fun and too cute. I remember when he did *Walk on the Wild Side* with Barbara Stanwyck. Everyone on the set was anxiously and nervously awaiting their first meeting. Larry had gained something of a prima donna reputation since his arrival on our shores and Miss Stanwyck, as everyone knew, was a tried and true professional; a real thoroughbred. Director and crew expected fireworks. Larry sauntered in, quite late, dressed in a brocade smoking jacket, his ever-present cigarette holder clenched between his perfect white teeth, a sweetly pungent odor of wine lingering about his breath. He hated doing this movie; he had not wanted to make it but he owed it to the studio, therefore he had no choice. However, he wasn't going to make it easy on 'the bloody bastards.'

Only his very closest friends called him by a rather odd nickname—Florence—and how Miss Stanwyck discovered this, no one knew. She put her hands on her hips, took her famous, legs-apart stance, fixed Larry with a steely gaze and growled, 'All right, Florence, get your ass in gear—we've got a picture to make!'

Larry's mouth fell open, he stared, everyone held their breath—then he threw back his head and laughed boisterously.

'Ah, my dear Missy,' he cooed, taking her hand and grinning broadly. 'How delightfully you Americans speak.' He kissed her hand and grinned roguishly, 'Well, shall we get crackin'?'

Barbara's nickname is Missy and no one calls her that without her permission, so it was her turn to gape. But only for a moment. She gave him a smack on the ass, grinned right back at him and said, 'Right—let's get crackin'.'

They worked wonderfully together during the entire shooting of the movie. Capucine, their co-star, did not fare as well, however. Larry detested her almost as much as he detested the script, and as he portrayed her lover in the film they were in many scenes together. I remember him complaining bitterly to the director that 'kissing Capucine is like kissing the side of a beer bottle,' and when the movie was completed he tried everything in his power to have his name deleted from the credits.

Hollywood, known for its stupidity, seemed always to cast Larry as a southern heel, and I feel that is one of the reasons his career did not flourish as it should have.

'Why do these clods insist upon casting me as a bloody bore?' he asked me one afternoon as we sat at my pool, sipping wine. 'The script looks good when I read it, then when the actual shooting starts it's just so much muddle.' He had made his big splash in *Room at the Top*, an English film starring Simone Signoret, where he played a cold, calculating young man who used women for social advancement and career connections. That part suited him perfectly as did his role in *Darling*, the movie that launched Julie Christie's career. Larry's favorite film, however, was *The Manchurian Candidate*, with Frank Sinatra. He simply loved working with Frank and had something of a schoolboy crush on him. ('What a bright, bright man,' he said to me once. 'I'm actually in awe of him.') But with these few exceptions, Larry's Hollywood career was a bust.

When I heard that he had been cast in The Alamo with the big Duke, John Wayne, I couldn't believe it. I somehow could not fathom Laurence Harvey with horse manure on his boots and a pistol strapped to his hip. He was not happy with the scripts that were presented to him and his personal life was unsatisfactory as well.

He was drinking too much and keeping late hours with unsavory companions. When I saw him in *Darling* I was shocked. He had aged considerably and looked tired and dissipated. It wasn't just makeup; I knew Larry too well— he was most definitely an ill man. I wished I could talk to him and find out what was troubling him, but he was spending much of his time abroad those days. I remembered when I had first met him—how he would bop over, unannounced, in the wee hours if the morning, insist that I go back to bed he just wanted to chat a moment— then, making himself comfortable on the other side of my king-size bed, he would 'chat' for hours bout his life and goals. Finally he would drop off and I would get an extra blanket to cover him for the rest of the night. He always lay down on the top of the covers and insisted that I stay in bed and 'not make a fuss' over him. It would have been good to have another of those intimate chats with Larry during his unhappy period.

I saw him again at Elizabeth and Eddie Fisher's second wedding anniversary party which was held at Au Petit Jean's in Beverly Hills, he came bouncing into the room, gay as ever, kissed a maitre'd, pinched a few asses on his way to our table, grinning boyishly at everyone. But I could see the pain in his eyes and the weariness of expression. We were sitting with John and Pilar Wayne and Larry came tip-toeing over, leaned down, and kissed Duke on the ear. Without even looking around, Duke muttered, 'Christ— it's that nut, Harvey.'

'Right you are, old man,' Larry grinned and sat down with us for a moment He became quite drunk during the evening and insisted that I sing a folk song with him entitled *Oh Shit!*—which I did. George Burns accompanied us by humming and throwing one-liners at the rest of the guests— 'I've got cigars older than this child,' indicating me. 'What's she doing out so late?'

Larry's fun and games and wild antics were becoming a bit of a bore to some of his old friends. He didn't seem to know when to stop. He made a complete fool of himself one night at The Daisy. George Jacobs (Frank Sinatra's valet), Mia Farrow, and Joey Tata (a young Italian actor), were having a sort of birthday party for George. Larry came careening through the dimly lit room, spied them, and immediately joined them, calling for wine. He became quite drunk and surly and used such bad language that even those sophisticated show biz folks were embarrassed and disgusted.

'I'd like to take a bite right out of you,' he slurred thickly to George, a well-built black man.

'Aw, you don't want to do that, Mr. Harvey,' George laughed uneasily. 'I'm too old and tough.' He slapped Joey on the back and said, 'Why don't you try this nice, tender young Italian here?' He was trying to keep it light, play it for laughs, but Larry was dead serious.

'No… don't want no young Italian kid… want you.' He moved in closer, swaying now with the effects of the grog and fixed George with a leer. 'I'd like to munch up your big brown body… all of it,' he mumbled as he almost fell from his chair.

This kind of conversation went on for some time with Larry becoming more frank in what he intended doing to George once he got him alone. It was clear that Mia was embarrassed and they all felt sorry for Larry; they had all been good friends and they were reluctant to ask him to leave. They tried to get him to eat something— 'Come on, Mr. Harvey,' George said. 'Just have a little piece of my birthday cake.'

'Rather have a piece of you,' Larry responded.

'Come on, Larry,' Joey coaxed, 'let us put you in a cab—you'd better go home while you can still walk!'

'Don't wanna go home—got no home—wanna munch up brown body.' He downed his drink and signaled the waiter for another.

'Let's get him out of here before he passes out or gets sick on the table,' George said, and he and Joey told Larry that The Daisy was closing and couldn't serve him another drink. They helped Larry to his feet and propelled him outside where they tried to get him into a cab. But Larry pulled away and went weaving down the street, alone, mumbling to himself. That was the last time any of them saw him.

'God, he looked terrible,' Joey told me the next day. 'His face was ravaged and dissipated and he seemed so damn unhappy—and alone.' He paused, then added thoughtfully, 'There's nothing anyone could have done for him. He seemed to actually resent our offers of help.'

I heard other stories of Larry and how he was rushing madly downhill to disaster. His homosexual activities became more notorious and his drinking became legendary. I had not seen him for several years, and whenever I read an account of his shocking activities I wished again that he would drop in on me for one of his 'midnight chats' maybe I could have helped.

Larry's drinking was completely out of control by this time but there were few rehabilitation centers in those days. The common consensus about alcoholism was that it was a matter of will power. If you wanted to quit drinking, you just did. If you didn't, you were a weak-willed bum. There were no Betty Ford Centers or Hazelden's to ease the addict into sobriety.

Larry Harvey died in 1973, still a young man, but aged from within. Just another victim of that lethal equalizer—booze.

other faces, other parties, other jokes

'Give the public what it wants,' is an old show biz adage that seems quite appropriate when it comes to the seamy side of our idols. The public greedily and with much horror and delicious shock eats up the star's misfortunes and smacks their lips for more. Even as they adore them and pay howling tribute, they cannot help but scream for all the gory details when they learn that one of the 'beautiful people' has taken an overdose of amphetamines or barbiturates, has had a miscarriage or divorce or illicit love affair.

Smart producers and screenwriters have taken advantage of this macabre curiosity, and television and movie screens are filled with violence, horror, sex, and loneliness, misery, and pain. In the olden days, movies were so wholesome and idealistic that studios refused to allow their stars to say 'damn' or show anything sexier than a bare knee. The ending in those old films inevitably had the chaste stars kiss and clench passionately, then slowly sink down and out of the frame as the music swelled on the sound track and a breeze played in the leaves of a tree and clouds glided symbolically across a stormy sky. In the sixties and seventies, in the first reel our stars are in bed making love, and then they go on to get acquainted for the remainder of the movie.

What happened to Hollywood? Growth. The founding fathers of the movie industry were a sharp, street-shrewd type who made it the hard way and ruled with an iron hand. They chose their stable of stars well and carefully and ran their lives both off and on the set. But they made one mistake. In their desire to own everything they failed to look ahead to the future.

The producers and heads of studios (Mayer, Cohen, Goldwyn) had hand-picked their stables, and they were as impressive as hell: Errol Flynn, Bette Davis, Clark Gable, John Barrymore, Greta Garbo, Susan Hayward, Humphrey Bogart, James Cagney—all the old tried and true thoroughbreds—the ones who showed up for work and put in a full day and took all the guff that directors handed down simply because they figured that was the way it was. They really had no identity; they were awed by studio power and the extreme changes in their lives due to the clever manipulating of those feared moguls. They were a part of the glamour mold and if their crowns set just a bit uneasily upon their heads, well, that, too, could be rationalized. They had been tapped by the finger of fate and they were the chosen ones.

In the early sixties, Old Hollywood was pronounced officially dead. Young blood was coming and taking over. Times were changing. It was a new era. Television was firmly established and was taking moviegoers away from the theaters and keeping them planted at home, watching the little black box. To draw the crowds away from the tube, movie makers started giving their films a big dose of sex and violence—something that television could not compete with. I won't even go into the Internet and streaming services!

Actors were definitely stars in the forties and fifties and they had fun—rather childish fun—but fun just the same. In those old days when 'dope' was considered to be a dumb person, some of the more ingenious stars took to stashing joints in the tops of the palm trees along Sunset Boulevard. When they were out on the town and felt like getting high, they would simply stop by one of their 'stashes' and pluck a joint and fly all the way home. It was good fun and nobody was ever busted or hurt by it.

When I recall the practical jokes that the stars used to pull on one another in those days, I have to crack up even now. One in particular comes to mind. There was a famous producer who went into ecstasy at the mere mention of an orgy. He was constantly talking about how much he would 'dig' being invited to an orgy and see all those young, luscious starlets romping around in the buff. One day Errol Flynn decided to play a joke on him. He told the producer of an orgy that was taking place that weekend and invited him.

The producer arrived, breathing hard, excited beyond belief that at last he was to attend an honest-to-goodness orgy. It was a grand, mansion-type home in Beverly Hills, and he was met at the door by a butler who somberly asked him to remove his clothes. The producer looked around the foyer and saw a great pile of clothes, coats and shoes stacked neatly in the corner. He hastily removed his threads and added them to the stack. The butler bowed him into the dining room, telling him that the other guests had already arrived and were having a bite to eat before the fun and frolic began.

Our would-be lecher strode naked into the vast dining area and there he encountered fifty or so guests, all dressed in formal attire, black tie and evening gowns, sitting down to a decorous dinner. You can well imagine his shock and embarrassment—and his vow to 'get that fucking Flynn' (who, by the way, was not at the party.)

Flynn had arranged it with the hostess to have the studio send over all the clothes and underwear and had personally paid for the butler (who was an out of work actor) to assist in the prank. This very same 'butler' also had another role in a practical joke that was the talk of the town for months. I've forgotten who originally put him up to it, but everyone in Hollywood talked of nothing else for almost a year.

It seems that this gentleman was very well endowed (some insist that he measured in at fourteen inches!) and perhaps all that weight pulled so hard on his brain that he was left a bit dim-witted. Anyway, he was broke and wanted to be an actor and actors had to attract attention—right? He was hired to entertain at a formal dinner party. Nothing too difficult, he was told, he simply had to walk through the crowd and serve hors d'oeuvres. He was outfitted in a waiter's uniform and given a large silver tray containing assorted canapes. Right in the middle of the tray he placed his very impressive penis, surrounded by parsley and all that garnish. He walked sedately through the room, holding the tray low, of course, and murmuring politely, 'Hors d'oeuvres, anyone?' Naturally it was a shock—and a hit so much so that hostesses all over Beverly Hills began calling to ask him to do likewise at their posh soirees.

When Jim Henaghan was working at Paramount Studios in the forties, a very amusing practical joke was pulled on him. He was finally given his own office and secretary in the writer's building and he had a certain amount of security. So he decided to buy a new car. He purchased a shiny new, bright green roadster and proudly parked it under his office window for all to admire. Around noon a producer friend of his called and asked if they could use Jim's roadster in the Alan Ladd movie they were currently shooting. Jim, thrilled that his new automobile would be in a movie, readily agreed.

He worked the rest of the day and when it came time to go home, no roadster. He called the producer and was assured that his car was on the way. He paced his office for a few minutes, looking out the window every so often until he saw a truck chugging slowly down the narrow Paramount street towing a pancake-flat green roadster! Jim almost fainted. He rushed into the street, staring with dismay at the totally trodden automobile and was told that in the movie it called for Alan Ladd's automobile to be demolished and flattened. Jim was still swearing and pulling his hair out when a laughing producer showed up with Jim's new car. (They had purchased a similar roadster for the wreaking scene.) Jim was too relieved to be angry.

In those days Hollywood was filled with characters who enjoyed good, clean fun and crazy, practical jokes. I guess it sounds childish to some that those superstars would behave in such a Peck's Bad Boy manner, but that was how they unwound after work. They considered the whole thing a huge joke—the fabulous fees they were paid to play-act, the awesome mansions they lived in, the fawning adulation of their fans—all of it was unreal and could end any day. Therefore, they hid their anxiety by poking fun at their lifestyles and the make-believe world that they indulged in.

One of Robert Mitchum's droll remarks is typical of the way many stars thought in those days. 'It sure beats working,' said the droopy-lidded actor.

People believed in miracles in those days because they saw them happening all around them. Some obscure stagehand (like John Wayne) would be tapped on the shoulder and whisked away to sudden stardom or a lissome blond teenager (like Lana Turner) would be discovered sipping a soda at the corner drugstore and be magically transformed into a sex goddess with a covey of servants and lovers to answer her every whim.

These suddenly rich and famous people enjoyed their fame and money with an almost fanatic pleasure—as if they suspected that someone would snatch it away as quickly as it was given. They spent money with a kind of frenzy;

chauffeur-driven limousines awaited them twenty-four hours a day; hairdressers and makeup artists were at their beck and call; lavish parties consisting of a thousand or more 'intimate friends' were the norm. They changed their names as easily as changing a pair of dirty socks and took on new lifestyles and make-believe backgrounds to go with their current identity.

Michael Romanoff was perhaps the best ever at making himself over. He hit Hollywood with a pompous attitude and a sincere belief that snobbery paid off. He told everyone that he was a true prince and proceeded to open one of the poshest restaurants that Hollywood was ever to know. Stars actually fought for the best tables and reservations were made weeks in advance for the mere pleasure of dining at Romanoffs. It was clearly understood that no commoners were allowed, and the movie people (with their own humble beginnings and insecurities) bragged to friends that they dined regularly at Romanoffs. Frank Sinatra and Humphrey Bogart had their favorite tables, and God help the poor waiter who unwittingly seated anyone else there.

When it was discovered that the bogus prince was just that, a fake, the son of a poor, common Brooklyn tailor and born Harry Geruson, all of Hollywood applauded his masquerade. Said one newspaper columnist, 'Prince Romanoff is Hollywood's only honest phony'—and Georgie Jessel quipped, 'Romanoffs is a nice little café—a man can take his family there for dinner for about $3,500.'

Unfortunately, Mike soon began believing his own publicity (a mistake that plagues most famous folks at one time or another) and his snooty, royal attitude was to become his downfall. He was forced to 'close my doors,' he told the press, 'because people right off the streets began coming in and demanding to be served—commoners!' He had class (and balls) because he refused to have anyone except the famous and super-rich in his restaurant, and when the times changed and the common folk realized that they too could rub elbows with the stars, Mike calmly locked his doors and closed down the most famous restaurant in Hollywood.

Another posh establishment was Chasen's. The late proprietor, Dave Chasen, was aware of the special needs of his famous patrons and made sure that they were not disturbed by autograph seekers while they dined. He was also aware of the fact that many stars were on strict diets and made it a point to carry such special foods. And if a director buddy of his told him not to let a certain star drink too much of the local grog as they had a heavy shooting schedule the next day, Dave would delicately escort the errant actor to the door. He was an understanding, nice guy type. Stories are told of some famous stars who had shaky beginnings that signed the dinner tab for as many as ten years—without one word of rebuff from Dave. 'They always paid me back,' he said, 'no matter how long it took.' (Schwab's, the famous drugstore in Hollywood, was another such eatery that allowed between-picture actors to sign the tab.) Chasen's always catered to the rich and elegant, the famous and infamous, and if they got sad or sloppy or drunk and let it all hang out, Dave protected their reputations.

More than once, when I dined at Chasen's, I was invited to the little room off the side of the main salon where I would see Barbara Stanwyck, drunk, crying, lonely, miserably twisting her old wedding ring from Robert Taylor as she lamented her unwanted divorce from him. 'Read what it says,' she would sob, thrusting the worn golden ring at me. 'He loved me, didn't he? See what it says?' I cannot recall at this writing just what the inscription was, but it had been twisted, stroked and handled so often that the words were all but gone from the metal. Poor Barbara never loved anyone after her divorce from Robert Taylor. They divorced in 1952, and she never married again. She took his death in 1969 very hard, and chose a long break from film and television work. She sat in her huge, impressive mansion in Beverly Hills, alone, drinking, living on memories. A forgotten product of the star system. (Two decades later, she won an Emmy for her amazing performance in *The Thorn Birds* miniseries.)

Elizabeth Taylor helped make Chasen's a household word because of her love for their special chili. When in Rome shooting *Cleopatra*, she would have Chasen's deliver, by airplane, a hearty serving of that heavy dish. I shudder to think what a simple bowl of chili and beans must have cost her!

Dave Chasen had a sincere love for his infamous clientele and told me an amusing tale of one of his more celebrated customers. He was opening a new room and the talented and wry James Thurber was among the chosen to the private party. Thurber, feeling very benevolent after a few tots of brandy, decided to show his appreciation by sketching a few of his witty and whimsical drawings on Dave's wall. He sketched a whole mural on the lounge wall and Dave was delighted. He pulled everyone into the room to show them his prize and was already planning how to turn it into publicity, and therefore more business. However, the next day when he arrived to begin the day's work, he found the walls bare. Not believing what he was seeing he ran through the restaurant, shouting for an explanation. It seems that the cleaning lady, thinking it to be the scribblings of a drunk, had washed the whole thing off! (It was reported that Dave cried for a week.)

Chasen's is long gone; it's a Bristol Farms grocery store. The Cloister, the Interlude, the Crescendo, Mocambo's,

Ellensburg Rodeo Queen

A rather prophetic entry
in my teenage scrapbook

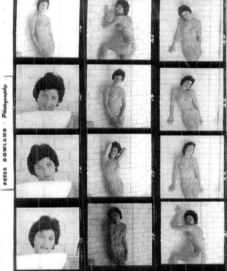

Shoot for Peter Gowland (one of Marilyn's
favorite photographers) and a publicity pic
for Zugsmith's AIP.

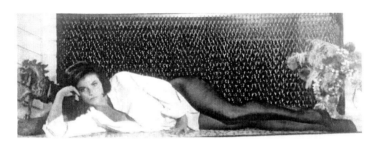

A Model Citizen

Above: Van Huesen shirt ad

Left: Posing with Jate

Lower Left: Cover girl.

Lower Right: From a feature spread in Swank.

Clockwise:

Me and Conway Twitty.

On the cover of The Ventures album.

An article I wrote after the scandal broke loose.

Probably typing one of Jim Henaghan's columns.

Me and Jim in Rome.

Wedding to Don Wilson in 1964
(Las Vegas)

Date night as newlyweds

At work and at play

Left and Below:

Halloween party at my place with Jack Chaplin, Arthur Miller, Ray Strait, and Andre Phillipe and Judy Garland.

More Hollywood wildlife. This is Zamba, the big cat owned by trainer Ralph Helfer, who starred in Fluffy, The Lion, and Napoleon & Samantha to name a few.

Clockwise:

Rusty with Jayne Mansfield. Me working out with Mickey Hargitay. Out on the town with Rod Taylor and Tommy Smothers.

Don and I celebrate our daughter's first birthday; me and Staci in 1970.

In the 1980s:

Lon and Rhoda Viser and Griff the Bear; me in Idyllwild; and with Staci

the Brown Derby, the Garden of Allah—they're all gone; torn down and replaced with high-rise office buildings, banks, or savings and loan establishments.

omar takes a drag, and i take the plunge

When I recall all the crazy, wonderful, outrageous nuts I have known and loved I can't help smiling even as I mourn their passing. All of them were loners of one kind or another. They all had a desire to live it all the way. They were right. They knew that they had to go out and grab any happiness they could because no one was going to hand it to them. We are born alone and we die alone. No one is going to chuck it all and leap into the casket with us when they are planting us six feet under.

One such person who was constantly taking steps to be and do just exactly as he pleased, was Omar Sharif. I met Omar at The Factory (not to be confused with Andy Warhol's in New York) in a most unusual way. He was sitting in the main room near the fireplace, watching Sammy Davis sing his heart out onstage. His long legs were propped up on another chair and he was leaning back, his huge, liquid brown eyes half-closed. I recognized him at once and pulled my girlfriend, Charlotte Ronan, aside. 'Charlotte,' I said, 'there's Omar Sharif. Let's go sit by the fireplace and order a drink. I've always wanted to meet him.'

'Okay,' said my gorgeous companion and we found a couple of chairs and pulled them up next to the fireplace.

I have to describe Charlotte for you. She is one of the most beautiful women I've ever known; five-foot nine, long, thick mane of red hair, enormous blue eyes, catlike grace, and the most ladylike manner of anyone anywhere. She reminds people of visiting royalty. Every time we went out together every guy in the place would find some excuse to walk by our table, she is that gorgeous.

Omar was no exception. He glanced up as we sat down, looked harder, did a double take, then flashed us that famous white-toothed grin of his. He offered to buy us a drink and, of course, we accepted. Soon we were chatting with him as we half-watched Sammy Davis. Omar seemed captivated with Charlotte and even a little shy as we spoke together. He fumbled in his pocket, took out a long, brown cigarette, and fired up. I thought I recognized the aroma and couldn't believe it. Certainly a world-famous movie star like Omar wouldn't be that stupid, to smoke grass in a public place? (Remember, this was the mid-sixties) But he contentedly puffed away, gaining confidence for the pass he was to make at Charlotte, until a waiter approached us and said, confidentially, 'Uh, excuse me, Mr. Sharif, you can't smoke pot in here.'

'Pot?' snorted the handsome Egyptian. 'My good man, I'll have you know that this is not that wanton weed you Americans seem to favor. This—' (and he flourished the brown cigarette) 'is a fine, old, and rare blend of Turkish tobacco.' With that he took another hit and fixed the young waiter with a scornful eye until the lad excused himself and made a hasty retreat to the kitchen.

The three of us broke up and I said, 'Listen, Omar, if you want to smoke in here, follow me—I'll show you where everyone goes.'

We wound our way through the flesh-packed room, behind the poolroom bar, and outside to the roof. There, overlooking the parking lot, was a flat area that held a couple of chairs, a few wooden crates, etc., scattered about over the rooftop, and here everyone came to smoke grass during the long evenings they spent at The Factory. Omar was delighted with the set-up but still insisted that he was smoking 'Turkish tobacco.' (Sean Connery was another novice that I broke in on the roof; not so much smoking as necking! It was all good fun and the dapper Mr. Connery is an excellent kisser.)

Another excellent kisser was Don Wilson, the founder of the rock group The Ventures – in fact, I married him! Don had seen me in some of those "nudie cutie" magazines before we met, but I had never heard Don's music. I was more of a Sinatra gal. Regardless, I got to know it when I appeared on the cover of The Ventures' album, *Walk, Don't Run Vol. 2.*

Don and I got married in Las Vegas on December 29, 1964, and I couldn't have been happier. That is, until 1966, when we had a healthy daughter, Staci Layne (Don liked the name Staci, and I chose Layne after my friend from my modeling days). But I guess all good things must come to an end… Don and I were divorced in 1967.

tommy smothers smothers me

My next plunge into the party scene began with the end of my marriage. It was the evening of August 26, 1967, and I was sitting in my Mercedes, waiting for a parking attendant to get to me. A tight throng of gawkers and star-gazers craned their necks and stared with awe at the thick stream of Rolls Royces, the cluster of shining Cadillacs, the softly purring Ferraris, Bentleys, and Maseratis. A gleaming Excalibur S.S. slid to a halt and a sleekly coiffed, expensively (but scantily) dressed starlet slithered out on the arm of an aging producer. Just another night at The Factory… or so I thought.

I was swept along with the crowd and carried up one flight in a freight elevator that opened out onto the restaurant and dance floor. As my eyes grew accustomed to the dim I realized with a start that I recognized almost everyone there. Natalie Wood glimmered in gold stockings, gold lamé dress and gold dust as she chatted with her escort. Patty Duke swaggered by looking like some refugee from a long ago USO Club in her Bonnie & Clyde slacks. Hairdresser to the stars Jay Sebring sat hunched on the back of one of the black leather couches looking small and lost as he fondled his beads and half-listened to the lush young lady who pressed herself against him. Zsa Zsa Gabor swept past me into the poolroom leaving a fluttering trail of feathers behind her like a molting bird as she preened before admirers; diamonds flashed and sparkled at her throat, fingers, ears, and wrists, blinding those nearest her. She paused moment, gazed appraisingly at the teenyboppers in micromini skirts, and murmured, 'I simply must shorten dresses, darling'—and the teenyboppers tugged at their skirts and wished they looked as elegant and sophisticated as Zsa Zsa.

Joey Bishop ambled by wearing the same wrinkled pants and soiled orange sweater that he had worn for the past three months, his hands stuffed deep into his pockets and a personality stuffed deep into some impenetrable secret place. He went to the pool table and began shooting pool with Richard Dawson, and I stopped to watch. I was wearing a purple dress that consisted mostly of tiny straps and bare skin. I glanced up just as this tall blond guy rushed up to me, sank to his knees before me, and kissed me on the belly button! To my surprise (and delight) I saw that it was Tommy Smothers and everyone in the room was looking at chuckling at his wild antics. I took his hand and helped his feet.

'You're the most beautiful girl here. My name's Tommy Smothers—who in the world are you?' He took my arm and led me to the bar, where he continued to stare at me even as he ordered our drinks. He invited me to a taping of his show the following evening and I accepted.

The rest of the evening Tommy and I were inseparable. We wandered through the huge, 13,000 square feet of private paradise, holding hands and gazing up, thirty feet, to be exact, at the steel-beamed ceiling, where row upon row of crystal chandeliers dripped their icy tear drops to the table-covered floor below. The blasting, blaring rock beat assaulted our senses, drowning out every word we spoke, so Tommy took my hand in a tighter grip and began elbowing his way across the floor that led to the poolroom in the back. It took us over an hour to reach it as we were stopped just about every three feet by friends or fans or just the surging mob. This was definitely the Pretty People's Playground—Tommy dubbed it the Star's Sandbox—and I saw more famous people there than I had seen at the Cannes Film Festival the year before.

The rollicking party finally broke up about five in the morning, and after a breakfast of eggs Benedict and icy champagne, Tommy walked me to my car and we kissed goodnight. As I drove along the winding Mulholland Drive on my way to my own white mansion on the hill, I thought about the meeting with Tommy. He was the first guy I had met since my divorce that I had been interested in. I hoped he felt the same way.

I didn't see Tommy when I arrived at CBS. I was met by a stage manager or some such person and taken to a seat in the front row so that I might watch the show. When Tommy and Dick came on (to a cheering, foot-stamping ovation) his eyes searched the audience until he found me, and he smiled and threw me a kiss. The show was hilarious, as always, and when it was over I went backstage to meet Tommy. 'Damn, you're the most sultry looking girl I've ever seen,' were his first words. (As our affair progressed, I learned that Tommy was always complimentary and flattering to his dates.)

We went to his dressing room where, after a fast smoke and a cocktail, he showered and changed clothes. Then we were outside in the parking lot and he was helping me into his tiny sports car. He lit up again as soon as we were under way and we shared it as we drove to The Factory. We had a marvelous dinner followed by coffee and Cherry Heering between kisses. 'Let's get out of here,' he said, and signed the check and steered me toward the door.

I was fairly flying from all the booze and now a joint really had me turned on. Then, suddenly, Tommy said, 'Oh, no—' and I looked up and saw a red light in the rear-view mirror. Naturally I panicked and had to swallow the short roach. Tommy casually rolled down his window and got his smile in place for the big, burly cop who was swaggering up alongside. I was suddenly very conscious of the heavy odor of marijuana in the small, smoke-filled car and prayed that the cop wouldn't recognize the aroma.

'What's your hurry, pal?' the cop glowered, and leaned down, almost stooping, as he looked inside the car. He sniffed once, frowned—my heart stopped beating—then a broad grin split his craggy face and he shoved his cap back and boomed, 'Well, well I've caught myself a celebrity!' He smacked the hood of the car with an open palm and the whole car shook. 'Tommy Smothers, ain't'cha?' He stuck his hand (which looked like a whole Virginia ham) inside the car and pumped vigorously at Tommy's rather reluctant clasp. 'I'll be damned. Me and the wife watch you and your brother every week. Wouldn't miss it' He reared back on his heels and roared with laughter. 'I sure do love the way you give them big shots in Washington a bad time. That was a real funny act you did on President Johnson a couple weeks back—never laughed so damn hard in my life.' He laughed some more to show us what he meant, then took out a pad and pencil and shoved it through the window. 'How about your autograph, pal? The wife'll love it.'

I could hear Tommy's sigh of relief as he quickly scrawled his name. 'Much obliged,' said the officer, tucking the autograph into his uniform pocket. He turned to go. Tommy started his engine. 'Say—just one thing more.' We held our breath and he turned back and gave Tommy a wink. 'Watch that speed, you hear?' He walked a few steps, still grinning, and called over his shoulder, 'And them funny cigarettes, too!'

Both Tommy and I almost died. We sat stone still until the cop had driven away (with a merry wave) then we collapsed into one another's arms, hysterical with laughter.

We went to my house and shot pool for a while and had a couple of drinks, but we seemed to be paying more attention to each other and less to the game. Finally he just threw down his pool stick, scooped me up into his arms and carried me to the bedroom. He kicked open the door— stopped, and stared. 'Jesus Christ,' he said.

I had just recently had my bedroom redecorated and it was a sight to behold. It was done in emerald green velvet and white chiffon. A round bed, eight feet in diameter, was draped in emerald velvet and completely circled in white chiffon panels that were held back by green silk braid. By pulling a green velvet cord the panels fell together, completely enclosing the bed, which was built upon a platform and surrounded by a sea of ankle-deep white carpet. Antique veined mirrors, crystal chandeliers, a sunken marble tub, twenty-four caret gold faucets, velvet-flocked walls, and plush furnishings completed my private boudoir. He sat me down and walked about the room. 'Is this for real?' he said.

I had to laugh. It did look like something out of the Arabian Nights. 'When do the dancing girls come out with their veils?' he asked as he pulled me down on the bed. I threw back the velvet spread and he whistled as he ran his hands over the heavy folds of the creamy white satin sheets. My pet ocelot chose that moment to leap upon the bed and fix Tommy with a level stare from her enormous yellow eyes. She flicked her tail at him, stretched a paw out, and gave him a token sneer. She looked like a young leopard lounging in the jungle, and I had to laugh at Tommy's expression. 'Who are you?' He asked at length, then immediately pinned my arms to my sides and held me captive on the bed. 'I'm afraid you're going to disappear into a puff of smoke,' he said, holding me closer. I felt my heartbeat quicken, and I pulled my arms free and put them around him and drew him nearer. I sneaked out a foot and gently prodded the cat off the bed—then turned my full attention to Tommy.

Wow! He may have been the slow one on his television show but in bed he was something else. He really had a beautiful body. Lean, muscular, smooth as silk—and he's a fantastic lover. We made love twice before we stopped to catch our breath, and I was hooked. Obviously he was, too, because that was the beginning of a very steady affair between us.

Hollywood was changing in the middle sixties and I seemed to be in on the ground floor. It was a heady time. Movie stars had taken to openly hawking for causes and political candidates, and grass had replaced booze in most swinging homes. The drudgery of workday life in Hollywood, which is boring at best, is intolerable to most artists after a while without some release from tension. It used to be that many actors drank and often lurched through long shooting sessions, sometimes at the end of the day literally staggering from the effects of booze. The lucky ones became accustomed to working smashed, and it seldom showed. But the lesser tipplers usually began to show signs of the grog after just a few belts and very often had to be sent home early—a great expense in shooting time.

Tommy and I were fast becoming what Hollywood calls 'an item.' We had a marvelous time together. Weekdays he stayed in town at a home he had in the Hollywood Hills, and on weekends he went to his apartment in Marina del Rey where he kept his sailboat. Mason Williams shared the Hollywood house, so Tommy usually stayed at my place during the week when he was rehearsing his show. It seems like I was always stoned, or at least high, during that time. Everyone was. It was like a replay of the twenties and Prohibition. The young, rich, famous set seemed determined to try every new drug as fast as it came out, even seeking a higher high. Perhaps it was the unpopular conflict in Vietnam and the confused state of our government that made everyone run as fast as they could toward a new kick.

Mason Williams was one of the writers on the Smothers Brothers Show and he also shared a close friendship with Tommy. When I first met him he was a shy, cherub-faced, slightly wistful young man. Equally adept at song writing and poetry, he also had a fantastic flair for comedy. But no one had ever looked quite deep enough to see the genius just below the surface. No one, that is, until Tommy took him over and turned him on to the better things of life. He gave it to him in one fast lesson, including how to convince a girl that two guys in bed are better than one. And Mason was an apt pupil. He let his hair grow-much longer than Tommy's. And when his pen moved across the paper now his words took wings and flew beyond the realm of fantasy into truth. But it was his truth and he didn't want anyone else singing his truth. He cut a record. He appeared on television. (No more behind-the-scenes for him.) First on Tommy's show, then others began calling and Mason was a star.

I remember the night we all celebrated his first album. We were at the Hollywood house; Tommy and I had just returned from Marina del Rey, where we had spent the weekend on his boat, and we were dirty and tired. Mason fixed something to eat while Tommy and I showered and slipped into some robes, then we turned on the tube to watch Tommy's show. We smoked, drank, and ate ourselves silly. I had some new grass that was dynamite and so, of course, I couldn't wait to try it.

Dynamite was too mild a word. The stuff was a grenade! We tottered upstairs to the balcony to watch the heavy rainfall streaking the windows: Deep thunder belched from the throat of the sky, and lightning cut the blackness in a jagged arc of brilliance. I flung open the glass door and stepped out into the rain. It pelted down, soaking me through in less than a minute, it seemed, but it felt incredible on my skin. I felt arms go around me and looked up to see Tommy stark naked—and he began to take my clothes off in what seemed to be slow motion.

Mason was standing nearby and there descended over all of us a feeling of incredible closeness. I put my arms around both Tommy and Mason and we stood for a moment and let the rain fall upon our bodies. I don't know who moved first, maybe we moved as one, but then we were inside and I dove for the bed and buried myself under the warm blankets. Mason threw me a towel and disappeared into the bathroom while Tommy tried to push me out of my warm burrow. We wrestled, giggling and making with the hip quips, higher than hell by this time. Tommy finally succeeded in pinning me to the mattress and then he kissed me and my body arched up to meet his, and the gaiety of a moment ago was quickly replaced with a surging passion like none I'd ever known.

We made love on a cloud that night. Soft. Gentle. Passionate. Deep. I don't know when Mason joined us, but in the soft gray room I saw his face close to mine and my arms were around him even as Tommy kissed me. Everything melded and interlayered and vacillated after that. It was a hazy, dreamy, unreal fantasy. A fantasy that quickly became reality.

Now I knew what all those men meant when they said there was nothing greater than making it with two girls at once. If it made them feel like a king, then you can well imagine that I felt like a queen bee! (Ladies, don't knock it if you haven't tried it!)

Summer was over and the thespians were returning to the studios for their fall shows. I was a bit at loose ends so I decided to go back to work. Besides, I had just about as much fun as I could stand!

'bobby kennedy wants to meet you!'

It was late fall of 1967 and even though Tommy and I were still dating from time to time, the magic was fading into a bad color print that bled at the edges. I threw myself into my writing and began working on a novel that I hoped would make me as famous as Edna Ferber—or as infamous as a female Harold Robbins. I was also doing fan magazine articles and, naturally, I had to be out on the town just about every evening so that I could catch some unsuspecting star in the act of being a star, and then do a story.

There was much unrest in Hollywood at that time. The new drug permissiveness and sexual promiscuity shattered the remaining barriers of exclusiveness for movie stars—

Old Hollywood was dead. The glamour was fading. Young actresses boasted (on national television) of their children born out of wedlock, while others openly lived with the lover of their choice without benefit of marriage. In the middle sixties, anything went. It was a time of change. Movie stars, political candidates, millionaires, and fallen kings were as available as the boy next door. I remember the commotion Bobby Kennedy caused when he showed up at The Factory with Frank Sinatra to have a look at the pretty people's playground. I was in the poolroom when I heard all the murmurings and whispering, and I asked a waiter what was up.

'It's Bobby Kennedy-over there with Peter Lawford and Frank Sinatra!' he stage-whispered, and I followed his pointing finger. It was so dark I couldn't see anyone, so I shrugged and went back to my pool game. I was not unaware of Robert Kennedy, boy wonder, next in line for the Presidency of the United States. Even though I was not politically minded, I would have had to be deaf, dumb, and blind not to notice the splash he had been making in the papers and on television.

Actually, I had met Bobby eight years before with his brother, John (aka, Jack). In 1960 I was dating Jim Henaghan. He knew Jack Kennedy quite well and invited me along on a dinner date with him. We met at Romanoffs Restaurant and Jack, charming, witty, sexy, spent most of the next four hours explaining, very seriously, why he would never become President of the United States. He said the people might like him (he admitted he had charisma) but they would never elect a Catholic President, or one so young, or so rich, or one who had a reputation of being a bit of a playboy. Jack and Frank Sinatra were close pals then, and I suppose a little of Sinatra's swinger image had tarnished Jack's Boston-Catholic image. It was a delightful evening, one I remember with fondness and more than just a little yearning.

The next morning Jack sent his car for Jim and I, and we donned the straw hats with KENNEDY emblazoned on the band (handed over solemnly by a silent chauffeur) and attended the Democratic National Convention at the Sports Arena. It was total bedlam. Thick smoke shrouded the entire room like a giant dark cloud; people dashed everywhere at once; voices shrilled out of nowhere, crying orders or just chanting for 'Kennedy'—I had never seen so many young, beautiful women (or so many showbiz folks) milling about all in one place—all wearing the straw hats with KENNEDY on the sweatband. It seemed to me a farce, a circus. I remember asking Jim: 'Is this the way a president is really elected?' I suppose I expected there should be some order or dignity. There was none. The crowd was hysterical. Even Kennedy aides seemed a bit hysterical.

Then I noticed this skinny, sandy-haired guy running around and giving a lot of orders to people. He looked too young to be of any importance, but men twice his age were doing his bidding. He was, I learned, the kid brother, Bobby. And he had single-handedly organized the entire campaign. Cute, I thought, watching him dash madly about, his shirt sleeves rolled up to expose golden hair on his suntanned arms. He reminded me a little of Audie Murphy or Dick Clark; the same baby face and look of innocence. I was introduced to him and don't remember being overly impressed. He was curt, abrupt, and his eyes were stony blue without a flicker of warmth. After a respectful moment, he excused himself and dashed off to disappear into the surging crowd.

Jim and I left for Europe soon after that, but I managed to follow John Kennedy's triumph via the newspapers. I was in Rome when he was elected President and if I had thought the Democratic National Convention had been an arena of bedlam and chaos, I was not prepared for the citizens of that otherwise sleepy little Italian city. They literally went crazy.

People poured into the streets like waters from a bursting dam; confetti blinded mc as I tried to make my way down the Via Veneto to Bricktop's Bar; monks danced in the streets; enormous crowds gathered in the square around the Vatican clutching rosary beads and offering prayers for the new Catholic president. Within seconds, it seemed, jokes sprang up about Jack Kennedy and his faith. ('Get me Father on the phone,' Kennedy allegedly ordered the White House operator. 'Is that home or Rome, Mr. President?' came the crisp reply.)

When I returned from Europe the Kennedy administration was going great guns. The Kennedy name had become magic. It stood for goodness, honor, integrity, and truth. The name of Kennedy stood for the new America. It seemed you could not say one without the other. It mattered not that he was rumored to have a Hollywood star for a mistress. It merely added to the legend. It was such a heady, romantic political era, and our leaders were a young, energetic bunch who gamboled on their sprawling green lawns in Hyannis Port and played touch football like a gang of roughneck boys. The feline and darkly attractive Jacqueline Kennedy set the fashion styles of the sixties and thrilled America with her whispery, little girl voice as she took us on an intimate tour of her home, the White House. Jack and Jackie soon began appearing on the covers of fan magazines as America's last gasp in gods and goddesses. If it seemed just a bit unrespectable for the President of the United States and his Lady to be gracing such publications, well, they were, after all, young, successful, and beautiful, and that alone qualified them.

Then a lunatic assassin sent John Fitzgerald Kennedy to a martyr's grave and the name was hallowed.

Four silent years passed. Then Robert Kennedy emerged and gave America hope once more. In fact, that was the key word of his campaign: Hope. Once again hearts were light and gay. Youth was the password. Hysteria the order of the day. The kid brother was doing all right. Already the legend was taking shape. His Hickory Hill parties had become infamous. Newsmen joyously reported that at least one dignitary was thrown fully clothed into the pool at every such gathering. Frivolity prevailed. It was rumored, with much smacking of lips, that Bobby was the paramour of another living legend—Marilyn Monroe. No one denied it. (In retrospect, it seems only logical that these two talented, beautiful, but doomed young people should have been drawn to one another.)

When John F. Kennedy was earning his legend in the early sixties, permissiveness was tentatively knocking at the door of puritanism. During Bobby's reign it flung open the portals and strode boldly through. In fact, Bobby came very close to being the first political hero to be busted on a narcotics charge. According to Heneghan it happened in a small western state, and the sheriff of that county claimed to have information that Bobby was holding a stash of marijuana in his hotel suite. An incensed red-neck type, he was all for making the bust when he received a visit from a 'couple of guys' who told him how very foolish it would be to bust the Attorney General of the United States, His brother might not like it.

I vowed to not only vote for Bobby, but to convince everyone else I knew to do the same. I simply adored him. He spoke on a gut level with people. He was intensely interested in everything. He wanted a safe world for his children to grow up in. I had read all the reports of Bobby's so-called ruthlessness, his tart, monosyllabic tongue, his complete disregard for President Johnson, his tight associations with show business people and rock freaks and acid-head poets, his utter obsession to get down in the streets and mingle with and touch the common people, even though it presented a security problem. And I loved every word. This was my kind of guy. What a president he would make!

I was thinking of all these things as I shot pool at The Factory that night. I must admit I was dying to meet the infamous Bobby. I knew Peter Lawford vaguely and was wondering if I should sort of amble over and say hello when I heard this loud hiss—right in my ear. Startled, I turned to find a waiter clutching at my arm. 'Bobby Kennedy wants to meet you! He invited you to his table for a drink!'

I put away my pool cue and followed him to a table in a shadowy corner near the fireplace. There were several people sitting there, but the only one I noticed had a shock of unruly, thick sandy hair and pale blue eyes surrounded by a million laugh lines (I don't recall ever seeing Sinatra or Lawford that night; I had eyes only for Bobby). He half-rose as I slid into the booth next to him, then he said with a sweet, warm smile. 'Hi, I'm Bob Kennedy—and you're Nancy, right?' My leg touched his as I squeezed into the already crowded booth and something like a shock quivered throughout my body. Oh dear God, I remember thinking, don't let me be turned on to the next president of the United States! I wasn't sure I could handle such an affair.

As I got to know Bobby I found him to be a soft, sweet person. He was even a little shy at times, and when this happened he would develop a stammer in his speech. I have a brother who stammers, so I was naturally concerned about what caused it. After some observation, I decided that Bobby only had this speech affliction when he was very fatigued or nervous or unprepared. Also, his hands would shake and tremble uncontrollably when he was angered or very concerned about some special issue.

When he spoke to me, he would sometimes duck his head and peek at me from beneath his shaggy brows, quizzically, and that slight tremor of voice was more pronounced. I was reminded of a small, tow-headed lad digging his toe in the dirt. He was not as articulate or well-spoken as his brother, Jack, had been. In fact, his speech sometimes held a rather rough edge, and he had a way of kidding himself—of kidding the world, really. His sense of humor was dry and laconic. As mentioned earlier, he was intensely interested in everything. When he discovered that I had been raised on a farm he fired questions at me like a prosecuting attorney. He had to know everything about what it was like living on a farm; what sort of hours the farmer put in; was it rewarding or just frustrating; did the children work as hard as he had heard; what kind of profits were made per year; was it a doomed and antiquated way of life; what was the fate of the farm animals; etc. and etc. Such curiosity I had never witnessed before, except, perhaps, in Errol Flynn. (Errol once said that his only true addiction in life was curiosity—not booze, dope, or broads, as rumored, but plain curiosity.) I got the impression that Bobby had this same unquenchable thirst for knowledge in every form.

I had campaigned for Bobby along with every other Kennedy fan in Hollywood and was in the throes of delicious agony as I awaited the returns that fateful June evening in 1968. I had been invited to the victory party (we were all positive that Bobby would win!) and was sitting in my dressing room applying my makeup when the telephone rang. It was Lloyd Thaxton, a good friend and fellow Kennedy supporter. 'Bob Kennedy's been shot,' were his first words. 'There won't be a victory party.'

'Oh, Lloyd, what a ghastly joke!' I said, knowing that Lloyd had a way with the practical joke. 'Look, I can't talk now—see you later.' I laughed at him and hung up the receiver. The phone rang again the moment I removed my hand. This time it was Griff the Bear. 'Kennedy's been shot!' he shouted, almost as if he were personally angry. 'Quick! Turn on the tube!' 'Which channel?' I gasped, knowing that if Griff told me it had to be true; we had been closer than brother and sister for years. 'For Christ's sake, Rabbit!' he choked with fury. 'It's on every fucking channel on the tube!' With that he slammed down the receiver and I rushed to the television set and turned on a rerun of Dallas. Same cast of characters. Same insanity. Same tragedy. Same confusion. Too familiar.

In the three or four days that followed I was completely numb. I had cried until my eyes were so swollen I could hardly see the television screen, but still I kept it on and watched, almost ghoulishly, it seemed, the repetitious reporting of the fatal shooting of Senator Robert Kennedy. I saw, again and again, Rosey Grier, Rafer Johnson and George Plimpton, struggling with the madman who had caused all this pain. I heard shouts of 'Get the gun! Get the gun! We don't want another Dallas here!' I watched the tear-streaked faces of the crowd as they wandered aimlessly about the big, gloomy Ambassador Hotel, almost as if they were waiting for Bobby to appear and tell them it was okay to go home now. Then the flag-draped coffin and the frenzied preparations for the last I plane trip. I saw people on television that I knew personally, looking grave and like stiff strangers—Andy and Claudine Williams, Art

Buchwald, Kennedy aides that I had met at rallies, and others. Silent. Taking Bobby home.

The plane looked impersonal as the casket was loaded aboard. The reporter who had been speaking softly and in husky tones was suddenly quiet. The door of the plane slammed shut. A whirring sound grew to a muffled roar. The plane lifted itself on lofty wings and filled the frame. The sky was incredibly blue, like a Hollywood backdrop, and there was only silence as millions of Americans said goodbye to their last chance.

I was sitting on the sofa with Quina, my housekeeper, and two-year-old Staci, who was cross-legged on the floor in front of the set. All was still as the plane climbed slowly and steadily into the clouds, then disappeared into a speck of nothingness. Staci turned her eyes to mine. 'Bobby's all gone, Mommy,' she said brokenly. Tears streamed down her cheeks. I was stunned. The Kennedy charisma and tragedies reached out to touch even the babies.

I had known Bobby for less than a year and he had touched my life as no other person, male or female, ever had. I was to recall the curve of his mouth, his sweet smile, the look of interest that turned on bright lights in his otherwise pale blue eyes, the feel of his strong hand on mine. I remember him as being broad-shouldered, lean-hipped, shorter than you would imagine, with rather a long torso. But vital. Oh, so very vital and alive.

I would not be voting in this election. Perhaps I would never vote. It was over for me when the Kennedys left this world.

Then a kind of stillness settled over the land. Strong men wept. Hope was gone. Hope was dead. It could not be resurrected.

A few die-hards clutched desperately at the last Kennedy, Teddy, and bumper-stickers proclaimed: 'Teddy in 72.' However, when baby brother stood naked before the people, he was found wanting. Politicians live on the narrow edge of ethics, and Kennedy haters (for there were those) took up their marking pens and listed everything from his being expelled from Harvard for cheating on an exam to the shocking Chappaquiddick tragedy, where a young woman, Mary Jo Kopechne, met her death in the icy waters of Poucha Pond.

The Kennedys have always surrounded themselves with canny advisors and perhaps they were the ones to issue a statement that Edward Kennedy would not be running for the presidency in 1972. Perhaps they figured this latest Kennedy locomotive needed a four-year cooling off period. Ted did play it cool from the sidelines—but he looked more and more like a take-over man for '76.

Then the kid brother blew it again. He and a buddy, Senator John Tunney, shared the headlines: TEDDY SAILS OFF MAINE WITH TUNNEY, TWO WOMEN. It appeared in a tabloid and fuzzy, pore-exposing photos appeared of the quartet as they struggled to get the sails up and remain anonymous. But this wasn't the staid fifties or the respectable sixties, it was the straightforward seventies, and where once typewriter keys resisted spelling out any Kennedy indiscretion, they now spewed forth in boldface type. The public wanted to know what the hell was going on. If Teddy and wife, Joan, had some sort of an arrangement which permitted him to scalawag about like a newly-nutted sophomore, then let them declare it. People looked up to this kid brother of their favorite President. To slam a Kennedy in print was as monstrous a gaffe as spitting on a baby suckling at its mother's breast. But if there was something behind the headlines, then the public felt they had a right to know.

comedy and tragedy unmasked

There were many tragic poets with vulnerable souls among our superstars. And they hadn't a chance of survival. That old villain, terrified, pompous, puritanical society was out there ready to shoot them down as swiftly as Al Capone armed with a machine gun. I've seen many friends of mine killed by society, murdered by an uncaring world, buried by the indifferent parasites that fed off them. Like Marilyn Monroe and Judy Garland. Like the sensitive poet, Robert Walker, who was masquerading as an actor. He wore his tragedy like a shroud and it was as much a part of him as his skin. He spent most of his young life in and out of clinics for his compulsive drinking problem and his melancholy. He was painfully shy, withdrawn, and sad when sober; drunk, he would spout flowery poetry, laugh, love, and drink until dawn.

He was married to actress Jennifer Jones, and when she walked out on him for David Selznick, he used it as an excuse to drink more heavily. He and Henaghan were old buddies and Jim has told me many funny and fascinating tales about Bob. As well as some sad ones. Jim was with Bob the night he died—or was murdered, as Jim claims. Bob had been on a binge for several days and was literally staggering from the effects of the booze. Jim had gone over to Bob's house to keep him company and they had downed a few belts of Scotch. Suddenly Bob began to weep and thrash about, smashing lamps and crying for help.

'Nobody's ever cared,' he sobbed, 'not a fucking one of them. They use me, devour me...'

Jim tried to calm him but Bob was out of control, sobbing and cursing. He had been under the care of a psychiatrist and Jim called him to come over as soon as possible. By the time he arrived a couple of Bob's friends had been summoned and they held him down while the doctor prepared a hypodermic. Jim said Bob was shouting and crying all the while, 'Don't give me that shot! It'll kill me! I've been drinking and that shot'll kill me!'

'I didn't know what the hell to think,' Jim told me. 'Bob was my best friend and I hated like hell to see him that way. The doctor said the shot would calm him, knock him out so he could get some much-needed rest. It knocked him out all right.'

Three minutes after the doctor withdrew the needle from Bob's arm, he was dead—at age thirty-two. The silent men carried him into his bedroom and stretched him out on the bed then shuffled outside and into their cars. Only Jim remained. He sat by the side of Bob's bed, weeping, talking to him about the times they had shared, then picked up his hand and held it tightly. He noticed his watch, and with tears blurring his eyes, he slipped it off and tucked it into his pocket.

'I always told you I'd steal your watch someday, you bastard,' he whispered huskily.

Success can be deadly-and it often is. Author Gene Fowler I once said (in a letter to Hedda Hopper), 'Success is a toy balloon among children armed with sharp pins.' How very true. I remember what Success did to Allan Sherman, the roly-poly comedian who became famous for his *Hello Mudduh, Hello Fadduh* albums. (He also did *My Son, the Celebrity, My Son, the Folksinger,* and others) Allan was a very bright man, almost too bright in many ways, because he was constantly trying to figure out why there wasn't more love and kindness in the world. This can be dangerous for anyone, but for a star it's sure death. He was a gentle, sensitive man, kind, generous, wanting love so badly he died for it. He could not cope with the vicious, money-grabbing producers and others he was forced to deal with; the grasping, greedy agents and coworkers; the publicity-hungry girls who used him to get their names in print; the head waiters and captains who deferred to him because they expected a big tip. It was all too much for this gentle poet who simply wanted the love of his fellow men. He was married for many years to his childhood sweetheart and they had two children, Nancy and Robert, but when Hollywood and fame and fortune beckoned, the marriage went down the tubes.

I met Allan in the middle sixties. He was living alone in a bachelor apartment in Hollywood and writing his first article for *Reader's Digest*. When he learned that I was a writer he flattered me enormously by asking (shyly) if I would check over his story to see if it needed any changes. I felt rather embarrassed to be put in the position of critic to one of the funniest men I had known, but I dutifully read the copy. It was great, not funny as I had expected, but rather whimsical and thought-provoking. That's when I knew there was more behind those black hornrims than just a fast-buck comic. We talked for hours that day and when we discovered that it had grown dark outside, he hustled me into his spiffy red Mercedes and took me to The Magic Castle for dinner.

That was the beginning of a long friendship between Allan and myself. As the years passed and I got to know him well I saw the pain he lived with each day of his life. He was not a handsome man, he was extremely obese and suffered from asthma, which required daily medication. Because of his obesity and his desire to find love, he constantly popped diet pills, as strong as they made them, to kill his appetite, then he would smoke several joints of marijuana (which increases the appetite) then polish off a dozen donuts, a fifth of Scotch, a couple bottles of champagne, and whatever else he could find in the apartment. He wanted to be slim desperately, but he just did not have the will power; food was his security blanket. When there was no one to hold or even talk to and the hour was late and he was alone, he turned to food and drink as a comforting friend.

He would use any excuse to get me over to his place in Hollywood for 'stimulating conversation,' he would tell me. However, I lived in the valley and had long since tired of the streets of Hollywood. One day he invited me over to help him decorate his new apartment. (He had just moved up two floors higher but in the same building.) He had purchased a large number of bookshelves and wanted me to show him how to put them up. (I'm famous for my carpentry.) We smoked some grass, drank some champagne, giggled a lot, put up the bookshelves (I did all the work while Allan sprawled on the thick carpet and regaled me with hilarious anecdotes of famous people).

He had the most interesting knick-knacks around his apartment and, of course, each one held a different memory for him, which he shared with me. He had a large glass block sitting in the middle of his kitchen table which was filled with everything imaginable; paper clip, credit card, condom, roach, champagne cork, etc. Whenever something he had represented a special event for him, he would drop it in the glass block. It was filled with Karo syrup and the objects would drift slowly like sand in an hour glass. It was fascinating to watch and even though I saw it at least a hundred times I was always able to find something new. Allan called it his scrap book.

Another treasure was a gigantic, tissue-paper moose head with antlers that touched the ceiling. It was painted in wild, bright splashes with a red bulb inside that lighted up the whole affair.

He was writing a novel about love, the lack of it, the need for it, the misuse of it, and each time I saw him he insisted on reading me the latest pages. It was really great and I regret that he did not live to finish it.

Allan's demise was typical. He died from a lack of love. And he didn't just sit around his apartment waiting for it to knock on his door. He went out seeking it. Unfortunately, it never answered his call. He told me of a very sad experience he had had at one of those 'encounter groups' where everyone gathers together and discusses their problems. Allan's was simple: Why doesn't anyone love me?

The doctor told them he wanted them to try an experiment. They were to stand in a circle, men in the center, women on the outside. The ladies would then circle the men and take the hand of the one they wanted to talk with that evening. Allan told me that it was the longest minute of his life. He stood there, eyes squeezed tight, hands held out, heart pounding as he heard the slow footsteps of the women walking past him—and past him, never stopping.

'Nobody took my hand, Nancy,' he said, pain and bafflement in his voice. 'Nobody so much as touched me.'

Poor Allan, he just wanted a human encounter, but no one cared. I'm sorry that I did not love him physically, as he would have liked, but we were close friends. I would always invite him whenever I had a dinner party or a gathering of any kind. He would bounce through the door, jovial, beaming expectantly, then, an hour or so later, he would be slumped on the sofa, breathing heavily, eyes half-closed, wheezing as he gasped for breath even as he lit another cigarette or joint. He was killing himself as surely as if he had put a gun to his head and pulled the trigger, but he didn't seem to care. I was aware of the envy in his eyes when he saw some good-looking stud, sexy and slim, making out with some sexy and slim chick, and I wondered why he tortured himself that way. Maybe it would have been better if he didn't hang around the so-called beautiful people; maybe it wouldn't have hurt so much. But he wanted to come to every party I had, insisted, actually, so that I always invited him.

All my friends liked Allan and thought him to be an interesting and intelligent person. Whenever Allan came over the party would turn into group therapy with everyone airing their opinions. I once asked Allan when was the last time he had gotten laid and he broke everyone up by replying, 'Laid? Christ, I haven't even seen my cock in over a year!'

Allan died in 1974. I was living at Lake Tahoe at the time and a friend of mine called and told mc Allan's body had been discovered that morning. His death was recorded as a respiratory failure and obesity, but I knew it was a lack of love. I'm sorry I was not in Hollywood when he died. I would have stolen his watch or at least his moose head.

Allan once expressed a desire to be buried like our mutual friend, Osmo, had been. Osmo was a tall, good-looking, blond dope peddler, but not your run of the mill dope peddler. He was a bright, witty, charming and talented artist as well. He was a flamboyant character, shoulder-length blond hair and drooping white mustache, bright blue eyes, and always a million-dollar idea popping into his head. Osmo had a few enemies (as most dealers do) and one night one of these unsavory gentlemen set fire to Osmo's house and he was killed.

A couple of days later a friend of mine, Vincent St. James, called and invited me to Osmo's funeral that afternoon at five o'clock in Malibu. I went with my daughter and two friends, Ron Bushore and Lee Silver, and I must confess to being a little startled at the scene. Just as

Osmo had not been an ordinary person, his funeral was not an ordinary funeral.

There were perhaps fifty or sixty people milling about on the beach when we arrived, hippies, children, young people, a couple of squares right out of Podunk, an elderly couple that appeared to be in their seventies (they owned the house that Osmo had perished in) and many people that I had known for years. Cosmo, Osmo's dearest friend, was stunned, red-eyed from weeping and shaking his head about the unfairness and violence of it all. We drank some wine together and swapped Osmo stories, then a young guy called everyone together and asked them to sit down, forming a large circle. At the head of the circle were two cases, one held Southern Comfort Bourbon and the other, Cold Duck Champagne—Osmo's favorite drinks. The 'preacher' then proceeded to open a bottle of each, take a drink, then pass it to the person next to him who did the same. A joint was fired up, clipped to one of Osmo's famous handmade roach clips and passed around the circle. Then a scoop of cocaine, using Osmo's coke spoon. It was so bizarre and yet touching that I couldn't help but notice the crowd. I saw the elderly couple, kind faces wrinkled with age, dim eyes lowered with sadness, as they drew jerkingly on the unfamiliar joint but determined to say goodbye to Osmo the way the rest of his friends were. A few girls were weeping softly, soundlessly, and if they didn't see the joint when it came to them the person next to them would gently hold it to their lips for them. Others were angry. Cosmo gritted his teeth and cursed the creep who had killed him as well as the cops who had done nothing about it.

We must have sat on that damp sand for over an hour, speaking about our departed buddy as we proceeded to get higher and higher. The cases of booze were almost empty now; the grass had long since been smoked; the sun was sinking behind some craggy rocks and the evening wind was chilly. Staci whispered to Cosmo, 'Where is Osmo? Can I see him?'

'He was burned up, little one,' Cosmo answered softly. 'He's cremated—all gone.' Just then everyone pointed to the sky and said, 'Look.' Everyone stared up at the small private plane that was climbing slowly in the sky. As if on cue everyone stood up as the plane circled low over our heads and dropped several dozen white roses and carnations, the delicate petals shivering in the breeze as they sank into the ocean. The pilot swept low, so low that we could see his face, and headed out to sea where he deposited his last package—Osmo himself.

As his ashes scattered and flew on the wind, the sun sank behind a mountain, coloring the sky a blood red. Cosmo thrust one hand high in the air, fist clenched, tears streaming down his cheeks as he shouted huskily, 'Goodbye, Osmo!' And one by one every person there raised his arm in the air, face turned up to the sky, and shouted, 'Goodbye, Osmo!' The wind grew stronger and whipped hair and scarves across faces and chilled the tears on cheeks but no one made a move to leave until the plane was a mere speck in the far distance.

It was the most beautiful tribute paid to a friend that I had ever witnessed and I was terribly moved by it. Later, when I was telling Allan about it, he looked very wistful when he said, 'What a marvelous thing-what a touching send-off. I would love to have a funeral like that, to know that so many people loved you—Jesus!'

'I wish I had balled him,' I said. 'That's my one regret; that I never made love to Osmo.'

'I think I've just come into possession of Osmo's soul,' Allan said seriously, looking wisely owl-like in his hornrims. 'You can ball me and I'll transfer the pleasure—'

'Allan, you nut,' I laughed, and our serious mood was broken.

i shoot down butch cassidy

In the fall of 1968 I had been assigned by the publicity department of 20th Century Fox to write a story on Paul Newman. The story was to accompany a set of photographs which were being shot on the location of Butch Cassidy and the Sundance Kid. They gave me a pad of paper and a pen and put me on a plane for Mexico City.

At the Mexico City airport I was met by a studio car and driven to some out-of-the-way place that apparently did not have a name because I never heard anyone call it anything. But smack in the middle of all this nothing— somewhere between the sagebrush and the foothills of some mountains-was a castle, and that's where the driver took me. When we got close I saw that it was a hotel (no town— just a hotel) called the Vista Hermosa, a monstrous rock and brick-faced establishment that had been built by Cortez to entertain his friends and torture his enemies.

The driver carried my bags into the lobby and left me there. I went to the desk, and on my way there, I noticed that the lobby was empty—except for one man who didn't seem to have any other place to go. While I was filling out the registration card, this fellow ambled over, stood a foot away from me, leaned over my shoulder and watched what I was writing.

Then I saw that it was ole Cool Hand Luke himself. Not exactly what I expected. Not as muscular, not as tall. Slimmer, frailer, but, well, beautiful. Yeah, beautiful—and I didn't mind him looking over my shoulder at all. Then reason took over and I remembered that I had been sent down there to work and that actors are as touchy as mink and have a tendency to tighten up on magazine writers, so I avoided his glances.

Besides, I was still wounded over Bobby's death and if Newman reminded me a little of him, well, I did not want to pursue it. However, I could not help but notice that physically he looked very much like Bobby; the same build, almost. The shoulders were wide, the torso long and well developed, and the legs short, rather stumpy. They must shoot upward at him, I thought, to make his legs appear longer. I made a mental note to watch which camera angles they used with him.

Paul's hair was thin and sandy-gray where Bobby's had been thick and lush, but the blue eyes were as wary and calculating, and the smile seemed as tentative and shy and warm. No, no, not again. I would not covet someone who could never be mine. I turned swiftly away and made my way toward my assigned room.

It was five o'clock when we met formally (by the pool) with a lot of people around. Paul Newman and I shook hands and we both said polite things and traded quips like strangers do. I felt his eyes on me-they were so blue and he was so magnetic—I knew he wanted to say something personal. Instead, we both gazed at the primitive beauty of the sprawling Mexican landscape. Big bulks of rock, toned red, russet, and brown by the slanting sun, rose majestically in the far distance. The sky was still very blue, bleaching to burnished silver at the horizon where the haze of the evening married it to the soil.

I sneaked a look at Paul as he talked easily with the others. He appeared vulnerable and boyish in his tan Levi's and moccasins sans socks. His ankles were slim. Then our eyes met and I found myself waiting, as he seemed to be, for the others to leave. And then they did leave and we were alone.

Paul put down his beer and ordered a Scotch, and I had a gin and tonic, and that happened quite a lot after that. I mean, he had another Scotch and I had another gin and tonic and it began to get dark and he said maybe we should have something to eat.

We went into the dining room, which was like a cavern spotted with wooden tables covered with red and white checkered oilcloth. We sat with some of the people from the picture crew, and word got out that I was a writer down there to do a story on Newman. He looked at me strangely for a moment—but only a moment, then his eyes softened. I think I was in love for a while.

After dinner everyone drifted away and we talked, and he got around to asking me if I was really down there to do a story on him. I said I was and he grinned and said, 'How about that?' and hit his thigh with his hand like they do in western movies and we both laughed. His eyes were very, very blue and he was deep and full of meaning for me now, and I couldn't tell it at the time, but we were both pretty drunk. So when he suggested that we go down to the cellar and look at the dungeons where the Spaniards used to torture the enemy, I couldn't think of a reason why not. And if I could have, I would have dismissed it from my mind.

The dungeons were dark and dank and tiny, and we decided to inspect all the passages. We crawled on our hands and knees, him leading and me following, down one skinny; passage after another until we were lost and in total darkness. But we didn't care. We stopped and laughed a lot and I remember thinking it was crazy but wonderful—who wouldn't give anything to be lost in a Mexican dungeon with Paul Newman. Then we saw a light up ahead, a narrow blade of white coming through a rock ceiling half-illuminating a cavern just ahead. It was a bit taller and larger than the others, and we went inside.

We stood amid the spider webs and dirt and it seemed very natural that he should take me into his arms and kiss me. I was willing, eager, and we stood for a long time in that dusty barren cave, me with my head tilted toward him, his mouth on my mouth, and he seemed to be quietly feeding from me and I from him—and I forgot who he was. And he let me go and said something about the stairs and led me to them and took my hand and guided me to a doorway that opened into the lobby. The lobby was filled with people and I tried to pull my hand away, but he held it tight and didn't seem to mind at all that everyone was staring at us.

It was late and he walked me to the block where our quarters were, through lush gardens, along pebbled walks, and we stopped in front of a building that turned out to be his suite. The moon was in the right place, sky-blue pink it was, not its normal green, but blue like his eyes. We stood with our arms around each other and the moon cast along shadow and it showed him towering above me. Then he chuckled and said something I think the French say, which is like an invitation, like 'Chez moi?' which loosely means, 'My place or yours?' and I thought about the morning and said mine. I didn't want some assistant director finding me in Paul's bed at six in the morning.

We sat like new strangers in my sitting room for a few minutes, nervous, like children, and then he kissed me and after a while he did something he really didn't have to do. He fell to his knees and clutched me tightly around the waist, his head pressed hard against my breasts, and he whispered, 'Please.' Like a small boy asking for a dime. He didn't have to say it because I had made up my mind a long time ago. Maybe by the pool, maybe at dinner, or in the dungeons. I took him by the hand and led him up the narrow stone stairway that led to my bedroom. He was a most tender and gentle lover and even though the last thing he said to me before he fell asleep was not exactly romantic, it was indicative of his fear, his big hang-up. He took a deep breath and said, 'Whew! It's heart attack time, baby!'

I had planned on staying a few days, getting my notes and returning to Hollywood. The few days stretched into a week and more. I guess I will always remember them. He was always honest with me. Not to a fault, though. He never mentioned his wife. But I felt he knew this was not just a casual thing with either of us. I suppose I was in love with him. I suppose he was in love with me. And the little things he did blinded me to the big things.

The things that rammed home later and hurt and made me unhappy.

Like the morning after the first night. He awakened me by throwing a handful of pebbles at my window, and we went to the hotel dining room for breakfast. We sat with some of the picture executives sharing a secret that we reminded each other of now and then by quick, tender glances. Then we drove to the new location in Taxco.

Whoever rationed out the rooms wasn't very clever. Paul was put in one of the two hotels the company had taken over and I was moved into another on the other side of town. He phoned me in a small panic after he had checked in. 'What are they trying to do to us?' he said.

'Us?' I said.

He waited a long time before he answered. 'Yeah,' he said eventually. 'How about that?'

We were together every night. And every day on the set we were like children. Wherever I sat, he moved my chair to the closest position he could find to where he was working. And between takes he let me know he liked me in little-boy ways. Like sneaking up behind me and dropping pebbles down the back of my shirt. Or putting his can of beer (he always had a can of beer in his hand when he wasn't in front of the cameras) on the arm of my chair so that it would fall off and spill when I moved. All sorts of silly, sweet, kid games. I enjoyed these little things as much as he did, because they said something we couldn't say out loud. Sure, I was aware that I was involved with a married man. I knew all about his 'happy marriage' and the fable about Hollywood's most well-adjusted couple. But if he had been all that happy at home he certainly wouldn't have made such a play for me!

We only mentioned his wife once, as I recall. It was when the conversation got around to astrology and I guessed his sign to be Aquarius. He was delighted that I was able to do that. Then I told him Joanne was Pisces and he was amazed. (Thereafter, he would bring people over to me on the set and ask me to guess their sun sign. He was always delighted and proud when I guessed correctly.) When I told him I was a Leo, he flipped. Leo and Aquarius together are like milk and honey. Pisces and Aquarius are like a hungry eagle and a lost rabbit. I thought for a minute he was going to say 'I made a mistake'—but he didn't—he just frowned.

It was wonderful in Mexico. Alone at night, learning things about each other, looking into those eyes, seeing a man extravagantly larger than life, who, with a can of beer in his hand, could still respond to Bach. Togetherness, secret togetherness, on the set every day. He seemed to be always moving my chair closer. And one day when the company was moving to another location site about a half-mile away, he led me to a horse and got aboard, then reached down and picked me up in those strong arms and sat me behind him and we rode to the new place, across the mesa together. Me with my arms around him, holding tight and wishing it were farther away. I didn't notice then, but he had a can of beer in his hand and he drank from it more often than he turned to smile at me.

The end of location shooting came to a halt. Gay with the festivities of wrapping-up we all drove to the Mexico City airport where we suddenly became a great deal more public. He signed autographs across the waiting room from me and I watched him as he moved like a movie star does among his fans, cool, a little impersonal, a little phony, and I had a lump of lead in my stomach because we were going back to a place where a secret is very hard to keep.

We boarded the plane and I was seated next to a girl reporter from a West Coast paper. As we fastened our seat belts she looked at me with a mixture of professional interest and naivete.

'Have you been sleeping with him?' she asked.

'Of course not,' I said, and added something silly like, 'What a terrible thing to say.'

'I would,' she said.

After a while everyone began playing musical chairs. Not literally, but that's what it seemed like. I sat with Robert Redford for a while, then with producer Paul Monash, then with one of the publicity men, and finally with Paul, and we stayed together the rest of the way home. As the plane drew nearer to Los Angeles I noticed that Paul grew particularly pensive.

We arrived at the Los Angeles International Airport and my lover of the small cave in the dungeons was gone. The man who had put his weight upon me in the darkness of the Mexico nights wasn't there anymore. A public image, with blue, blue eyes and a sensual mouth drawn tightly now against the invasion of the hordes of fans, moved quickly among them and the studio people and never looked my way. I knew I would never see him again.

Then, just before he grabbed a couple of bags and walked swiftly toward a waiting car outside, he strode toward me, not really looking at me, and muttered, 'I've got your number' and he left me.

It was a week before he called me. 'Nancy,' he said. 'Newman.' I said, 'Hi, there.' And we talked stiltedly, like people who had known one another somewhere before.

The next time I saw him was at the cast party when they wound up the picture. I was escorted by a friend, but most of the time I sat and looked at Paul across the room as he squinted his eyes with an expression of tremendous interest and self-assurance and seemed absorbed in conversation with people he couldn't care less about. I noticed, but they didn't, that his hand trembled and he held himself rigid until he had put down a half-dozen drinks. Then he began to act normally and with confidence—the movie star at the wind-up party. Now and then he would amble over to where I was sitting, and each time (playing it with slightly glazed eyes now) he would appear surprised that I had come.

Later on, they darkened the room and a projector was turned on and they began screening what they called out-takes, scenes from the film that have been cut, in which actors blow up or can't remember their lines and swear or act silly. (This was the days of actual film, and nothing was digitized.) Everyone laughed as though they had never seen them before. I felt a warm hand on the back of my neck and it moved toward my cheek and caressed me, and I leaned my head back and pressed his hand against my shoulder and didn't want to let go. He was not uptight there in the darkness and I realized we were still a secret thing. He hadn't forgotten our nights together in Mexico. He still loved me.

I didn't quite know what to make of our affair. Was it wrong to be so involved with a married man? Or, I should say, a married screen idol married to another screen idol. I knew if he had been happy with Joanne, happy like they said in the magazines, it wouldn't have happened between us. With his hand against my cheek I turned and put my lips against his arm and felt the warmth of him against my mouth. I felt a little chill as I smelled the liquor that fortified him against the confrontations at the party and I was uneasy. I remembered that night in Taxco when it had stormed. We lay side by side in his room, passion subsided, and lightning ripped the sky from black to electric blue and thunder rumbled down from the peaks of mountains and Bach blared on his stereo and we didn't speak.

Paul came to my house often after that. He would telephone and say (in case my answering service picked up) 'Nancy? This is the Sundance Kid.' He would giggle about how cleverly evasive he had been, and it was all great fun. He had portrayed the character Butch Cassidy in the film; Robert Redford was the Sundance Kid.

He usually came into my house carrying a beer or a bottle of Scotch or (most often) a drink already mixed and in some crazy container. A couple of times it was an enamel pot that held about a quart of booze-the sort of pot they use to toilet train babies. Sometimes it was a large peanut butter jar. He seldom wore anything but Levi's and moccasins and he'd sit formally for a while, sipping his Scotch straight from the potty. Then he would come to me and kiss me with a bone-crushing hug.

We talked a great deal at first. About where we were in relation to life and what we wanted, what we needed, and as time went by the chills of doubt came oftener. Love, making love, becomes a heavy-handed thing after a while, as passion, greedy passion, turns to forced lust, and the prettiness wears thin and the bones of the affair are bared. And I looked at Paul more closely during those days as December slipped into January and January into February.

He went away from me often and we seldom spoke about it. He would say, 'I won't see you for a week or so. I have to go someplace.' It was usually New York—or some place called Connecticut. I knew what was in Connecticut. She was there. The lady who lived with him and raised his children.

Once he left her at a party and came to my house. Once he missed a plane he was to catch with her because he was in my bed. Once he told me he loved me—but how many times can you say 'Once he—'

After the first time he said he loved me, it seemed easier for him to repeat. But I never said it back to him because I was insecure, of course. How can you be secure with a man when you don't even know his telephone number? I think he really believed that I liked the solitude of my life as his mistress because he told me once that I was lucky to be happy alone.

I think it was late spring when I realized how sordid the thing had become. He asked me to go to Aspen, Colorado, with him and a friend to ski for a few days. 'It'll be okay,' he said, 'my buddy is bringing his lady of the evening along with him, too,' *Lady of the evening?* What the hell did that mean? Why didn't he call me his girl? His strumpet, his hidden sweetheart? Then I knew why. He was really a square. He was sinning—and he was always drunk. I never saw him fall down, but I seldom saw him for an evening that he didn't put away a bottle of Scotch-after a lot of beer, of course. I began noticing it more and more, and I wondered why he was doing this thing to himself. Not just the booze. The whole thing. The sex, the arcane meetings, the remorse that started before he made the phone call to see if I was going to be home.

I remember the time I had gone to The Factory and he came in with Joanne and about four of their six children. He danced with his nine-year-old and looked over the top of her head into my eyes. That night he came over after midnight and we made love until dawn and he said tiredly afterwards, 'Oh, you're heart attack time, baby.'

'What do you tell your family when you walk in just as they're sitting down to the breakfast table?' I asked that morning as he dressed to leave.

He flashed me the famous Newman grin. 'I tell them Daddy's been making movies all night.'

We drifted apart some after that. He was making a movie called *Hall of Mirrors* (the title was later changed to *WUSA*) with her. When he came back to Los Angeles he came to see me and he was jolly at first, clowning around and telling his corny jokes like he always did. Then he glowered at me and said, 'I mustn't be happy. I'm playing Reinhardt, and Reinhardt is a dark man—a man in a black mood.' And he played Reinhardt when we made love. Maybe it was habit now. And later I noticed that the red in his eyes dimmed the blue, like in a bad color print. He told me he was looking for contentment, blurry contentment, I suppose. Or maybe in his guilt he was looking for death. He constantly told me I was his secret sanctuary.

The affair was straining at the seams now. He showed up one day in his puny little Volkswagen with the Porsche engine that could jog along at about 150 miles per hour. He had an eight-band stereo in the car that was big enough for Carnegie Hall. And he played it as though that's where he was. He scrambled into the house carrying his Scotch-filled peanut butter jar and giggling at the fun of it all and he looked at me as if he were about to do something naughty for the first time. He grabbed me, not spilling the booze, and swept me into my bedroom and took me boisterously, like a kid tossing baskets into a backyard hoop. Afterwards, he lay back for a moment and laughed happily, and when I looked into his face I knew if someone had cried 'Cut!' he'd have stopped because he really wasn't having that much fun.

But the scene was not over. He dragged me by the hand out into the driveway. 'You didn't hear the real volume of the stereo,' he said, and he tumbled me into the Volkswagen and turned on the stereo full blast. Lights began coming on all over the neighborhood. 'Turn it down,' I said and he shook his head. 'Look,' I said, 'I want to show you the new house I'm moving to. Let's drive there. It's right off Mulholland.' Anything to get him out of my driveway with his blasting music.

He placed his drink on the floor and started the motor. 'Tell me where to go.' I sat beside him in terror as he whipped the bug around the curves, kissing the edge of the grades that fell into a deep canyon. Me in a negligee—him in Levi's and no shoes or shirt. I tried to be casual as I directed him but I wasn't. All the fun elements were gone and I was terrified. Not only of the crash I expected momentarily but of being found at the bottom of the deepest gorge—half-naked with a married movie star.

We finally reached my house and pulled to a stop in front. 'Do you think you'll be able to find it again?' I asked. He looked at me strangely and his voice sounded different as he said softly, 'I'll never forget.'

It was fun time again. The dark, brooding Reinhardt had been played out and he was the bright-eyed, corny-joke-telling Paul once more. He burst into the new house, giggly and all male, holding the jar of Scotch. He liked the new house but thought it too large and pretentious for me. He suddenly looked at his watch and jumped to his feet. 'Gotta go,' he said. 'I have a dinner date with my kids. That's the only appointment I have to keep. Be back later—' and he was gone.

My roommate, Tove Rosenkilde, shook her head and smiled. She seemed to have a quieting influence on Paul and they got along well together, often getting into deep, intellectual discussions. But even she had to admit that he was becoming a handful.

He came back later and still had the jar in his hand, replenished, I'm sure. I was in the bedroom and Tove was watching television. He took one look at her, let out a whoop, and made a lunge for her. She ran and he chased her all over the house until she burst into my bedroom and asked me to call him off. He seemed determined to find out if Danish girls were the same as American girls. He was almost incoherent and so drunk he staggered against the wall, bumping paintings sideways and stumbling over furniture. It was turn-off time for Nancy. I was going to kick the habit. It wasn't just that evening that had done it. It was just that every time he came to see me he was drunk and got drunker as the evening wore on. He was not even able to perform successfully in bed and most nights I lay awake beside the gorgeous body and face of superstar Paul Newman, bored and watching television as he snored in a drunken stupor.

He called. Often. And I would let the answering service pick up, then listen in to hear his voice saying, 'This is Mr. Cassidy.' I had nothing to say to him. Then a mutual friend told me that he was living apart from his wife and that he had told his kids for the last time that 'Daddy has been making movies all night—' So when he called again I spoke with him. He told me how much he missed me and how he wanted to be with me again—like it had been in Mexico. I was almost ready to believe him when a friend showed me a copy of the Los Angeles Times. There was an advertisement, half a page in size, and a rather lonely ad because all the type was clustered in the center of the space. It said: '(I) Recognizing the power of the press; (2) Fearing to embarrass an awesome journalist; (3) Terrified to disappoint Miss (Joyce) Haber and her readers, we will try to accommodate her 'Fascinating Rumors, So Far Unchecked' by busting up our marriage even though we still like each other. Joanne & Paul Newman.'

I was stunned. He had actually taken out that ad the same day he had called me for a date! He called again the next afternoon asking if we could get together that evening. I told him I was getting married. (I wasn't really, it just seemed a cleaner way to break off with him.) He didn't miss a beat. 'Great,' he said. 'Congratulations.' Then he did miss a beat. 'Hey could we get together a couple more times before you do it?'

I hung up the phone and lay back against the sofa cushions and thought about the anatomy of an affair and the morality in a sexually permissive society. It's all right to go to bed. It isn't even bad if you get caught. But it is immoral to be a part of a deceit. I was a part of that ad. I was the woman Joyce Haber didn't mention in the item. And while I may be sexually impetuous, I would not be an active part of a public deceit that will make a good man out of a swinger—a doting father out of a rake. Paul's life-style seemed to me one big deceit and I wanted no further part of it.

The man I had loved and laughed with in Mexico was dead as surely as if I had buried him there. I made a mental note to send flowers.

lightning strikes with rod taylor

A few weeks after that devastating experience, I went to The Factory with my roommate. We were shooting pool in the back room when I fell someone behind me. Turning, I saw this tall, muscular, blond guy who looked very familiar. I mean, not only did he look familiar to me but he was looking at me in a very familiar way! I let him have his look then turned back to the pool table. Maybe it was because he was watching (which made my skin tingle), but I ran five balls before I missed a shot.

'Hey, that's pretty good shooting,' he said, walking right up to me and grinning down at me.

'Thanks,' I replied, and went to sit down in a chair. He followed me and leaned casually on the arm of the chair staring into my eyes, and his were almost as blue as Paul Newman's but with a mischievous twinkle in them that really turned me on. He seemed bigger than life, towering over me, so close I could feel his warm breath on my face. I leaned back a little and he leaned toward me, the grin broadening.

Then some people came over and started making a fuss over him and I realized with something of an electric shock that it was Rod Taylor! I mumbled something about it being my shot, slid under his arm and hurried to the pool table. I kept my back to him as I shot pool but I could feel his eyes on me-and that damn tingly feeling was with me again. *Oh no,* I thought, *not another movie star!* But, let's face it, they look different from plumbers and mailmen. I sneaked a look at him and he was still staring at me even as he joked and talked with the people surrounding him. We both seemed to know in that instant that we would know each other better before the night was over. (I am a lady of snap decisions!)

I finished my pool game and walked to the bar to join a group of friends. He was right there, gazing down at mc with those mischievous eyes that made me blush. I wanted this man.

'Mind if I join you?' he asked as he sat down close to me and our legs touched. I could feel the heat of his body through his clothes. Then our eyes really met—for a good three minutes and I found myself waiting, as he seemed to be waiting, for the other people to disappear. But they had no intention of leaving and not witnessing this electric play between Rod and me. He solved the problem by taking my hand and saying goodnight to the others. I don't remember if he asked me if I wanted to leave, but I know that he wrapped my mink coat around my shoulders and hustled me outside, his arm strong and possessive around me.

The moment we stepped out of the club onto the sidewalk, flash bulbs popped all around me and I leaned against him, feeling his strength. He wasn't rude to the photographers or fans, but he didn't waste any time with them either. He helped me into his silver Rolls Royce and we sped away.

I didn't ask him where we were going and he didn't say. We just drove through the velvet black night, our hands moist and warm, entwined with each other. When we made a sharp turn and climbed a steep hill, I saw a huge, stately white house that gleamed like a castle in the moonlight, and I knew we were home.

He eased the Rolls into the garage and the motor purred to a halt. Then he turned toward me and I eagerly fell into his arms. When his lips touched mine it was like an electric shock—I mean, like something burning. We strained together, unmindful of the steering wheel jabbing into our ribs. We necked like a couple of kids in Daddy's parked car—and after a long while we drew apart and he ran his hand through his thick, curly hair and grinned at me in that sexy, yet boyish way. 'I think we'd better get out of this damn car while I still can.' he said.

He pulled me out of the car and led me through the door into the living room. His home was lush, lavish, expensive, immense—the great white mansion on the hill. We went to the bar where he made drinks and then a couple of guys walked in and he introduced us. I later learned that Rod was never alone. His producer, director, manager, friends, and flunkies were constantly hovering around him, ready to do his bidding. But this time Rod seemed not at all pleased at having so much company, so he invited me into a large building adjoining the main house, which was a combination bar, playroom, and projection room. It was a vast area, long, wide, big, with a wall-to-wall screen at the far end. He told me he had a movie that he was exceptionally proud of and asked if I wanted to see it. He had written the screenplay, produced, directed, and starred in the flick, he explained. Of course I wanted to see it—no matter that it was after two in the morning. We snuggled up on the sofa together, drinks in hand, and watched the credits unreel.

Charm flashed across the screen and as the credits continued to roll he wrapped me up in his arms and caressed me in a rough, yet tender way as he pointed out several shots and locations in the film. Soon we were wrapped up in another kiss that took my breath away. If I had thought that Newman was frail, even too tender, Rod was made of steel as he bent me backward on the sofa, his body covering mine. The kiss grew in intensity and everything seemed to haze together as our clothes magically fell away. Flesh burned into flesh and our breath came hard and fast as the music score of the film mounted and grew to a crescendo of drums that beat in time with our movements.

It was such a wild feeling. A storm had just come up on the screen—lightning flashed and thunder rumbled and the black night of make-believe was highlighted in muted color and crashing drums as rain pelted down from the turbulent skies. It seemed so appropriate, a storm on the screen and another one raging on the sofa.

When both storms had subsided we lay quietly, side by side, and watched the cowboys round up the stampeded herd of cattle. Then there was a close-up of Rod there on the screen, bigger than life and in Technicolor, and I turned to look at the real Rod Taylor's face—close, tender, just inches from mine, and I felt like I was in some weird fantasyland.

We smoked a cigarette, finished our drinks, and after a while began making love again. Only this time it was easier, slower, dreamier—and less like sex-starved animals.

The sun was peeking over the Hollywood Hills when Rod finally drove me home. We kissed long and deep and he asked me how long it would take me to get ready for dinner. I thought for a moment that he planned on coming inside to wait!

He called for me at seven that evening and we went to the Tail of the Cock for dinner. Of course, every female in the restaurant found some excuse to walk by our table and ogle Rod, but if he noticed he paid no attention. His eyes were for me alone and I must admit that I loved the envious stares from the ladies as they paraded by.

After about a month of seeing Rod almost every night, the gossip columnists had us engaged and then secretly married. At first it was fun to read that bunk and laugh about it, but soon it became a bore. It seems that every time someone in the public eye finds someone he can be comfortable and happy with, the gossip columnists try their best to blow it. Rod was going through a lot of shit at that time-both professionally and personally. His ex-wife was giving him a bad time and he was having trouble getting the right roles because the parts he wanted to play were hard to land. I knew it bothered him. I mean, here he was, Rod Taylor, superstar and one hell of a fine actor, and he was losing parts.

I could never understand that about Hollywood. They have a great actor, good-looking, oozing sex appeal, marvelous personality and easy to work with—then they give the juicy roles to some pretty-faced newcomer. I have seen Rod in countless films and he was great in every one of them. He was what is known as an actor's actor. He was admired and congratulated by his peers, but the roles he should have been playing, went to somebody else. You figure it out. Remember him in the *V.I.P.'s*?—he stole that movie from everyone who was in it, including that old pro Dame Rutherford.

If Rod was hot about other actors getting the parts he should have gotten, he never let on. Oh sure, we talked about it a lot, but he was never petty or jealous about the new pretty face that was currently making it. He was always happy, laughing, teasing—the most perfect lover I've ever had.

He made me (and most all women he came in contact with) feel special. I know that I felt cherished and protected and loved with him. He never left any doubt in anyone's mind that I was his lady. He was a two-fisted drinker, a barroom brawler, successful in his chosen field, and a magnetic lover—what more could any man wish to be? After Newman and his moods, I was in for a real treat during my eight months or so with Rod. We went out often. Usually to the Luau (one of Rod's favorite spots) and almost every time we had dinner there some big, burly dude at the bar would cast an eye in Rod's direction, get a little drunker, then finally swagger over and say something like: 'You don't look so damn tough to me, movie star.'

Things like that really happen to actors. If they are known on screen as a tough-guy type, they're fair game for any drunk who happens to spot them in a bar and decides to invite them outside. Rod never turned down an invitation. He would try, as nicely as possible, to discourage the bum or talk him out of it, but if they persisted, he obliged. And the challenger usually went away with a shiner to remind him of just how tough this particular movie star was! Sometimes some joker would call the cops and then the scene got real cute. I remember once when the sirens wailed and the red lights flashed and a whole army of cops leaped out of their black and white chariot and fell, en masse, upon Rod. They had him by the arms and were tugging him God knows where, when suddenly one cop said, 'Oh, sweet Jesus—it's Rod Taylor!' And every other cop there dropped their arms and stepped back a respectful five feet or so. I cracked up and so did Rod.

I simply adored being with Rod. I think we would have fallen in love and set up housekeeping together if we hadn't been such good friends. We loved each other, there was never any doubt of that, but we were not in love with each other. We had such a merry time just laughing it up, doing crazy things, making love until the small hours of the morning; we exercised together, played together, and even tried writing a screenplay together. (It was a disaster!)

I think, looking back now, I'd have to say that Rod Taylor was the most complete man I have ever known. He was wonderful both in and out of bed. I was working on a novel that was quite important to me at the time, and every time Rod and I had a date he asked me to bring along my manuscript so he could see how much I had completed. He would take the pages, pour us a drink, and then sit down on the sofa and read every line. This impressed me more than anything else. I mean, what other actor, or other person, for that matter, would show so much interest in what someone else is doing? Most people in show business are notoriously selfish and care only about what they are doing at the moment. But Rod was different. He was an honest critic as well. He would frown over my pages, reread them, and finally tell me how to fix them so they would read smoother and more realistically. He was a marvelous help to me and showed me many tricks with a shooting script. I don't think there was anything about the movie industry that he did not know.

I suppose it's my fault that Rod and I broke up at last. Marijuana had made its debut in the Hollywood circles and I was an early (and eager) advocate of the weed. Rod was not. He is an old-fashioned man in many ways, one who believed anything that is called 'dope' is bad for you. I don't think I ever saw him take a pill of any kind, not even an aspirin. Anyway, he told me I was crazy to be smoking that wanton weed known as marijuana and that it would destroy my mind and ruin my talent. He said I was wrong, dead wrong, to think I could handle it. We quarreled and I walked out in a huff.

Of course, whenever he called I would go to him and we'd have another fantastic evening together. I was sad to hear it when he passed away in 2015, but my memories are most fond.

two affairs to forget
Whenever I think of the creeps I have known (and, surprisingly, there have not been that many) I cannot help

but think of two of filmdom's most respected citizens: Ben Gazarra and James Farentino.

I met Ben Gazarra at The Factory one evening and we shot some pool, had a few drinks and some good, stimulating conversation and I guess both of us knew that we were very much attracted to one another. We left early and went to my house, where I mixed drinks while Ben raided the refrigerator, then we sat on the sofa and talked, laughed together, really digging one another.

He was extremely charming and polished in his approach and we necked on the sofa like newlyweds until we both said at the same time, 'Let's go to bed,' and he scooped me up in his arms and carried me into the darkened bedroom. I lit a candle and he kneeled down and took my hand, gently licking my fingers even as I tried to get out of my clothes. He stroked and kissed each part that I uncovered, telling me over and over again what a beautiful and fabulous woman I was, how difficult it was for him to find someone who was the least bit intelligent, and on and on.

I thought, *my God, don't tell me he's falling in love with me?* (He was really an excellent actor, folks!) I was thinking, good heavens, the poor man hasn't had any loving for months to respond this strong and passionately, and I immediately took care of that problem.

I've always had a thing about Italian men and Ben did not disappoint me. His lips and hands were every place at once until I felt like there were two other guys in bed with us. We made love until dawn, then Ben looked over at me, grinned, and said, 'Come here, fox,' and tucked me under his arm and we fell asleep that way.

Upon awakening, we made love several more times, talking quietly in between, sneaking trips to the fridge for nourishment, and, all in all, just having one hell of a grand time of it.

A couple of nights later I was at The Factory again and saw Ben standing with a group of people in the pool room. I was headed that way, so I paused and said, 'Hi, Ben, how are you?'

'What the hell do you want?' he snarled, his otherwise handsome face looking ugly and surly. I was taken aback, but I put my hand on his arm and said, 'Hey, I just wanted to say hello, how are you—that's all.'

'Well, you've said it, now get lost. I'm with my friends.' He angrily shook my hand off and turned his back, cutting me dead.

I stood there for a moment, not believing the scene. I mean, here was a guy who, just two short days ago, had spent twenty-four hours at my house, professed love and passion for me, ate my food, drank my booze, used my home, soiled my sheets, and he didn't even have the common decency to respond to a simple 'hello.'

I tapped him on the shoulder and when he turned, scowling in a most ugly manner, I said sweetly, 'Ben Gazarra, you are a prick.' Then I walked away and went into the poolroom where I saw friendlier faces.

The only other creep I had a sexual encounter with is the boyish James Farentino. We had met several times and talked together. I knew he was married and I wasn't even that attracted to him, but he was cute and fun and we had some conversations. We always kidded around if we saw one another. Then one night we were both a little bombed and we stumbled together into a back booth; giggling and necking and carrying on, mostly in fun. We were both young then, of course, and were acting like a couple of crazy teenyboppers.

'Wow,' he said, running his hand through his crisp, curly black hair. 'Baby, you're really turning me on—let's go home and fuck.'

'Let's do it,' I laughed, and we were off. We got to my house quite late and fell into bed almost immediately. We made mad, passionate love until dawn, doing everything to each other that was humanly possible, and Jim promised me a million thrills from then until we were both too old to appreciate them. I declined any kind of relationship because, quite frankly, I was not into being the mistress or the other woman anymore. And also because by this time I had sobered up sufficiently to realize who I was with, and I discovered that he really didn't turn me on all that much. He wanted to spend the day and (hopefully) the next night, but I told him I was leaving town for a couple of days so he would have to split. He seemed a little hurt as he left, kissing me hungrily and with much intensity, making me promise to let him know the moment I got back in town.

About a week later I ran into him at The Factory and saw that he was with a group of friends, drink in hand, chatting about show biz. I wasn't even going to say anything because I didn't want to get into another scene with him but he looked right at me as I started to walk by. I gave him a little wave, said, 'Hi, Jim' and continued on my way.

'I don't know you,' he said loudly, loud enough for his friends to hear. Then he did something really stupid. He reached out and grabbed my arm, pulling me close, shoving his face next to mine. 'I don't know you,' he repeated. 'What the hell are you trying to do—break up my marriage?'

'What are you talking about?' I said, pulling away, but he followed a quick couple of steps and grabbed my arm again.

'I don't know you, lady, I'm a married man—got it?' He shoved his face in close, sneering menacingly and squeezing my arm awfully hard. 'You leave me alone, you understand?'

I was completely and utterly shocked and disbelieving. I really could not accept what was happening. He had a death grip on my arm, still leaning in close, glowering at me.

'Saying 'Hi, Jim,' is going to break up your marriage?' I said in genuine bafflement. 'Hey, man, you'd better have your head checked out.'

'Don't start any trouble,' he warned. 'I'll tell everybody I don't know you.'

'Cool,' I said. 'You'll be doing me a favor.' And with that I shook him loose and walked away.

Can you believe it? What a character. All this crazy, stupid conversation for one simple roll in the hay when we were both feeling horny. You don't break up a marriage for something like that. Besides, it was a one-nighter for me; I had no eyes to make it anything else. If he wanted to play around he should at least have had the class and the balls to be cool about it. I certainly did—and still do, quite frankly,

I really can't stand dopes who want to play the bigshot in public and the rake in private. I've never been the type to blow the whistle on anyone and I'm also very friendly. When I see a guy I've been to bed with I usually manage to say 'hello'—it only seems polite.

With the exception of those two guys, all the other movie stars I had anything to do with were really super guys and considerate gentlemen. I have had brief affairs with married men, and when we ran into one another in public they were always warm, friendly, and seemed genuinely glad to see me. If they were with wife or friends they would introduce me, knowing, I suppose, that I had enough class not to blow it for them. Messrs. Farentino and Gazzara, however, showed their own lack of class by snubbing me. If they were truly all that sophisticated they would obviously pick a paramour who would be discreet in public. The very fact that they panicked when they saw me proved their ignorance and insufferable boorishness.

orgy to the death

The little man held the yellow, cotton-covered ampule almost lovingly in his hand between thumb and forefinger, almost as though he wanted to squeeze it and release the amber fluid so that it would flood and saturate the cotton and fill his nostrils with the pear-scented gas that would send his mind soaring in ecstasy, blow it reeling into a private heaven. 'It's in there,' he said softly. 'The highest high I know.'

'What is it?' I asked.

'Amyl Nitrate,' he said. 'An Amie.' He wanted badly to squeeze it now. Wanted to go with the fumes on a trip, but he withheld the pressure. 'It accelerates your heart beat,' he said. 'Opens you up so the blood roars. For a few seconds you are on the precipice, a step away from death. If you dig Amies, you'll really dig dying. That's the next stop.' He frowned slightly, sadly. 'I've been on the edge so many times. One day I'll go over—the whole trip. Maybe soon. I don't think I'll really mind.'

A month later, Jay Sebring went over the edge. He flew higher than the highest high of the Amie and died from multiple stab wounds, a hood over his head, tied with knotted rope to the body of a beautiful woman, Sharon Tate, in the most bizarre murder in the history of Hollywood.

Jay Sebring, barber, little man with a craving to live it all the way and a passion to die, collapsed into a tiny bundle of his own dead flesh; the blood that once roared seeped into the carpet of a plush home never to flow again, silent forever now, near the corpses of the celebrated people he needed to be around. I miss him. (But he would have loved it, for his greatest social deficiency was that he was a name-dropper.)

The conversation about the Arnie had taken place at The Factory, the ultraelegant former machine shop that then served as Hollywood's escape hatch for the jades who sleep on satin and drive to their restless occupations on kid leather in their Porsches and Rolls Royces. He slipped the Amie into his pocket and helped me from the bar stool. We went into the dining room and sat beneath the crystal-dripping chandeliers and ate silently. We didn't speak much because we didn't need to. We communicated mentally as we had for several years. We were friends.

Over the coffee table, I watched him as he fidgeted tensely. He was a handsome man with a sad-eyed look about him. Short in stature, he looked like a boy who hadn't fully grown up. But in those eyes that never twinkled, beyond the glaze of secrecy, there lurked an almost animal urgency that could account for the success he had achieved in just a few years. His background was wretched. He had been a junkie, hooked on heroin, confined for cures in several cities, by occupation a barber in whatever shop in whatever city would have him until he came to Hollywood more than ten years before. In Hollywood his good looks and his cool had brought response from a number of fairly important people. One particularly was Jim Byron. Jay had worked on Byron's receding hairline and styled it in such a way that the press agent was no longer fretting about his baldness. And he was grateful. Together they came up with an idea that was to make the little barber himself a celebrity. The going rate for a twenty-minute seat in a clipper's chair at that time was two dollars.

'The only think they understand in this town," said Byron, 'is price. Make it expensive and they will buy it. I'll raise the money and you open a shop, and charge fifty bucks a trim.'

'A styling,' said Jay.

'That's what I meant.'

Ten years later the man sitting across from me was a tycoon, a millionaire with shops in three cities. One of them, in San Francisco, was backed by Abigail Folger, who was one of the bodies on the lawn that night of horror in Benedict Canyon.

When we finished our coffee, Jay led me by the hand through the bar area of The Factory and down the grilled lift to the entrance. I had brought my own car, so he signaled for the parking attendant to bring it and moved toward his own Porsche, which was parked at the curb.

'Follow me,' he said.

'Where?' I shouted—but he was already in his car so I pulled out behind him. We drove over Sunset Boulevard, skimmed along the deserted Strip and headed for the canyon in which he was soon to die.

The road up Benedict Canyon is narrow, rutted, and dark. His home squatted at the top of a flat mound like a black angular frog perched on a hillock. A twisting set of steps led to the front door, and as I parked I saw Jay waiting for me on the bottom step. Above him the stars were eerie in the darkness, lighted only by the muted glow of the moon. I trailed after him as he led me to the front door, and I felt the night air hang about us, ominous and heavy. I always got a chill when I walked into Jay's strange, Moorish-Spanish house.

Inside, he flicked on a light, and we went into the living room.

'Can I get you a drink?' Jay went to the fireplace and turned on the gas. Immediately, flames leaped high, casting tall shadows on the wall but doing nothing for the chill that lived there.

'Get comfortable,' he said, taking off his jacket and finding cigarettes and a lighter on the coffee table. He lit two, handed me one then reached into his pocket for the little vial of cocaine that he always carried with him. I wasn't shocked. I had seen him go through the ritual before. He produced a small slab of silver, hollowed out on one end like a demitasse spoon, and dipped it into the cocaine, scooping up a small amount. Holding one nostril shut with an index finger, he sniffed the white powder into the open nostril—then changed, and filled the other nostril.

Without speaking, he dipped into the vial again and brought out another ration and held it for me. I pressed first one nostril, then the other, and inhaled deep of the stuff on the spoon. Satisfied that I taken it, secure that I was now in his bag, Jay gave me one of those rare smiles.

Rising, he hurried up the stone steps (the interior of the house was all stone, brick, and rough wooden beams) to the kitchen, returning a moment later with a bottle of some exotic and obviously rare liqueur. He filled glasses for both of us, lit a joint, and settled on the floor, resting his arms on his knees. The flames from the fireplace flashed mosaic patterns across his sad-handsome face and I was silent, waiting for him to speak. He said nothing, but I knew he had some to tell me so I waited.

He reached to a gadget behind him and turned the flames up higher in the fireplace. Suddenly, dim lights flickered on outside the windows, casting the living room in long, trembling shadows. Jay filled the spoon again, four times—two for him and two for me. I made no protest.

The strong drug was coursing through my bloodstream now, spinning my brain and sending my pulses pounding. The sticky liqueur burned my throat and the heavy, sweet odor of marijuana cloaked the room. I leaned back against the cushions, closed my eyes and put my feel upon the coffee table. I felt the butt of a cigarette against my lips and took a long pull, not surprised to find that it was a fresh joint. I felt Jay lean against my leg, resting his head on my thigh, and I stroked the curly dark hair, wanting to say something that would reward me with another smile.

'You're my friend, aren't you.' It wasn't a question. The low, soft voice was muffled against my leg and I nodded. He felt the nod and his hand caressed my arm. 'I know I can talk to you. You've never put me down. You don't put anyone down.' He stopped speaking but the gentle pressure of his fingers continued up and down my arm. 'You're kind—'

I bent my head and kissed his closed eyes and his arms went around me and he held me so tight I couldn't get my breath. 'Don't leave me tonight.' His eyes were dark with emotion, fathomless sadness in their depths, and I said, 'I won't leave you, Jay.' I felt his body relax in my arms, like a child reassured that nightmares aren't for real, and I got my reward. He gave me one of his smiles. I think we both knew he had so few left to give.

Then he began talking and he told me about his fears and his dread of life. 'People knock what they don't understand,' he said. 'They think it's got to be bad if they don't dig it.' Then he looked into my eyes, and there was pain and anguish in his voice when he said, 'We all have different needs.'

'I know, baby—that's just the way it is.' I stroked his head some more. He took my hand, and still holding it, reached to the coffee table for the liqueur bottle. He seemed especially concerned about the order of things. First came the liqueur, then the little vial of cocaine, then the joint of marijuana.

'Jay, no more—' I turned my head away as he held the coke-filled spoon under my nose. My protest sounded as weak to him as it had to me, and I dutifully sniffed in the white powder. 'What the hell,' I mumbled, but if he heard he gave no sign. I felt my body begin to relax and unwind, and I dug it.

Jay reached to the coffee table again and leaned to me and kissed me. 'I'm going to pop an Amie,' he whispered against my mouth, and then there was a popping sound and he was holding something moist under my nose. 'Breathe in,' he ordered softly. 'Breathe in deep' And he pressed the Amie tight against my nose until I could breathe in only the fumes, no air. Immediately a feeling like nothing I've ever experienced filled me. I felt my head, my brain, expanding, filling with the nearness of him. His lips came down on mine, crushing, hard, passionate, and the nitrate swirled through my body, my veins, my blood; then I was lifted, flung upward with such a frighteningly beautiful force that I lay prone in its power, letting my body and soul expand, fill with an intoxicating, churning, vacillating, mind-blowing high. I could actually fill my body with his. My pores opened to allow him entry. There were no barriers. We were swirling, flying, winding, floating above the whole ugly world in a private paradise that only we could share. That only the two of us, now, at this moment, could feel. My body seemed to come apart, to unravel and expand into coils of sensual, animalistic wantoness. It was an exquisite blending, a melding of the flesh that needed nothing to bind it together. Just raw, animal emotion. We had no bodies. We were tossed up and out of our bodies, twisting, turning, climbing high, higher-aspirants to ecstasy. But the ecstasy was withheld.

Our blood returned, reluctantly, to throbbing veins, and we drifted, floated, fell softly to the carpet and felt the coarse weave, and we found our bodies waiting there for us. And we slid into them and we both knew we had been to another place.

We talked. We talked about everything from his hang-ups to my work, and we scooped into the vial more and more often. We were both on the floor now, sprawled out in a languid fashion, staring with drug-glazed eyes into the hypnotic flames that seemed to dance and leap for our pleasure alone. He told me about his desires, his needs, and I wasn't shocked when he painted pictures of girls bound and straining against their bonds as he caressed their half-nude bodies. I was fascinated with the picture and I asked him to tell me more. I wanted to know why he dug it. But he couldn't tell me. He could only suggest that I try it and see for myself.

I think it was curiosity. Maybe it was boredom. It could have been my own latent sense of doom. I stood up and he pulled my jeans off and stood back and admired my body, clad in a pair of high-topped boots, black bikini panties, a see-through blouse and no bra. He left the room, returning a moment later with a beautiful vest of gold chains which he slipped over my blouse. He then draped a gold chain belt about my waist, the many links falling around my hips. He stared at me for a full minute then ran up the stone steps again. He was gone for some time and I sat back down on the sofa and relit the joint which was now a short roach. I was so high I felt as if I was being lifted by invisible hands and held aloft as I surveyed the room below me. I heard Jay's footsteps, and I looked down from my perch in limbo and saw him standing there. A funny half-smile rested like a frightened dove upon his lips, ready to take flight the moment I said the wrong tiling. But I couldn't say the wrong thing for I couldn't speak.

My little friend, Jay Sebring, was showing me his soul. He wore a black silk Japanese robe that stopped where his thighs started. A wide leather belt accentuated his ridiculously small waist; high-heeled black boots hugged his calves and stopped at his knees, standing away from his thin legs. He looked like a waif in borrowed G.I. boots. The robe was very carefully opened two inches down the front. He wore nothing beneath it

I didn't know what to say. I don't think there was anything to say. I smiled and hoped that my eyes were understanding. He gave me a look of gratitude and poured us another drink. When he offered the silver spoon I did not refuse.

'I love your perfume,' he said. 'It's Joy, isn't it?' I nodded and he continued. 'I love beautiful fragrances. I have more than a hundred different kinds that I have collected from all over the world. Would you like to see them?' I nodded again, not really trusting myself to speak, and heard his high-heeled boots clumping up the barren stairway and into his bedroom. He was gone a long time and I waited, curious now and perhaps just a little sorry that I had allowed myself a peek into his tortured world.

'Oh, Jay,' I breathed, looking up in surprise as he entered the room carrying a large, hand-carved, mirrored tray edged in gold. It was literally covered with tiny, exquisite glass bottles and jars. Each one held a different fragrance. Some were liquid, some lotions, and some thick, smooth cream. He took all the caps off and the odors blended in a potpourri of scents; sickly sweet, pungent, strong, exhilarating.

'I want to rub them on your body.' He didn't ask. He got to his feet and disappeared again, returning this time with a length of rope. 'Will you let me tie you?' He was a small child asking for a treat that he was afraid would be refused. I nodded, and he looped the rope loosely around my wrists, asking, 'Is it too tight?'

'No, it's all right.' I tried to catch his eyes, but his head was bent and he fumbled with the slim white rope. 'Jay.' My voice pulled him up and those dark questioning eyes were upon me. 'I don't like pain.' I made my voice steady and tried to convey to him, with my eyes, that I would not allow it to happen. 'I want to make you happy, to do what brings you pleasure, but I won't allow you to hurt me.' The eyes penetrated. I licked suddenly dry lips and tried again. 'I'm not knocking it. I don't put anyone down for it—it's just not my thing.'

'I understand,' he said at length. He raised himself and kissed me, and his lips were warm and dry. He looped one end of the rope over a beam above the fireplace and tied it, asking if it was too tight. I shook my head and watched as he secured the other rope to another beam on the other side of the fireplace. I was standing on the rough stone hearth in front of the crackling fire, my arms outstretched, wrists bound with thin white rope that stretched to wooden beams on either side of the fireplace mantle. He stood back and admired his handicraft. I looked down at myself and felt— What was it? Pride in my body? Pride in my ability to bring that sexy and passionate look to his eyes? Was I turned on by this new and bizarre scene? I didn't know. I only knew that I wasn't frightened. That I trusted him. And I was curious and anxious to see what he would do next.

'You're so beautiful,' he murmured, and his eyes swept my body with such desire I felt as if I had been touched. He sank to his knees and ran trembling hands over my thighs, my legs, my leather boots. He was so gentle it felt like a butterfly wing and I writhed against the hand, wanting it to be harder. But he stopped caressing me and reached for a bottle of perfume. He poured a large amount into the palms of his hands and moved slowly toward me and spread it over my breasts and belly and thighs. He worked it in slow, circular motions, spreading, massaging, working the perfume into my flesh. He filled his hands with another fragrance and massaged it into my skin.

Again and again he reached to the coffee table, coming back each time with yet another scent, a cream, a lotion, a liquid, and he spread them over my body, onto my transparent blouse, between the chain links of my heavy gold vest, over the draped gold belt, and slithered them down my perfumed and slick legs. A lotion rested like whipped cream on the tops of my boots and glistened like satin in the eerie glow of the flames. It mingled with the perspiration of my body and shone wet and gleaming and still he did not stop. He caressed and massaged and spread layer upon layer of perfume onto my now reeking body. Then he took out a hairdressers' plastic bottle with a spray head and he squirted me all over with warm water. The heat of the water sent the fumes up to my nostrils.

'Please, Jay, it's too much,' I pleaded. The odor was reeling my drug-churned head. I was afraid I would be sick. 'The fire's too hot.' My voice seemed to come from another place, and I was surprised when he moved quickly and turned down the flames. Then he stood and surveyed his masterpiece. His eyes were seeing a beauty that only he could see. I was sorry that I was unable to share it with him. I guess I was even envious of his secret world. My wrists had begun to ache and my head was pulsing with the emotion of the evening and Jay was suddenly by my side, loosening the ropes, rubbing my wrists, and whispering, 'Are you alright? It wasn't bad, was it? It wasn't bad.' And he kissed my reddened wrists and smoothed my hair back from my damp face and wiped the perspiration from my forehead.

I sank to the floor and asked him, 'Why?'

He lowered his head and the flames made the dark sweat-curled hair glow auburn. He scooped up a spoonful of cocaine and sniffed it in jerkingly. He held it for me, and he did not answer me. Instead he said, 'Can we do it again as soon as you've rested?'

I knew my answer would be yes. I had committed myself to this point and it would have been unfair and cruel to stop him now. We shared another joint, a glass of wine, and he asked anxiously, 'Are you alright? Can we do it again?'

I watched him go through the procedure that I knew now, and I smiled sadly at his bent head as he wrapped thin white rope around my ankles, stretching my legs apart until I was standing in a spread-eagle pose. Then he began again with the perfume and warm water. Every so often he would stop and offer me a cigarette, holding it while I dragged in the smoke, and he asked me how I felt, if the fire was too hot or the ropes too tight. He seemed very concerned about me. And more and more often he left the room, staying away for longer periods of time and when he came back he always carried a new 'toy' with him.

First it was a small gold bell on a black leather thong which he tied loosely around my waist, the bell resting on my pubic mound. Thereafter, whenever he left the room, his voice would float back to me: 'I can't hear the bell. I want to hear that bell ringing.' And, smiling, amused, I would do a bump and grind, pleased at the thin tinkle of the bell and his voice saying, 'Fine—fine—keep it ringing—that's just fine—'

One trip he returned wearing a black satin hood that covered his head and shoulders. Two holes, edged in black leather, enabled him to see his way into the room. In his hand he carried a small whip with several thongs of leather, each tipped with a knot. He sank to the floor, staring, the whip la in his hand, and I began to get frightened.

'No, Jay, not the whip,' I said, and pulled against my bonds a little to see how much play I had. I was helpless.

The ropes were rather loose around my wrists but tied tightly to the beams and the loops were too small to allow my hands to slip through. My legs were beginning to tire and I tried to shift my weight. It was impossible. I was immobile. 'No whips, Jay,' I said again, peering into the black holes of his hood. I searched for his eyes, knowing that if I could get him to look into mine he wouldn't hurt me. But I couldn't see into the bottomless pits that were now his secret way of seeing me.

'I won't hurt you,' he said and I was shocked by his voice. It was hoarse, deep, and his breath came fast from behind the satin folds of his hood, fie flicked the whip, snaked it out of nowhere and it just brushed the gold bell and set it to ringing. I flinched and maybe I cried out for he suddenly clasped me around the hips and buried his face in my stomach. 'I won't hurt you—please-' His voice was muffled, sounding of pain and unshed tears and I longed to free my arms and hold him to my breast and tell him everything would be all right. But I was frightened. Frightened about the strange sensations I was feeling, the pity I had for him, the newness of being high on cocaine, the bizarre, strangely fascinating emotion of being tied and bound, spread-eagled in front of a roaring, leaping fire, the curious desire to see into his hood, into his soul...

'It's all right,' I murmured and he raised his head and for an instant I caught a glimpse of his eyes and they were shiny and they were not the eyes of my friend. The whip snaked out of the shadows and flicked the bell again and I gasped. This time I seemed to have lost my pity for him and I was just frightened. He had hurt me. He promised me he wouldn't. I felt the whip again, harder this time and I shrank away from it. But not before it had licked a red path across my thigh. 'No, Jay, no!' I pulled back as far as I could and felt the heat of the fire and I screamed. I felt the tears in my throat even before I cried out again. My body writhed against the bonds that held me helpless and I began to sob. 'Don't—don't—oh, God, don't!'

Jay cried and began tearing the hood from his head and clawing at the ropes on my wrists and ankles and freeing me, and I was crying and saying,

'Oh, Jay, Jay—you frightened me.'

And then I was free and he was standing before me and there were tears on his cheeks and he kicked the whip from him and turned his back and wept. I put my hand out to touch him and I moved a step closer. As I looked at the thin stooped shoulders, wracked now with the effort of his sobbing, my eyes fell upon the discarded whip. And next to it, there on the floor, gleaming dully in the dim light, was a long, curved butcher knife! My heart leaped in my breast. My voice was stuck captive in my throat. He leaned his head in his hands am I turned away from him.

I don't know if he heard me. I didn't try to be quiet, grabbed my things and fled out of that dark house. I ran gasping for breath, tears blurring the stone steps and my heart beating a wild tattoo against my ribs, and I didn't look back, don't remember getting into my car, but suddenly I was turning onto the brightly lit Benedict Canyon and my legs were sticking to the leather seats and the thick, sickly sweet odor of perfume assaulted my nostrils, and I put my head on the steering wheel and cried like a baby.

I saw Jay a number of times after that and I spoke to him often on the telephone. He always asked me back to his home saying one time: 'You still owe me a couple of hours. You cheated me.' But I knew I could never go back to that dark house where the chill lived.

I saw him again at a real swinger of a party where all the wild ones showed up. I was practically sucked into the room by the force of the swinging, rollicking crowd and fell into Jimmy Boyd's arms.

'Hey, sweetheart, how are you?' Jimmy had to shout in my ear to be heard above the deafening roar of the acid rock that blasted throughout the darkened room. But then another pair of arms swung me away and Tommy Smothers kissed and hugged me and passed me into the waiting arms of Nicky Blair, and then I was handed into another pair of arms. I made my way across the room in this fashion and found myself on the patio where I sank into a chair and ordered a drink.

Producer Jimmy Harris slumped against the wall, his eyes restless and sober as he surveyed the undulating bodies of the dancers. Nearly naked starlets writhed suggestively against the quivering paunches of sweating movie directors, and married stars whispered promises and propositions into the ears of other married stars. I saw one hero of the silver screen, broad-shouldered, lean-hipped, virile, dancing methodically with his mini-skirted date, but his eyes caught and held those of a limp-wristed young boy-and the boy twitched his hips in acknowledgment. I knew it would be only a matter of minutes before he traded in the mini-skirted chick for the slim-hipped boy. They're all here tonight, I thought, looking around the patio and into the living room. Hungry-eyed starlets moved restlessly through the crowd looking for somebody—pathetic kids of pathetic movie stars, show girls, models, hookers, hippies and has-beens—a real Hollywood potpourri.

Keely Smith sank into a chair opposite me and I said, 'Well, it looks like it's going to be one of those parties.'

'God—aren't they all?' Keely sighed wearily and leaned her elbows on the table. Tommy Smothers appeared with his date, Judy, and the three of them got into a heads-together, back-stroking conversation and I decided to mingle.

I stepped into the dimly lit poolroom and saw Dick Dawson leaning on a cue stick. I wasn't surprised. He can be found with a pool stick in his hand no matter where he is—the star-studded Factory, Daisy, or Candy Store, or an intimate dinner party—waiting for someone to challenge him to a game. 'Hey, Dick, how are you?' I went into his arms for my kiss.

' 'ello, Luv, 'ow are ya?' He hugged me tight, then motioned toward the pool table. 'Shall we 'ave a go, Ducks?'

'Why not?' I took a pool stick and saw Ron Joy slouch by, disappearing into the darkened living room. I wondered if Nancy Sinatra was with him and peered into the black, but all I could see were shadowy silhouettes, moving, grooving, a swaying sea of bodies.

Jack Haley Jr. claimed my pool cue and challenged Dawson to a game.

I started toward the bar and someone shoved a joint of marijuana into my mouth. But I didn't see who my benefactor was, for Kenny Spaulding scooped me up, flung me around, and kissed me. 'Hey, baby, how the hell are you?' But he didn't seem to know who 'baby' was, nor did he wait to find out. A slinky model-type pulled him away and they were swallowed up into the black room, taking my joint with them. Dino Martin brushed past me headed for the pool room with a couple of just-getting-there actresses trotting adoringly after him.

Suddenly, in the flesh-packed room, I found myself in Jay Sebring's arms. We kissed and shouted into one another's ears and I heard him say, 'Meet me in the bathroom,' but I was swept away by—Jimmy Boyd again and lost sight of Jay.

The rest of the evening was a giddy haze of debauchery. A beautiful young lesbian stuffed me into a corner and kissed me wildly upon the mouth as she blew marijuana smoke down my throat. The son of a famous star, himself a musician, was necking with the son of a famous actress, and when his wife walked into the room I was hastily shoved in as a replacement necker. I stumbled across two people having intercourse on the floor of the dark, sunken living room and the man reacted angrily, claiming I had trod upon his thing. The air seemed supercharged with an undefined electricity. Even the servants seemed to sense it. They hurried about the room, packing their rented silver trays and left-over lemons and limes. They seemed anxious to leave and let the Beautiful People get on with whatever it is Beautiful People do in private.

After a while the party began breaking up. I was getting my coat when Jay appeared and took my hand and led me to the bathroom off the master bedroom. He produced the little vial and, against my wishes this time, forced me to breathe in the wanton powder.

'Stick around,' he said. 'The squares are leaving and the good things will happen.'

'Like last time?' I asked.

'No—better,' he said. 'The whole bit-whips, ropes, and Amies. You dig Amies…'

'No, Jay,' I said. 'It's too frightening.'

I started out of the room but he held me back. 'Sharon would like to meet you again,' he said.

I looked a question. 'Sharon Tate,' he said. 'She'd dig you. She's back, you know. We have great parties.'

'Orgies,' I said. 'Good night, Jay.'

He looked genuinely rejected as I left.

He called me the very next day. 'Come on over,' he said. 'I'm having a little get-together later with Warren Beatty and Julie Christie. It'll be fun.'

'Can't make it,' I said—but he had another suggestion ready.

'How about next weekend? It's Steve Brandt's birthday and John and Michele Phillips are throwing a party for him.' He paused. 'Sharon will be there.'

'Jay, I really don't dig that crowd,' I said, 'I'm sorry, but I'm just not interested.'

But he wouldn't be put down. 'You've got to meet Gibby,' he said. 'You know, Abigail Folger, the coffee heiress.'

I had to smile at the name-dropping. 'Who else?' I asked, knowing that's what he wanted me to ask.

'A very groovy writer, friend of Gibby's, Wojciech Frykowski,' Jay said, warming up to the conversation now and speaking very rapidly. 'And, of course, Mama Cass and Bill Doyle and probably George Hamilton and Herb Alpert, Andy Prine, Joe Namath—' He was reeling off names faster than I could remember them. Obviously on an upper, I thought Jay didn't usually speak so quickly. 'There will be a couple hundred people there. Come on—it'll be fun.'

I wondered how many would be left for the fun and games after the squares had split for home but I didn't ask. I finally convinced him that I couldn't make it and he reluctantly hung up the telephone.

The last time I spoke to Jay was early in August. He called me about eleven at night. 'Remember what I spoke to you about the last time I saw you?' he asked.

'What?' I said.

'Sharon,' he said. 'She's got a great pad. Lonely. Safe. Great people. Only small groups and nobody talks. Won't you come—please. I promised you would.'

I hesitated. It was the small boy asking for the sweet again. I looked toward my kitchen. My maid was cleaning up the dishes. She held a butcher knife high in the air and shook water from it, and the lights flashed brilliant along the curved blade. I shivered with fear, remembering the knife near the ropes at Jay's house. I hung up the telephone without even saying goodbye.

Less than a week later, Jay Sebring was dead, one of the victims of a senseless orgy of carnage that also left the bodies of Sharon Tate, Gibby Folger, and Wojciech Frykowski. He died near the celebrated people he loved so much, his life's blood seeping into the thick carpet of a plush mansion while the hawks of death pussyfooted through the house and gardens, chuckling over the gawky, awkward clumps of stiffening flesh they had littered about until the clean fragrance of dawn sent them to some other place.

tripping along in Hollywood

Yeah, I had embraced the inner circle of Hollywood's jet-swinger-set who were all into one kind of drug or another. The sixties brought drugs right up front where they could be analyzed and experimented with, and the stars were the first to publicly announce that they found drugs to be safer than booze.

Articles appeared in national magazines reporting that this star or that one smoked grass, lived with whomever they pleased, and scorned marriage and the Establishment. These new stars did not bother to drape themselves in diamonds, furs, feather boas, tuxedos, silks, and satins; they turned up for interviews wearing faded blue jeans, sometimes holding a baby on their hips that had been born without benefit of its father's last name. And these wide-eyed little tykes were not hindered with names like Clark, Debbie, Carole or Jimmy—their handles were Sunshine, Freedom, Earth, and Star. Morals were lax or nonexistent.

Everyone smoked grass, snorted cocaine, gulped tabs of mescaline and LSD and were quick to tell the squares what they were missing. It was, after all, the age of Aquarius, and there was a new world a-comin'—the sixties were the ground floor of tomorrow. Anyone could climb aboard for the trip if their heads were in the right place. And if parents the world over wept when they saw their children taking to the road, what could they do? The young people were following the stars.

I do not mean to give the impression that the then-current crop of movie stars invented or even introduced drugs to Hollywood. Drugs are as old as time. No one 'discovered' them or even came up with new ideas of their power. Our culture did that for us. It does not take greatness to come up with an idea; sometimes it's simply that the idea's time has come. And so it was with drugs. If a fall-guy must be produced, then let us submit our government of that era.

Vietnam was a dirty word in most cities of the world during the sixties and early seventies, particularly with the younger set. The kids under twenty-five who reveled in permissiveness of all kinds and stumped in the streets or attempted to invade the Pentagon or burgle draft board offices of their files. And, in a way, this was true of Hollywood, where causes are often the only meaningful part of a drab fairy-tale life—playing a cowboy or a spy or a hillbilly hick from dawn to dusk in an endless episodic dream of unreality.

But Vietnam soon became a beautiful word in Hollywood. It came to mean a paradisic location from which came the greatest, headiest, most soul-satisfying grass known to heads—from messenger boys to superstars and producers. When our boys in uniform began returning home they brought with them a new type of potent grass, called ganja. And it came well-advertised with a snappy, fatalistic slogan originated—not by a bright young man on Madison Avenue—but by one of the hordes of smokers who gasped in its numbing, stunning fumes before going out on a patrol from which they might never return. Huddling in a group as they checked their weapons and grenades, a squad leader would flip away his roach (because there's plenty more where that came from) and shout to his buddies: 'Let's go, men! Let's die high!'

In Hollywood, where patrols were not real anyway, the players don't want to die-they just want to get high. High enough to get through the day and ease the boredom of the evening ahead. (Like, what do you do after you've put your clothes back on?)

So where do we all go from here? The bum, the groper for fame, the business types in their plush front offices, the superstars (and those who write about them), the hookers, and the hippies. You fly along on the prevailing wind, that's what you do. You don't unwind after work. You blow your mind. Drugs had gotten out of hand. No longer were folks using it for relaxation—they were abusing it in the worst possible way. Dope seemed to suddenly become a monster, a raging flood, gobbling up everything that stood in its path. The younger set, those in Podunk as well as Hollywood, were grabbing at happiness with both hands and thumbing their noses at the Establishment and the government. They needed pulling up. They got it in one fast lesson. It happened like this.

On the night of August 8, 1969, peace appeared to be residing in Cielo Drive, an off-shoot of Benedict Canyon in the Bel Air section of the sprawling city of Los Angeles. Peace was appropriate, because *cielo* is Spanish meaning sky or heaven, and L.A. is, after all, the City of the Angels. But—*Aparecio coma llovido cielo* (He appeared out of a clear sky). A killer came to call, to disturb the peace of paradise.

The next morning five bodies were discovered littered about the vast, sprawling grounds and living quarters of Roman Polanski's rented mansion. His wife, actress Sharon Tate, her ex-lover and hair stylist Jay Sebring, coffee heiress Gibby Folger, a Polish dope peddler named Frykowsky, and Steven Parent, an innocent victim of a society gone berserk. Immediately cries were heard: 'Drugs!' 'Sexual permissiveness!' 'Black magic!' 'Decadence!'

In a one-sided press interview, during which no questions were permitted, the bereaved husband said, a week after the murders, that he was badly shaken by the implications in the press and the speculation in Hollywood that his home had been a scene of a sex and narcotics orgy and that his lovely, dead wife had engaged in odd practices that night and at previous times. And he capped his statement by inviting newsmen to come to a macabre exhibition of the home, still blood-covered, and the room and furnishings that had been intended for the child that had been the sixth victim in its mother's belly.

The statement, coming with the invitation, was farcical and only lent credence to the observation that somewhere in the whole bizarre atrocity there lay a typical Polanski movie plot with all the grisly touches. It was said of Polanski that, if the murders had not involved his wife and friends, he would have more than likely bought it and filmed it.

Polanski's bald and bold picture of his home and friends as gentle, ordinary people, bruised in death by reckless wagging tongues, was considered utter nonsense. The home was notorious in underground Hollywood as a palace of illegitimate roistering. Roman Polanski's reputation as a mad genius director, famous for being able to give a weird twist to a shot of a pair of nuns walking to mass, probably did not help the rumors. Besides, since no one had the least clue as to who had done the grisly deed, Polanski seemed a likely candidate.

When it was finally discovered that Charles Manson and his gang of hippie killers were responsible for the multiple murders, all of America was thrown into shock. In the past, they had carefully avoided believing that such a thing could happen in their society—to their children. They were forced to look back, and, perhaps for the first time, they realized that their children were not following.

The murders, then, became a slap in the face. They were the very encapsulation of truth about violence and revolt in our young people today. With one senseless act, America was shown, quite vividly, that tomorrow is promised to no one. In Hollywood, this was a pretty bitter pill to swallow. Tomorrow means: the release of your latest movie, residuals from that television commercial you did last month, better scripts, more money, bigger homes, fancier cars. But in less time than it took to read an account of the murders, hate-obsessed Charlie Manson showed these affluent and influential people just how swiftly they could be eliminated. And their drawing power at the box office would not save them, nor would their bank account, beauty, or brilliance.

Hollywood was faced with the task of seeing what it had become. Movies were filled with blatant sex, horrible violence, vomit-inducing shockers that sent the squeamish screaming into the night. There were those who admitted that the depraved younger generation were definitely influenced by these corrupt, degenerate films.

Hollywood looked at itself. And it saw.

the gorgeous and the grotesque

In another part of Hollywood, a tiny fingernail slice of moon slid through a shutter of a huge decaying mansion on a hill and fell across a tiny figure. It was white and bloodless in death, its body stiffened in awkward angles. The neck was thin and scrawny, showing pale blue veins bulging against the pallor of death. The face was ghastly. Yellow eyes protruded from red-rimmed sockets, an expression of horror frozen in the amber depths. Colorless lips were drawn back in a silent protest of rage, the empty mouth slashing a dark cavity in the ashen face. Thin tufts of dead hair matted to the skull in ragged patches—exposing two small dun-colored horns.

It was dressed in swaddling clothes; rough, hand-sewn garments that clung to the thin body and wrapped about the head forming a hood. It lay in a crude coffin, the lid of which had been slid halfway back to expose the little corpse inside. A candle stood on the lid, its dim flame haloing the coffin, somberly illuminating its grotesque occupant.

A sudden gust of wind in the airless room snuffed out the candle and pitched the room into blackness.

'God, no—no! Murder! Death!' A woman's voice, pitched high with terror, sliced through the dark room and there was an audible gasp from the assembled hippies. There was a thud as a body hit the floor and someone quickly relit the candle. Princess Lida Ramu, queen of the hippies, self-ordained witch, and believer in the unknown, lay stiff and rigid, a thin rope of saliva at the corner of her lax mouth. She was in a trance and recounting the horrible murders that were taking place that very minute in Benedict Canyon. If there had ever been any doubt that Lida the Witch had the power, that doubt no longer existed in the minds of her guests that sultry August evening. She writhed and moaned and repeatedly murmured, 'They're dead! Killed! Murdered—all of them—dead!'

The next morning the papers were full of the bizarre and macabre murders that had taken place in sedate and pompous Beverly Hills. Even the Los Angeles coroner, Thomas Noguchi, no stranger to bloody, grisly crimes, was shocked by what he found at the Tate home. The bodies were hacked, slashed, and repeatedly stabbed, their sexual organs mutilated in a most grotesque manner. Sharon's swollen belly, carrying an eight-month-old unborn child, had been deeply cut with an X—and one of her breasts had been removed. Jay's sexual organs had been severed and reportedly stuffed into his mouth. He and Sharon were bound together with a thin white rope—the kind Jay had used to tie me up that evening less than a month before.

Rumors ran wild in Hollywood's underground news media. Whispers had close friends of Sharon and Roman claiming they knew the murders would take place weeks before they actually happened. They no longer hinted at black magic, but openly accused the victims of being members of a depraved cult which worshipped the devil and was fond of inflicting and receiving pain.

Hollywood was in a spasm of fear. Celebrities hired private detectives to stand guard around the clock. Guns were purchased in astonishing numbers. Huge, fearsome watch dogs were snapped up by still others who lived in the area and a kind of gray quiet settled over Los Angeles.

For weeks, months, police searched and arrested and questioned countless suspects-but they still remained baffled and without a lead of any kind.

Suddenly, four months after the rampage of death, police announced they had solved the murders. Sketchy information appeared about a band of hippies who lived in a rundown western town (Spahn Movie Ranch) and were led by a mystical, bearded Pied Piper, Charles Manson.

Once again fear careened throughout Hollywood and Beverly Hills. The Beautiful People were still terrified. Had the police really captured all of them? Were there some in hiding, perhaps, who felt an obligation to carry on the carnage against society and the Establishment? Being rich and famous doesn't always exclude one from the same fears the commoners feel. In this case, the rich and affluent were the hunted.

Manson told police that he had commanded that everyone in the Tate home be murdered as a warning to all the hugely successful entertainers that had acted without compassion to those trying to break into the ranks of show business. It seems Charlie Manson had aspirations toward becoming a singing star, but all the Hollywood doors had been closed to him. Seething with rejection, hating those who were too beautiful and successful, he decided to eliminate them one by one, until the powers that be recognized his talent—and his needs. Everyone wants to get into show biz! Even a demented madman like Manson.

Susan Atkins joined the ranks of the infamous when she spilled her story to a grand jury in the hope of escaping the gas chamber. She told of a communal family that consisted of some thirty hippies who lived in a derelict, rundown movie ranch and followed, blindly, the orders of a small, long-haired, demonic Mahdi-Manson. She said that six or seven members of the family took part in the killings on orders from Manson, but that he did not participate in the murders himself. Miss Atkins said that Manson had ordered everyone to dress in black clothes, to take their knives and drive to the home of Sharon Tate, and to kill everyone there. He wanted to 'teach the Establishment a lesson' and show the world that their gods and goddesses of the silver screen were mere mortals after all.

Now, of course, the world knows the intimate details of the mad, hate-obsessed Manson—but this has not stilled the fear. Rasputin-like, Manson was a spiritual leader in every sense of the word, and millions of Americans had to face that fact—even as they cringed in revulsion. He was worshipped by his followers and referred to as a 'high priest,' 'God' or 'the Devil'—he was called both 'Satan' and 'Jesus', and the American public was forced to face the fact that he was the very image of the revolt and violence that had become fashionable with the young people—with their own children. They were forced to ask themselves how our society could have produced a Charlie Manson—a creature of violence, capable of inflicting numbing cruelty upon others; a sick, twisted reject who set himself up as a leader and commanded his subjects in acts of horror and death.

In 1970, I had been assigned by a magazine to get the story on Manson, so I contacted my friend Osmo, who told me, 'I think it was June or July when I first met Manson.' He lolled against a tree in my backyard and lovingly stroked his shoulder-length blond hair as he methodically drew on a joint. His eyes were dreamy, his attitude relaxed. 'I went out to the ranch with a cat called the Kid. He was hooked on some chick who lived there-Squeaky, I think her name was. (Lynn Fromme, a member of the family who had been taken into custody, questioned, then released—her nickname was Squeaky.) Anyway, the Kid was strung out on smack (high on heroin) and when we got there he shot up again and just went on the nod and crashed. He had the wheels, so I was hung there until he came to. Then this chick comes out, ya dig, and says, 'Hey, wanna drop some acid?' and I didn't have anything else to do, so we each popped a tab and sat down to wait for it to hit.

'I had just dropped a couple of days before and was still on from it, so this hit me right away. I saw an old car parked in front of the house and I climbed up on the roof and sat down, watching this chick, ya dig. She was wearing this skimpy little dress and she sat down on the porch steps and let her legs fall open. She wasn't wearing any panties and she reached down and kinda played with her pussy for a while, then got up and disappeared into the house.

'I was really coming on to the acid now and didn't think about how long she had been gone, but there she was again, sprawled in the doorway on the porch steps and holding a big, motherfucking knife! *I made it*, she says, smiling real funny-like. Then she opens her legs and shoved the handle of the knife into her cunt. So I sit there on top of the car and watch—what the hell. Then she says, *Charlie really digs knives. He makes us all carry a knife and we have to make them ourselves, too.* She bent her head and smiled that funny grin and watched herself masturbate.'

I learned that the Kid and Manson did not get along. Most hippies don't get involved in hard drugs like heroin and the Kid, although just barely nineteen years old, had been hooked on the stuff for years. He was no stranger to Manson's group, however, and had married one of the girls in the family. The Kid told me that it wasn't just a handful of hippies and drifters who believed in Manson's powers, but even the rich and influential were affected by him. Timothy Leary, self- appointed king of drugs, once sent a limousine to the ranch with orders to this driver to pick up Manson and drive him straight to Leary's lair. The feisty little guru reportedly told the driver to 'Fuck off. If Leary wants to see me he can come out here.'

A sexually permissive attitude was the order of the day. Girls were passed from man to man each night and were made by Manson to fuck anyone he told them to—even occasional strangers who wandered into the ranch. Girls were given to men from the so-called straight world as gifts—when he wanted a favor in return.

Another female member said: 'We made love at least once a day, usually more, with somebody. Sometimes Charlie wanted to see us girls making love to each other and just said, *Go in there and fuck that dude—he's a friend of mine.* And we did. Nobody could refuse Charlie anything. He was beautiful.'

Manson may have been of a generous nature with his girls, but he did not deny himself in the process. More than one told me that they witnessed the scrawny little guru when he called in one or more of his girls and commanded them to perform bizarre sexual acts with him—while he sat chatting with guests!

'There was just no morality at all,' Osmo told me. 'This chick who was jacking off with the knife when I was there, was a pretty little thing, but dingy as hell. She had dropped acid so many times and experimented with so many mind-expanding drugs, she was really strung out in the brain. While I was sitting there watching her, somebody yelled, 'Hey, Pig, come in here and suck my cock'—and without a word she got to her feet, pulled her dress over her head and walked naked into the house.'

Two occasional visitors to the Spahn ranch, Cosmo and Valentino, belonged to a different type of 'family'—this one presumably founded on kinder, more gentle factors. The high priestess of his little group is none other than princess Lida Ramu, the good witch of the west.

'Lida's a real trip,' Cosmo told me once. 'She won't put up with any bullshit or any phony establishment freaks. She just goes into a trance, man, and drains them—I mean, she literally drains them of every ounce of energy. She really freaks people out who bug her sensitivity—like, dig, she and a friend made this wax baby, like the one they used in *Rosemary's Baby*, with the horns and everything. She was going to present it to Roman Polanski as a warning to stop with all those creepy-crawly movies about the unknown and that junk, dig.'

'Hey, man, there's more,' Valentino mumbled from the depths of his long, shaggy beard. 'What about all those cats who think the baby was meant as an omen to Sharon Tate that her own baby would be born like that? Because of Polanski's eerie movies about sadomasochism and the devil and all that there.' His head dropped back to his chest and disappeared into the matted patch of hair and beard.

Bits and pieces, gathered from reluctant sources, hinted that the grotesque wax figure in the crude coffin was a symbol of Polanski's blatant display of black magic; that his wife was doomed to give birth to a deformed baby—a baby who would be a tool of the devil—a baby who must be put to death before it reached life.

Others argued that the baby played no part in the murders. It was Sharon Tate and Jay Sebring whose time had come and who had to be put to death as a warning to the affluent. This was determined by a mad, dwarf-like demon who needed to lash out at the Establishment with a psychotic, horrifying violence.

I heard from a few family members that Sharon had paid a visit to the Manson ranch with Abagail Folger and that Manson had flipped over the blond goddess. But he was short and dirty and his ravaged face held strange, penetrating eyes, one of which was turned at an angle, giving him a cock-eyed look. Sex goddesses sneer at trash and Sharon was no exception. She put down Manson's timid advances with five well-chosen words: 'Fuck off, you little creep.' Manson seethed at this public slap in the face. How dare she, this blond, leggy creature, refuse his hand offered in love and friendship? (Since then, more reliable sources revealed Manson and Tate never met and that Manson sent his minions to the mansion because he thought music producer Terry Melcher, a former tenant, still lived there.)

While meeting and interviewing the principles in this most bizarre of Hollywood crimes, I was often shocked at the many hang-ups of the so-called Beautiful People set.

I remember talking to Joe Hyams and his wife, Elke Sommer, about their ghost—and not quite believing what I was hearing. It seems Joe and Elke had finally managed to get enough money ahead (movie stars are notorious spenders) to buy their dream home in Beverly Hills. They hadn't been there a fortnight when they began to see and hear strange things. It wasn't long before they were convinced that they had a ghost sharing the mansion with them. At first they thought it rather elegant to have one's own ghost haunting one's own mansion. Then it began to get on their nerves. Elke thought it was haunting them because they had come by their fortunes too easily. Guilt, I learned, is a major hang-up among most show business folks. Most of them cannot accept the fact that they earn more in one week than the average Joe earns in a lifetime. Result—guilt. And from this guilt there results a most complex personality.

In writing my article, I speculated on this theory of famous folks and their hang-ups and remembered, with fondness and some amusement, the famous, infamous, rich, and royal folks that I had known and loved. It reminded me of what F. Scott Fitzgerald said to Ernest Hemingway:

'Rich people are different from you and me.' To which Hemingway replied, 'Yes—they have more money.'

And more hang-ups, I thought, remembering my numerous encounters with these very special people. I remembered how I had become one of them and had believed, as they did, that sex, booze, whips, and dope was fun.

when the party is over

When I got divorced, I asked for three things: My daughter, child support, and alimony for two years. I figured I'd be earning plenty on my own within two years, and everything would be fine.

But in 1970, I was forced to undergo a radical double mastectomy… and my life was never the same. Back then, women didn't talk about things like that. It was almost shameful. In the mid-seventies, former First Lady Betty Ford, millionairess Happy Rockefeller, and newsperson Betty Rollin finally broke the ice. This was all very interesting to me as I was naturally curious about how other women felt about their ordeal. However, in almost all cases the women were married and pretty well settled into their lives. There were not very many young, single women writing about their experiences and I knew that cancer doesn't just strike mature, married ladies; I was just out of my twenties.

One night in the fall of 1970 I was making love with my current man, and he was caressing my breasts when he suddenly raised himself upon an elbow and said, 'Did you know you had a lump here?'

I didn't really think anything about it. I mean, you read about how a woman finds a small lump and she immediately panics, calls in the relatives and starts writing her will. Well, that's not the way it happened with me. I just thought it was probably a swelling from all the exercise I had been getting lately or maybe it was one of those little fibrous cysts a woman sometimes gets in her glands. So, I just murmured something about the lump being my pulsating passion for him and pulled him back into my arms.

It wasn't until a couple of days later that I thought about what he had said. I checked myself in front of the bathroom mirror and sure enough, there was a little hard marble-like swelling in my left breast, near the armpit. I still wasn't frightened but I told a couple of girlfriends about it and they convinced me to go to a doctor. The first one I saw told me it was probably nothing, gave me some antibiotic for a possible infection (from my previous silicone injections? He said no, it was not that) and sent me home.

Three months later my left breast was swollen and red and very painful. This time I really did have an infection of some kind but I responded to the medication and was fine again in two or three days. Things went on normally for the next eight or nine months and I was not aware that several more lumps had formed in both breasts. To make a long story short, I went to the doc, was put in the hospital the next day, and operated on the following morning,

When I awoke I no longer had my lovely 38-C's. I had been sliced from armpit to armpit and stitched up like a Thanksgiving turkey with two drains inserted into my body beneath each breast—or the place where they had been. The drains were long, thin rubber tubes which were inserted up into the cavity of each breast and into the incision to drain out the old blood. The blood would flow through the tubes and empty into a clear plastic cup with a lid. It looked a little like a dish of Jell-O by the time my blood had drained off for a few days. Those awful drains and the long needle inserted into the back of my hand was the most painful part of the surgery.

The doctors came in, examined me and began changing the bandages and I almost flipped when I saw all the blood, those ugly tubes and awful black stitches. My chest was totally flat, the nipples tuckered up as tight as hard little raisins, blood caked in the creases, one pointing straight up at me, the other one over to one side, almost under my arm. I turned my head away until the bandaging was completed. I had had to sign a release the night before stating that I wouldn't hold the hospital responsible if they 'lost' my nipples in surgery.

My first visitor, my dear old friend Griff the Bear, almost made me pop my stitches with his get-well card. He had scotch-taped two Playtex Living Nipples from a baby bottle to the card and said those were my spares. And right then and there I knew it would be okay with my friends. I didn't give much thought to men and how they would react.

In fact, I didn't give much thought to anything for over a week. I just lay back, rolling over every four hours to receive that lovely injection the nurses brought like clockwork. I think I was still stoned when I left for home nine days later. And the

prescription I had had filled kept me in a state of rosy relaxation for another week or so.

Then one day I woke up and I wasn't stoned anymore and I looked down at my raw, ugly chest, the thick black stitches marring the white skin like something out of a horror film, the twisted nipples cocked at odd angles from one another, one almost hidden by a flap of skin that tucked under my armpit. The scar looked like an axe murderer had been at me. I fell across the bed and cried until I couldn't catch my breath.

My roommate Wendy, and Griff, rushed into the bedroom and tried to comfort me but I was absolutely hysterical. I cried for three days until Wendy became worried about me and called a doctor she knew who prescribed an antidepressant drug. It worked and in a couple of days I was able to joke, 'Well, I went in looking like Jayne Mansfield and came out looking like Twiggy. Guess I'm fashionable, huh?'

I've always had many, many friends around me, people dropping by at all hours, shooting pool, swimming, whatever, that my life was no different than it had ever been. Only now we talked a lot about my operation and how lucky I was, and so on. When I finally did get around to noticing men again, I naturally turned my attention to the guy I had been dating before the surgery.

He and I went to bed as easily as we always had but he was very concerned with touching me or not touching me. His hands would tremble as he neared my breast area and then he would quickly put them around me, stroking my back. He asked me several times if I was all right, did it hurt to hug me, things like that, and I was put off by it. It made me more conscious of it and I found myself joking in an effort to cover my embarrassment and sadness. The joking stuck and I discovered that it was the only way I was going to be able to handle the loss of my 'fantastic tits' as they had been dubbed by many photographers and lovers.

Six months after the mastectomy I went back into the hospital to have silicone implants put in. The only thing that had kept me going those past months had been the knowledge that I could have my breasts reconstructed as soon as I was totally healed and there was no danger of infection.

I spent only five days in the hospital this time and came out with a cute, pert little set of 36-B's. I was at my slimmest, 105 lbs., and found that I liked the new image of myself as sleek and lean, rather than sexily voluptuous as I had been.

For the next year and a half, I must admit that I really went wild. I guess I felt that I owed it to myself. I had gone through a devastating experience which was not only mind-blowing and painful, but as expensive as hell.

Like most restless young women about town, I had never given a thought to life or medical insurance so I was stuck with an enormous hospital fee. I was unable to work for two months and I fell behind in my house payments, which resulted in a foreclosure and forced me and my daughter out on the street. I rented a smaller house and forced myself back to work.

Life was beautiful, I was alive and I had a brand-new set of boobs that felt as natural as my real ones had felt: Soft, pliant, the skin over them smooth to the touch, the implants soon felt like a real part of me. If any nagging doubts about my sexuality entered my head I would immediately cover it with a wisecrack.

I remember one night I was going out to a party of some sort and my date, eyeing my sheer blouse and bare breasts, remarked, 'Why not? The way you dress everybody in town has seen them!'

'Oh, no they haven't,' I replied. 'These boobs are brand new—no one's seen them before!' The jokes were still pulling me through.

About a year and a half after I had the implants put in, I developed an infection in one side and discovered a number of hard little lumps all over my pretty new boobs... on both sides. There were several under each breast along the scar, solid as a rock and stuck fast to the scar tissue, and many more along the edges of the implant, all the way around both of them.

I was terrified of calling the doctor. I would die before I lost my breasts a second time, but after a week both breasts were so swollen and red and painful I had no choice but to make an appointment. The doc gave me pills for the infection, instructions to apply cold compresses to the swollen area—then he told he was afraid the implants would have to come out. He made the arrangements.

I went home, got roaring drunk and smoked everything I could get my hands on. By this time, I was well acquainted with the procedure; the awful drains, the slashed chest, black, ugly stitches and the pain.

I was out of the hospital in five days and back at my typewriter in less than a month. The bills wouldn't wait for me to take the required time of six weeks to heal properly. I medicated myself to get through it all.

I still found myself clinging to the men I had known for a long time and who knew all about my boob history. But I'm friendly and optimistic, and soon I was going out, meeting new people, new men. I met a really super guy, Jerry Morris, and was attracted at once. He knew nothing about my background and I was suddenly faced with telling a stranger about my deformity. I couldn't just tell him without a lengthy explanation about the implants, infections, etc. I thought maybe I'd just go ahead and keep on my padded bra and try to discourage him from touching me *there.*

But that didn't seem like a very good idea. He was sure to find out, and what then? What if it turned him off so much he wouldn't want to continue? That wouldn't be fair to either one of us. I knew I should tell him up front so he could back out if he wanted to, but I didn't want him to back out. If he didn't want me anymore it would just kill me. For the first time since all the surgery had begun, I was faced with the truth. The awful knowledge that I was deformed, maimed, scarred, whatever you wanted to call it, and this gorgeous man might reject me because of it. For a woman who had always been very secure (smug, some said) in my sexuality and attractiveness, this was a devastating blow to my ego.

I solved the problem by pouring more wine and lighting another joint. If he was stoned enough, maybe he wouldn't notice.

Then I suddenly blurted it out, as quickly as possible, just hitting the highlights. Whatever his answer would be, I wanted to know right now and get it over with. Jerry didn't say a word until I was finished speaking then he slipped his hands up under my gown and unhooked my bra, letting it fall off my shoulders. He bent forward and gently kissed each puckered, cock-eyed nipple then raised his lips to mine. There was such an expression of sweetness and gentleness in his eyes, and when we made love he caressed me with passion, not afraid that he would hurt me, but with all the lust of healthy male animal. He whispered the most beautiful things; I was lovely, a sexy, a whole woman; and if he didn't mention my fantastic tits then neither one of us noticed. (Thank you, Jerry, for making the most difficult moment in my life so easy.)

I was planning on having the implants put back in after I had healed sufficiently and there was no danger of infection. The six-month waiting period passed quickly and I was full of enthusiasm, rushing to the hospital to hear the good news of when I could be admitted.

I was to be admitted, all right, but not for the eagerly-awaited new boobs. I had developed more lumps in my breasts, dozens of them that drew the flesh down to my chest bone sticking it together in hardened lumps that looked and felt like old candle wax that had long-since melted.

I would have to have what the surgeon called a mini-mastectomy, a thorough cleansing to rid my chest area of all cysts, lumps and scar tissue before my body would tolerate the foreign objects, or implants.

I was devastated for a while then my optimism rose again and I even convinced myself that it was a good idea: I would finally be free of all the old tissue that seemed prone to fibrous growths and all the toughened skin, once and for all, and when I was ready to have the implants put in, there would be nothing for the lumps to grow on.

The hospital trip was easy and familiar to me. The morning of the surgery I awoke promptly at six in the morning, knowing that a nurse would soon be there to prep me for the operation. I rolled over without being told for the injection that was to calm me before being wheeled into the operating room and the granddaddy shot, sodium pentothal.

I woke up sometime that afternoon, groggy, nauseous, glanced down expecting to see two nice little mounds under the bandages.

I saw nothing. I was still as flat as a board. Flatter, it seemed, as the bandages were wrapped tight to my bony chest. Time for the doctors to make their rounds and I listened mutely as he gently explained that there was simply no way to remove all the lumps at one time. He couldn't leave me under that long while he fished around for all of them. I would have to come back in six months for another cleansing mastectomy.

My life seemed to be divided into six month periods of agony.

I was dry-eyed, then he left and I remained that way when I was released five days later, I didn't even cry when I got home. I sent my neighbor out for some vodka and proceeded to get righteously ripped. I stayed that way for the next month. If depression set in when I was alone, I'd pick up the phone and invite some new cutie over who was currently infatuated with me.

That's when my drinking started getting out of hand. I found that as long as I was drunk and had some young lover in my arms, dazzling him with racy stories of my past glories, I wasn't depressed. In this foggy state of mind, I cast myself in the role of sexual guru.

Kids from ten to thirty, old friends, and older friends started dropping by my house almost daily, knowing that there would be a party of some sort going on. I would sit there, holding court, amusing everyone with my witty stories, expounding on life and strength, sex and love, pain and happiness, because who knew better than I what it was all about? When I had had enough of the group therapy, I would look around the room and simply pick the guy I wanted to stay after the others had left.

Now romantic encounters were a very simple matter; I did not have to go through the embarrassing, stammering explanation of my boob history. Everyone knew, as it was usually one of the main topics of conversation. Men were naturally curious about how a woman would have the strength to carry on her normal life after losing such an important part of herself. They related it directly to a man losing his testicles, and I could feel their genuine sympathy. Women were naturally frightened, wondering if it could happen to them.

There were those who simply did not mention it, but they would constantly remind me that they knew what I was going through by complimenting me on how well I was handling such ugly fate. Others were openly sympathetic, wanting to talk about it and even to see what my ravaged chest looked like. As I was still stoned much of the time, this macabre request didn't upset me. I even rather liked the attention and the look of horror on their faces when they stared at my wasted chest.

I was still just flat. I mean, I hadn't had the final injustice that would come later.

At this stage I was still able to wear a regular padded bra or a regular pair of department store falsies.

The six month wait over, I went back to the hospital for the next step in the exorcising of Nancy's lumps. I did not look when the doctors changed the bandages. I had this very queer, fatalistic feeling and the most gross, sick jokes flitted through my mind about my deformity. Making fun of myself before anyone else could had become a way of life with me. My sense of humor had pulled me through some very difficult situations and I wasn't about to give it up now. I had a feeling I was going to need it more than ever, so I lay in my sterile hospital cot and dreamed up funny gags about my operation.

I was driven home by one of my closest male friends, Lon Viser, and the moment I was inside the house I unbuttoned my robe, lifted off the wide bandages and looked. It was far worse than even my twisted sense of humor had imagined.

I was used to being flat for the past few years. Flat I could handle. I wasn't too sure I could handle concave, however, and that's exactly what I was. There were two deep, lopsided holes in my chest as if all the meat had been scooped out, scraping the bone itself and totally emptying the chest cavity. The skin was stretched super-tight across the hard ridges of bone and scar tissue. It was discolored, purple, red, traces of dark bruises, the swollen incisions crisscrossed with black thread, the knots bulky and stiff, scratching my arm whenever I tried to move it. The wide bone that runs down the middle of my chest protruded out, causing the flesh on either side to fall away, disappearing into the shrunken holes. It looked like a couple of muffin tins without the muffins.

'My God,' Lon cried, staring horrified 'What the hell did they do to you? It looks like you were chopped with a hatchet!'

Not a terribly discreet way of putting it, but I had to admit it was shocking. I forced a laugh and retorted 'It's better than a poke in the eye with a sharp stick, I reckon!'

And that was the way I felt. I just figured, *Oh well, I'm used to it by now. I know I'm not going to die, I know that I have super friends and a darling daughter who loves me very much. I have all the support any person could ask for.* I was luckier than most so-called whole people in my relationships with others, so I figured there was nothing to worry about.

Being concave opened up a whole new area of witticisms I could toss off at parties, 'Are you sure the Bionic Woman started this way?' I found that I not only could handle 'flat' I could handle 'concave' as well.

As I began healing, however, I found that concave wasn't going to be that easy. First, there was the matter of bras. I couldn't wear falsies anymore because the large holes spread up toward my throat and the falsies stopped about two inches short of the cavity. You could look at me from the side and see daylight through my bra.

I found a place in downtown Los Angeles that sold prosthesis and I made an appointment for a fitting, I had pretty much convinced myself that I was destined to remain deformed for the rest of my life so why not go all the way and get the damn phony tits to go along with my phony sense of humor?

I was now thirty-six years old and much of my shining optimism had given way to nonchalant acceptance. I hated the damn prosthesis from the first moment I put them on.

They felt like they weighted twenty pounds each and the dense foam-rubber material irritated my still-fresh incisions. They were very expensive and were not sold as a pair. Each one cost seventy-five bucks, but I felt a bit consoled by the fact that there were also some there with a price tag of over a hundred-and-fifty dollars each. I was getting a bargain! The special bra that they fit into cost twenty-five bucks, and I had to have at least two. Two was all I could afford as my income was in sad, the sad shape.

Once fitted out with the prosthesis something happened to my head. The super-strong lady who could handle anything and make light of it was suddenly filled with such self-pity, I was shocked. I found myself bursting into tears at the slightest provocation. Melancholy would sweep over me with such force that I felt like I was shrouded in dark clouds and would never see the sun again. I cried all the time and I didn't want to see anyone.

I moved to Lake View Terrace, far away from my old, familiar neighborhood where everybody knew me. I much preferred being alone with my booze and grass and the dull, droning, reliable boredom of television. I managed somehow to get some work done, just enough to feed myself and Staci, using her child support to make ends meet. My world was foggy and just a little off balance, and I liked it that way.

I became such a recluse that when friends called to ask me out they would begin with, 'I know you never leave your house, but...' I was amused by this and dubbed myself a hermit and fed the rumor with new jokes about my aloneness. But every so often, my natural optimism would arise and I would throw a party and get in on like I used to.

The self-pity I had been feeding for the past few months changed into a sort of embarrassment. When someone would tell me how strong I was and how well I was coping,

I would feel guilty and ashamed because I knew that it just wasn't true. I wasn't coping with anything. I was escaping. I wasn't a cute, eccentric recluse. I was a coward. I wasn't even pretty anymore; I was bloated, puffy, and always suffering from a hangover. I wasn't having beautiful love affairs; I was having drunken, stoned orgies that I couldn't even remember clearly the next day because I had reached the point where I was blacking out a lot.

Again, I felt self-pity. Not because I had lost my breasts. Because I had lost my self-respect and pride. Self-pity turned swiftly to self-disgust. Now I stayed behind locked doors for another reason. The person I had become made me sick with shame. The sort of people I hung around with, I wouldn't have looked at twice a few years before. My writing career that I had been so proud of, now consisted of quickie little sex books that paid just enough to get me through another month.

I'd always been a big drinker. But now I had to face the ugly fact: I was an alcoholic.

drunk in hollywood

In Hollywood, the players didn't want to die—they just wanted to get high. High enough to get through the day and ease the boredom of the evening ahead. The drudgery of work day life in Hollywood is boring, and it's intolerable to most artists after a while without some release from the tension. In the olden days, it used to be that many actors drank and often lurched through long shooting sessions, sometimes at the end of the day literally staggering from the effects of booze. The lucky ones became accustomed to working smashed (Holden, Bogart, Tracy, Clift) and it seldom showed on camera, but the lesser tipplers usually began to show the signs of the grog after just a few belts and very often had to be sent home early a great expense in shooting time.

The very first time I ever saw anyone drink alcohol before noon, I was a teenager and having breakfast with then-President Dwight D. Eisenhower. I was there on the arm of Henaghan, of course. It was barely seven o'clock in the morning and the Commander-in-Chief had a little bit of food with his vodka. I had been shocked then but as the years went by, I became quite accustomed to seeing my friends and lovers drink their breakfast. I never dreamed that the same fate awaited me as well.

The statistics are staggering on the number of alcoholics in the United States and they are not all drinking alone. They have a booze buddy stashed somewhere, an alcoholic just like them, who feels, somehow, that if they share their addiction with a loved one, then it's all right. I shared the addiction of alcohol and, in some cases, chemical dependency with a glittering array of world-famous celebrities. I was young, impressible, in awe of their fame and talent, trying to emulate them and be just like them.

When I was friends with Judy Garland and she used to lock herself in my guest room for days at a time, ringing for the maid only when she wanted another bottle of gin, I had thought it was hilarious. *What a whacky, fun-loving broad, that Judy,* I remember thinking. In those days, the late sixties, people were still not aware of the dangers of alcoholism.

During my affair with Paul Newman, he never once showed up at my house without at least a fifth of scotch and a twelve pack of beer. Most often, he had already mixed a drink so he could sip it while driving to my place.

One of my favorite drinking buddies was Errol Flynn. He drank hard and hearty and didn't apologize for it one whit. 'You know, little one,' he sighed. 'After thirty years of debauchery I've drank enough booze to destroy a dozen healthy livers, smoked enough nicotine and marijuana to pollute Des Moines and had enough sex to make the Marquis de Sade look like a virgin!'

Rod Taylor was a very heavy drinker, capable of putting away huge amounts of liquor almost nightly. Shecky Greene, Phil Foster, William Holden, Allan Sherman, Richard Burton, Laurence Harvey, Jack Carter, John Wayne, Jayne Mansfield, Marilyn Monroe, Janis Joplin and many, many more acquaintances of mine were all on intimate terms with the bottle and most of them died an alcohol-related death.

Booze seemed to enhance the brilliance of my writer pals, Jim Henaghan, Robert Ruark, Richard Condon, John Huston, Clair Huffaker, Hemingway, Saroyan and Fitzgerald—literary giants and legendary drunks.

In Rome, I sat with King Farouk on many different occasions and watched him polish off two full bottles of wine with his meal, then drink a fifth of cognac with his after-dinner expresso. Henaghan had arranged for us to have a private audience with the Pope and when we entered the Vatican, we walked right straight into a bar. At the end of the foyer was a small area where wine and drinks were being served, in case a visitor needed some liquid courage before facing His Holiness, one supposes.

Back home in the States in 1961 at the beginning of the Age of Aquarius, Camelot, the sexual revolution, ERA, draft dodgers and drug permissiveness, I was to witness firsthand the devastation of alcohol and drug addiction.

Many friends of mine did not make it to the seventies, dying in some drug or alcohol related death, their brilliant careers screeching to a sudden halt long before they should have.

When I was in the deepest depths of my despair, I knew that alcoholism was not new, but recognizing it as a serious disease rather than a minor character flaw, was relatively new. I feel that had the public known in the golden era of Hollywood what they know now about alcoholism, we would have had many of our brightest stars for much longer.

In the seventies, Alcoholics Anonymous had the highest success rate in treating the insidious disease, but they still could not cure everyone. AA teaches what they call Higher Power, i.e. God. If you turn your life over to Jesus Christ, they say, you will be saved from the demons and live happily ever after. AA tells an alcoholic to simply put their faith in God, give Him their burdens and they will forever be cured of this life-threatening disease.

If that was all there was to it, then why hadn't it worked for me? Why couldn't I have kicked my addiction alone, just me and God, on any one of those horrendous days or nights when I was literally on my knees, sick and puking, half dead, and begging God for help?

It couldn't work, of course, because alcoholism is a disease, not a religious or moral issue. How can an addict believe that God will help him if he doesn't believe in God? How can he have faith when all hope is gone? Perhaps he doesn't believe in Higher Power at all. Maybe he is an atheist or an agnostic. Does this mean, then, that if an alcoholic does not believe in God he will never be cured? What of the hundreds of clergymen who suffer with alcoholism? They would have a direct line to God, it would seem, and yet they cannot heal themselves of this fatal disease.

I swam through the seventies on a river of wine and vodka. By the eighties, I'd stopping drinking wine. Now, it was just vodka... and more of it.

snake pit

Jarring, unfamiliar sounds awakened me. I opened my eyes, confused by the activity in the large room, the strange odors and noises, the brightly-glaring overhead lights that made my pounding head ache even more.

I lay on a cot, one threadbare blanket thrown over me, a caseless pillow beneath my head. The bars on both sides of the cot were locked into place, giving me a convict's view of the room and the hallway outside an open door. Stringy-haired, dull-eyed patients shuffled past in paper slippers and tattered hospital robes with the word COUNTY stenciled across the back. Many had black eyes, swollen mouths, missing teeth, bandaged heads and broken arms or legs.

My gaze swept the interior of the room and I saw several other women in identical cots. Some were strapped down with wide leather bands that buckled around their wrists and ankles, holding them spread-eagled, the locked cuffs secured to either side of the cot. Others sat quietly, blank-faced, rocking gently back and forth or moaning softly.

It was eerie, chilling. I squeezed my eyes shut tight, hoping that when I opened them I would be home in my own bed with only the dull ache of a hangover that I had come to expect on each waking morning. This couldn't be real. It had to be some horrible nightmare.

Screaming, cursing and violent sobbing shattered any illusions about where I was. I watched four policemen and two doctors drag a woman into the room and dump her onto the cot next to mine. Deftly, they strapped her down, holding her writhing body as still as possible while a nurse injected her. Then they left her there, still screaming obscenities, her face contorted with madness, until the sedative took effect.

It was a horrifying scene but one that I was to witness many more times during my stay in the Los Angeles County Hospital where I was a patient in the drunk ward. The blazing overhead lights were never turned off and the door never closed. The nurses were all stone-faced, icy-eyed, showing no compassion for the tortured souls who were their charges. They had seen too much of that kind of misery and it no longer moved them.

I lay flat on my back in the narrow cot, my brain churning, afraid to ask what day it was. Afraid to admit where I was. What I was. But I knew: I was a drunk in a drunk tank.

Dear God, what had happened to me? I had had it all. Success, wealth, beauty, an abundance of love and a dazzling life style that had been the envy of all. I dined with royalty, made love to movie stars, hobnobbed with presidents and lived the good life for twenty-five years.

My daughter had been attended by a live-in nanny and my closets were filled to over-flowing with designer originals. I had so many diamonds and other precious gems that friends feared I would become a target of jewel thieves. My furs outnumbered the days in a week and I slumbered without a care upon a round king-size bed with custom satin sheets.

Then I went through six agonizing years of surgery. I couldn't work, couldn't cope.

Now I had nothing. I wanted to die: Just end it all. The pain, the horror of living life as an addict. If there had been a weapon available, and if I had had the strength, I would have killed myself at that moment. But I was too exhausted to move. My limbs seemed paralyzed and my brain was sluggish, my thoughts confused. I knew I didn't really want to die but I was scared to death of living.

I also knew if I continued to drink, I would have no choice. And I still wasn't sure I was ready to give up booze. I could not imagine a life without alcohol. Hell, I couldn't imagine a day, an hour, without alcohol. Face the real world without a buzz on? Unthinkable! Deal with the stress of everyday life without a buffer of booze to cushion the hard knocks? No way.

A piercing shriek caused me to jump a foot off the cot. I held my breath, trying not to look as another crazed addict was being strapped down across the room from me. The stench of urine, feces and vomit assaulted my nostrils and I shuddered, burrowing my face in the pillow. I gagged, wanting to throw up, but my stomach was empty, my mouth bone-dry, and I could only tremble in agony as hard, hurting cramps ripped through me. Where the hell was that buffer of booze now that I needed it? Jesus, I was dying for a drink!

I wasn't able to stand up until the next day, then I barely made it down the hallway to the pay telephone. I called Chris Casanova, my live-in lover (a boy, really, fifteen years my junior), even though I wasn't sure he'd be there. There were too many missing weeks in my fragmented mind.

Chris answered the phone, drunk as usual, and told me that I had been depressed for weeks, that I had drifted in and out of consciousness, going on crying jags that lasted for hours, calling all my friends (those who would still speak to me) and begging them to help me, to please take me to a detox center, a rehabilitation program, anything that might save me from my desperate addiction to alcohol.

The reason I was in the hospital, Chris explained, was because I had suffered a seizure. We were watching TV, drinking as usual, and the next second I was on the floor, jerking spasmodically, my eyes rolled back in my head with only the whites showing. My tongue lolled, spittle foamed at my mouth and Chris was certain I was in the throes of death.

He quickly called the paramedics who arrived in time to revive me—then Chris and I had calmly finished off a bottle of vodka. He said he couldn't remember when my friends took me to the hospital, but thought it must have been several days ago, maybe even a week.

As Chris told the story, I began to shake, trembling so badly that a nurse standing nearby quickly shoved a chair under me just as my knees buckled. I was put back to bed and sedated.

I awoke again at three in the morning with a blinding headache, my mouth as dry as sand. The lights blazed unrelentingly. The restless snores, grunts and groans of the other patients grated on my raw nerves like fingernails across a blackboard.

I wanted to go home and be with Chris, feel his arms around me and know that I was safe. And I never wanted to see another bottle of vodka again as long as I lived.

I checked myself out the next day and Chris picked me up. I smelled strong liquor on his breath when he kissed me and I tasted it and wanted more. But I was through with booze forever. I really meant it.

darkness

When we got home, I tried. I really did try so damned hard. But there was Chris, sipping a tall, cool one. And there was me, sick as hell, shaking apart, knowing that all I had to do to stop the pain was to walk into the kitchen and pour myself a drink. Chris, happily smashed by this time, delighted in having his drinking buddy home again. He was so loving, so solicitous as he held me close and sighed, 'God, honey, I can't stand to see you suffering like this. I love you too much. All you need is a couple of stiff drinks and you'll be just fine. Come on, baby, have one with me. I won't let you have anymore. I promise.'

I stared at the drink he held out, at the beads of moisture that sweated on the glass like teardrops, at the bright yellow lemon wedge that floated on top of the ice cubes. I reached for the glass, my hands shaking so badly I couldn't hold it. Chris took my hand in his, gently tipping the glass to my lips. I swallowed until it was empty.

The very next day I was back to a fifth and a half of vodka and two weeks later I suffered another seizure. Again, the Paramedics came. Again, I was hospitalized, this time at USC Medical Center in Torrance. It was a grim repeat of Los Angeles County Hospital. The same humiliation, self-disgust, guilt and the sheer mental and physical agony of withdrawal.

This time when I was released I didn't even try to pretend. I knew what I needed. When Chris picked me up we drove straight to the nearest liquor store and drank a pint of vodka between us, there in the parking lot, before starting the long drive back to our apartment in the San Fernando Valley.

Everyone knew we were alcoholics and we had each been fired from our jobs weeks ago, we lived on unemployment and money borrowed from his parents. We became reclusive, leaving our apartment only to walk my dog, Shaunti, and to drive to the liquor store. But it soon became a real bore walking the dog, waiting for her to sniff everything in sight before doing her business. It took too long. So we combined the two activities.

Shaunti was included when we went to the liquor store and I would walk her while Chris went inside for our daily purchase. The three of us became more neurotic as the weeks passed and even the dog began to pick up the bad vibes and unhealthy atmosphere. My fourteen-year-old cat, which I had raised from a kitten, sensed the decay and ran away. My best friend of seventeen years dropped me like nuclear waste, refusing even to answer the many letters I wrote her, begging for help. I was estranged from my daughter due to terrible things I said and did while drinking. It literally broke my heart, causing me to become even more isolated from the world.

No one wanted anything to do with Chris or me and we didn't give a good Goddamn. But me and Chris didn't need anybody. We just wanted to be alone with our old pal, Smirnoff.

A handful of friends stood by me in spite of it all. They tried so hard and I, God forgive me, lied to every one of them. I took advantage of their love, promising them that I was getting help, I was attending AA meetings. But that was my brain on booze and I couldn't stop.

The morning was still dark, cold and rainy as I grasped the edge of the kitchen sink and vomited into the garbage disposal, the sour bile from last night's vodka causing my body to shudder with convulsions. Blood from strained vessels in my throat, broken from the hard, dry heaves that racked me, speckled the sink. My forehead was clammy with icy sweat, my legs trembling so badly I could barely stand and more than once I sank to my knees, pressing my face against the cold porcelain of the sink. Fluid streamed from my eyes and nose and the steady pulsating in my temples matched the heavy, hurting pounding of my heart.

I raised my hands to wipe my face and saw large magenta bruises on my forearms, the result of alcohol poisoning running rampant in my system. My entire body was covered with bruises in every shade from the darkest purple to the palest yellow as they passed through the stages of healing.

I was never without at least a dozen or more bruises. Hardly a day went by when I did not trip over the furniture, bounce off the walls or doorways, or just simply fall down in a drunken heap sprawling over whatever object may have been on the floor. My equilibrium was shot, making it impossible for me to even walk around my apartment without holding onto something for support. I fell so often and suffered so many injuries and yet I never felt them. Nor could I remember later, seeing the cuts and scabs, how they had gotten there.

As I made my way into the bathroom I felt a pain in my inner thigh and looked down to see a large, nasty burn. I vaguely remembered it from a few nights previous. I had nodded off with a cigarette in my hand, burning a hole deep into my flesh before the intense pain finally jarred me out of my stupor. I had smeared butter on it and forgotten it. Now it was a flaming infection that oozed purulence and sent shooting pains through my groin and down my right leg. I stood naked in front of the full-length mirror on the bathroom door, staring at the pus-dripping sore, at my bloated, discolored body with the dehydrated skin stretched as taut as a drum.

I am five feet three inches tall and have always been rather vain about my perfect size six figure. I was dubbed 'The Face' by local photographers and voted 'The Girl I'd Like Most To Photograph' by the entire foreign press. I easily walked away with the crown at every beauty contest I entered.

Now I ballooned up to the size of a baby blimp, one-hundred-and-eighty-five pounds of ugly fat from a steady diet of vodka mixed with sugary soft drinks. Empty calories that settled on my small frame all but obscured me. My once-oval, fine-featured face was now the size of a basketball. My bright green eyes were dead-gray, opaque, hidden in folds of fat. The capillaries in my nose and cheeks were red and broken, and my hair was dry and brittle thin.

I was no longer Nancy Bacon, successful writer, former model, well-adjusted single parent, a woman content with her life and who had fulfilled all her dreams and fantasies. I was a caricature of the pathetic old lush, the skid row bag lady with milky eyes, a red nose and big, bloated belly. Quickly, I pulled a nightgown over my head, hiding the wretched reflection in the mirror.

It was four-thirty in the morning, Thanksgiving Day, 1986. I was cold sober for the first time in over a year. Sober, sick and scared to death. I had to have a drink or I knew I would die. Just shake and jerk apart in a million pieces and die. There was nothing alcoholic in the apartment. No perfume. No cough syrup. No shaving lotion. Chris and I had long since consumed those desperate antidotes. I began to panic. Our morning liquor store did not open for another hour and a half and my stomach knotted with cramps just knowing I'd have to wait.

I sat on the sofa, watching TV, but my full attention was on the clock above the TV. I swallowed three Valium, wanting so damn bad to believe that they would stop the shakes and unfrazzled my jumping nerves. I prayed aloud, with tears streaming down my face, beseeching God to please help me, please drive the demons from my brain, please, please not let me take that first drink of the day.

An hour later I popped my last Valium and still I shook so badly I had to wrap my arms around myself and hold on tight to stop the spasms. The Valium did not come through for me and neither did God.

At five-forty-five I stood in a line of winos and bums, waiting for the liquor store to open. The store was in a very rough, seedy neighborhood, a slum, where it was not uncommon to see gangs of Latino youths rolling the drunks for what little they could find.

I always took Shaunti with me on those early morning vodka runs and I covered myself completely in shapeless caftans, head scarves and big, dark glasses. In spite of my dreadful condition I was still embarrassed to shuffle along in a line of smelly drunks, shivering in the pre-dawn chill, dying a little inside with each step that took me closer to the door. I was often the object of curious stares, sly, knowing glances that filled me with apprehension. People always stared at me, but in the past, it had been with appreciation, approval and envy.

A rude, bony elbow in my back prompted me along and I stumbled inside the liquor store, tears stinging behind my dark glasses. Humiliation was a new emotion for me but one that I was to become all too familiar with.

Thanksgiving and Christmas decorations festooned the streets and store windows as I drove quickly back to my safe neighborhood. My hands shook so badly by this time that it took me a full ten minutes to get inside my apartment. Tears of frustration blurred my vision. Sweat poured off me even though it was cold and raining. My breath came in short, heavy gasps, a tight lump in my throat almost choking me and my heart began to palpitate wildly. Terror filled me. I saw myself dying right there on the front door step while I tried to make my useless muscles respond to one simple command: the lock.

Insert the key and turn.

I could not do it. I had to put down the bag of vodka and mix, my purse and Shaunti's leash, grasp my right hand in my left and try to hold it steady while I very carefully, very slowly stuck the key into the hole before my muscles spammed again. It took several tries before I managed it.

At this point in my addiction the electrolytes in my brain had begun to burn out, slowly and steadily leeched from my system, destroyed by booze. My central nervous system was shorting out, continuing to trigger itself without any outside stimulus. It was like stripping the insulation from an electrical cord.

I fell through the door and tore the cap off the vodka, taking a huge swallow straight from the bottle. Immediately, the burning lump in my throat disappeared and I was able to breathe normally. My heart still fluttered and beat erratically but I didn't care. I could swallow again. So, I made myself a tall one and settled back down in front of the TV to watch Macy's Christmas Parade. But I couldn't see the images at all because tears blinded me.

I took the bottle of vodka into the living room with me so I wouldn't have to get up and go into the kitchen when I needed a refill. The ordeal at the door with the key had exhausted me. I covered myself with a quilt and stared dully at TV, listening to Bob Eubanks and Stephanie Edwards describing the floats, their voices hearty and holiday bright. Methodically, I poured myself another drink. No mix this time. No ice. Just vodka.

Tears blinded me. I couldn't stop crying. My life was in shambles. My career as a writer gone, my health shot all to hell. I had no money, no job and a very serious addiction to alcohol that I knew was fatal.

dawn

My next clear memory is of a bright, sunny Saturday morning in early January, 1987. I was being driven to The Clare Foundation, a sober-living facility in Santa Monica with strong emphasis on personal counseling. Lon Viser, whom I'd known since he was photographer and I was a model, had literally scraped me off the floor and was taking over.

Although I downed a pint of vodka that morning just to get ready, I was still shaking so much I could barely speak. I couldn't even take one step without Lon holding me upright. He had to sign me in as well because I had lost my ability to write. I slumped in the corner of a sofa, half-dead, unable to return Lon's goodbye hug, unable to call him back when he turned to leave. I completely panicked. I wanted to scream his name, beg him not to leave me there in that frightening place, but I was mute with terror.

The first two or three days were a blur of pain as I alternated between freezing chills and hot flashes. Diarrhea cramps sliced through my stomach like a sickle, making me nauseous and filling my mouth with sour bile. I suffered insomnia and my brain became a jumble of dark, painful memories, of deep remorse and paralyzing guilt. It was physically impossible to eat. My throat was swollen almost shut and I could not raise a forkful of food to my mouth; everything shook off before it ever reached its goal. I felt like an infant. I couldn't do anything for myself. Not even go to the bathroom. Two male patients escorted me, one on either side, so I wouldn't topple off the toilet. I was too sick to be embarrassed.

When I was finally able to go to the TV room with the others, I had to be helped there. When I sat down, I couldn't get up without someone hauling me to my feet. I survived on orange juice, honey and hot water, a combination that nurses and patients swore by. It helped relieve the shakes by replacing the sugar in the system that had been deleted by alcohol. I was also prescribed a strong muscle relaxant for delirium tremens (DT's) which helped me regain my equilibrium.

Everyone at Clare's had chores to do. We woke at seven every morning and promptly began our assigned tasks, vacuuming, doing laundry, dusting, mopping, cooking breakfast. I was detailed to clean the women's toilet before breakfast. It was the only job I could manage without dropping and breaking something.

After breakfast, we had two hours of free time before being called together for the first therapy meeting of the day. I spent that time curled in the room, watching old movies. The first time I saw Paul Newman's image flash across the screen in living color, so handsome it hurt to look at him, I was stunned, shaken to my very soul. My life had been hedonistically full, a cornucopia over-flowing with abundance, sun-kissed and blessed.

What, then, was I doing in a shabby detox center in a seedy part of downtown Santa Monica, crushed like a broken doll in the corner of an old sofa that reeked of vomit and urine?

Because booze had kicked me square in the ass. I couldn't plead ignorance. I had been friends and lovers to some very famous alcoholics all my life and most of them had suffered alcohol related deaths. Yet I had continued to drink, confidant that I could handle it. And as I sat crumbled in the corner of that worn sofa, I still wasn't sure I could stay off the sauce. Or even wanted to. I still believed, somewhere in the back of my brain, that I wouldn't have to stop drinking. I would just get my coordination back, dry out, poisons from my system and then resume drinking completely.

I was at Clare for a week when a biker showed up, a big, burly dude adorned with tattoos and wearing a sleeveless Levi vest sans shirt. He watched me all day and I could tell by his eyes that he was high on something.

I didn't suspect liquor because all patients were thoroughly frisked before signing in. Our belongings were searched for contraband of an alcoholic nature—perfume, cough syrup, anything with booze in it. Late in the afternoon the biker joined me on the sofa, withdrew a pint of vodka from his vest and offered me a slug. The bottle was open, right under my nose, and the pungent aroma spun my head around like a dervish. Saliva filled my mouth and there was a sudden humming in my ears.

I almost took it. I wanted to. Just one drink. But I didn't. I got up and left, joining some other patients at the card table. The biker followed me. He had poured his vodka into a coffee cup and added some grape Kool Aid to disguise it. Everywhere I turned, he was there, offering me a drink, a sly, knowing grin on his lips.

When I tried to escape to my room, he followed me down the hall, grabbing my arm and twisting it viciously behind my back. 'You fucking bitch,' he snarled, shoving me against the wall. 'Too fucking good to have a drink with me, huh? I've been watching you. You act like some kind of high and mighty cunt, but I could have you just like that!' He snapped his fingers and took a pull from the coffee cup. 'I can rape you anytime I want to, bitch.' Now his voice was slurred, nasty, his eyes mean, shiny slits as he tightened his grip on my arm. 'I'll just take your ass into the laundry room and do it! Ain't nobody gonna hear anything with all them machines running.'

He started pulling me down the hallway and my throat was paralyzed. I couldn't scream and I wasn't strong enough to pull free. I lost my balance and fell. He was dragging me toward the laundry room. He just kept on pulling me, as we came abreast of the men's toilet, a patient asked me what was wrong.

The moment of distraction saved me. I scrambled to my feet. The biker quickly dropped my arm and I don't know how I got the strength or balance, but I was out of there, running straight to the administrator's office. To hell with being a squealer. I told him what had happened and within twenty minutes the biker was gone. The Clare Foundation did not waste their time on boozers who were just there for free food and shelter.

I was shocked to learn that all the patients there, some thirty-five or forty, were homeless street people. The main topic of discussion was where the best detox centers and free shelters were. Each had stories of the shelters they stayed in over the years and they exchanged addresses, information and phone numbers of future shelters that might take them in when they were released from Clare. Most state-run detoxification centers allowed patients to stay for two weeks only, then they were required to pay forty-five dollars per day for their room and meals.

My colleagues at Clare could not afford even forty-five cents a day, so as their time drew near, they scrambled like frenzied mice, looking for another hole to hide in. Most had spent the last several years moving from one shelter to another, drying out (sobriety is a requirement if staying free of charge) and then, once they hit the streets, they'd be back on the bottle. The women turned tricks and the men committed petty crimes or panhandled to get money for their habit. After a few weeks of staying mostly drunk, sleeping in parks or doorways, they stumbled to another free shelter and begged admission. Many of them died between moves.

At one sharing session, everyone was talking about where they would go next, after Clare released them. I mostly listened, as I had nothing to offer. This was my first and only experience with a detox center and I swore it would be my last. A man I had befriended turned to me and asked, 'Where are you going, Nancy, after you leave here?'

'Home,' I said, 'to my apartment in Northridge.'

In a hushed tone, he repeated, 'Home? You have a home?' A dozen pairs of eyes stared at me incredulously and the word *home* just sort of hung heavily in the room, sounding eerie and haunted.

I felt a chill close around my heart as my gaze traveled about the room, taking in the wasted, used up lumps of humanity. Home. Home was a bottle. Death was what I smelled in this shabby little room. It was then and there that I quit drinking, for once and for all.

The thing about being sober is that you remember everything you drank all those years to forget. I was never drunk enough to drive those memories back into the black hole of forgetfulness where they had lived these past years. The memories stayed, refusing to be banished. They danced and shimmered in vivid color just behind my closed eyelids. Beautiful, glorious, happy memories of a fantastic life that played out like a breathless, enchanted fairy tale. A life worth remembering.

That is what got me through. I had to live up to my own memories, my own life. When I got home, I changed everything. I left Chris. I apologized to everyone I'd hurt. Slowly, my friends and family returned. I moved far, far away from Hollywood, taking nothing but Shaunti and my typewriter with me. And, eventually, I got my writing career back.

The all-powerful, wisecracking, super-bitch who can handle it all by herself is gone—and I don't miss her a bit. God, when I think about it now, it must have put a lot of people off, but I guess they didn't want to shatter me by telling me what a fool I was making of myself. I love them for understanding. My daughter and I reconciled, and our bond is stronger than ever.

All in all, I've had a great life.

afterword

Much of this memoir was written in the mid-seventies, and was published under the title *Stars In My Eyes, Stars In My Bed.* (The publisher folded shortly after it was published, so the few surviving copies are very scarce.) In keeping with the jargon of the time, I've decided to leave in words like ball, grass, chick, and teenybopper in this version. The less star-studded, sensationalist parts of my story—how I got started as a bit-player, my mastectomy and alcoholism—are collected from previously unpublished manuscripts I wrote in the seventies and eighties.

I am seventy-seven years old at the time of this writing, living happily in the beautiful Pacific Northwest. I've never lost my passion for prose. I still ghostwrite and cowrite memoirs. My most recent book is a collaboration with Barbara Williamson, the pioneer sex goddess and cofounder of Sandstone Retreat. It's called *An Extraordinary Life: Love, Sex, and Commitment.* The next book I plan on writing is a deeply personal one… even more intimate than this one. I call it *The Wilder Years.* It's a (barely) fictionalized account of my life, exploring my abusive childhood and beyond.

I'm proud that my daughter Staci has followed in my keystrokes and become an accomplished writer in her own right. Look for an excerpt from her own memoir, *So L.A.*, at the end of this book.

acknowledgements

Thank you to my computer-savvy daughter for taking the reins on this project and shaping this book: from scanning and piecing together yellowing old pages and fading photos, streamlining, editing, minor rewrites, and designing the cover, to getting my whole story out, available, and directly to you.

Without Peter Viser, there would be no book—no *me*— had he not brought me back to health after I stopped drinking and left everything behind. I'm so grateful for his love.

I wish to thank some very special, dear women in my life. Beth Sinclair has not only been a lifelong friend, but she's gone above and beyond everything ever expected in helping me through very tough times. Gwen Michaels has been wonderfully thoughtful, kind and generous. Linda Rose has been a great help in reading this manuscript through to make sure all the t's are crossed, all the i's are dotted, and the p's and q's are minded. Carrie Lundgren physically scanned my entire paperback, and all of my unpublished manuscripts written by typewriter decades ago.

I must acknowledge my remaining sisters Wanda Harmon, and Barbara Wheatley. Through our ups and downs, they've always been there for me. The same is true of my ex-husband, Don Wilson; even though we were only married a few years, our daughter united us forever and fifty years (*fifty years?!*) after our divorce, he's still there for me when I need him.

Last but far from least, I gratefully thank my supporters Mark Wheaton, Craig Martinez, Jon Condit, Shirin Behnia, Stephanie Paris, Anne Retamal, Curt Lambert, Lisa Johnson Mandell, Renate Andrasevits-Reed, Shawn Adler, Joe Edmunds, Kaci Hansen, Rob Brantz, Ricardo H. Fujisawa, Traci York, Colleen Scott, and Tonjia Atomic.

So L.A. – A Hollywood Memoir
by Staci Layne Wilson (excerpt)

While my parents were feuding, I was riding. I'd disappear for hours on my new pony, Smokey. He was glossy black with one white "sugar foot," a wide diamond between his eyes, and a small one between his nostrils. Smokey's muzzle was soft like velvet, and smelled of warm clover. His eyes were deep chocolate brown.

Mom's friend Beth gave him to me because he was getting fat and lazy with nobody to ride him. Basically, he was the equine equivalent of Dom Deluise. That casual handoff would result in one of the most enduring and profound friendships of my life. Smokey was the best thing that ever could have happened to me at that time. He was kind, wise, patient and well-trained. He seemed to adjust himself to my riding ability, only going faster after my balance improved. I never fell off, and before long I was riding him bareback all over the neighborhood.

Poor Smokey had to bear the indignity of wearing cone-shaped birthday hats, groom's outfits (he got married more often than Mickey Rooney), silly ties of various style and fashion, and even goofy alien antenna affixed to the crown of his bridle. He accepted my "dress up" phase with his usual quiet dignity, and even gave the cats and my pet rats rides on his back at my behest (not at the same time… even the long-suffering Smokey would have drawn the line there, I think).

Tarzana was zoned for horses in some areas, but it was mainly a residential neighborhood. We had to ride across a lot of sidewalks to get to roads with dirt shoulders. And even further, to get to the golf course. My friend Laurie would borrow a horse named Punkin and we'd hit the green and try to get in a good gallop before the groundskeeper ran us off, yelling and shaking his fist in the air. We were the bane of the block.

One time, I rode Smokey across a neighbor's newly-paved driveway. I was hoping the old dude wouldn't figure out who did it, but there was only one newly-shod pony in the area. When the neighbor came knocking on our door, I'd just finished cleaning all the wet cement out of Smokey's hooves. My mom shrugged and invited the red-faced man to come out back and take a look. "It couldn't possibly have been our pony. See how spotless his hooves are?" Mom had my back.

My friend Laurie's mount Punkin was a Hollywood horse, of course. The palomino was already well into his teens when I came to know him, but he was still sound and going strong. Laurie wasn't lucky enough to have her own pony like I did so she made do by exercising some of the neighborhood horses for their owners. As soon as the man with three beautiful beasties moved into the corner house down the way, Laurie and I made our move and before long we were fast friends with Black Lightning, Fire Queen, and Punkin.

We were thrilled when we learned that Punkin had actually been a stand-in for our favorite TV star, Mister Ed! Punkin also starred in an episode of *Green Acres*, called *Horse? What Horse?*, which aired during the first season in 1966. Punkin's golden coat had faded to a pale yellow and his once muscular body had become flaccid with age, but to two little girls he was a dream come true. One of our favorite things about Punkin was how he would "talk" like mad whenever we pointed to his muzzle. We delighted in showing off this trick to all of our friends. Punkin loved Cheetos, and he always got that special treat after performing for us.

Smokey and I shared lots of adventures — I loved riding him to the window of the Pup 'n' Taco fast food drive-thru and seeing the smiles on the faces of the cashiers. (What health code violation?) At Halloween we'd go trick-or-treating. And we didn't even have to do it in a mall or a parking lot. This was old-school, door-to-door, baby. I could ride Smokey right up on the front porches. One neighbor looked at the pony and quipped, "That's one helluva costume, kid!" We even made the newspaper when we went out as a unicorn and princess in outfits my mom made by hand. My first boyfriend, Stan, was in a Prince Charming costume and he rode double on Smokey with me. Smokey loved Halloween because I always split my candy with him.

Our pets were like members of the family. My mom had this mink coat she wore a lot, and she would let my rat, Squeaky, ride in the pocket. I'm guessing the climate in The Valley must have been cooler in the 1970s because you'd have to pay me big bucks to wear so much as long sleeves these days! We also had a squirrel named Twinkles. I found him as a newborn, eyes still sealed shut, lying at the bottom of one of the tall palm trees in our yard. Mom showed me how to feed him with an eyedropper, and we kept him until he was old enough to fend for himself. Setting Twinkles free was hard on me, but occasionally he'd come back to visit and have a snack — all the squirrels loved our plum trees. We also had a vegetable garden that my mom tended. (Who better than the editor of *Confidential* magazine to dig in the dirt?)

Yes, our pets were spoiled but it's nothing like today. The dogs didn't get their bones in Bento boxes, and the cats didn't have their own Instagram accounts. They were lucky if they got flea collars. Spaying and neutering wasn't a thing yet, so we'd have assorted litters of kitties running around the house, climbing up the curtains, and swinging from the chandelier. When the kittens were old enough to be weaned, it was my job to round them up in a cardboard box, stand in front of the grocery store and yell, "Free kittens!" And you know what? It actually worked. Well, there was one time it didn't — so, I found a car that looked like it belonged to someone well-to-do and, grateful it was unlocked, I placed the leftover fuzzballs inside. (Don't fret, kitten-crusaders! The car was not hot inside.)

In spite of all the horseback riding I did, I was actually a very indoorsy kid. With my bright red hair and skin whiter than a fish belly in skim milk, I was a prime target for all that carcinogenic California sunshine. The smell of Solarcaine haunts me to this day, but back then all moms thought dousing their kids in that chemical haze was a healthy way to heal second-degree burns.

I loved to stay in and read. The librarians would see me coming and say, "There go all the books!" I couldn't get enough of *Nancy Drew*, or *The Black Stallion* series. When I was older, I'd read everything from Judy Blume to Jackie Collins. I read my mom's copy of Erica Jong's *Fear of Flying* when I was about 12. Probably should not have known about "the zipless fuck" at that age, but I was like a sponge for knowledge. I wanted to know everything.

Back in 1974, I was more into age-appropriate fare. I read *Mad* (I loved the new-movie satires, and I had all of Al Jafee's books), *Cracked*, *Bananas*, and *Dynamite*. *Dynamite* was like a cross between *People* and *Highlights*. Hawkeye and Radar from *M*A*S*H* appeared on the cover of the first issue — in the 70s, kids looked up to older stars. Even our "teen heartthrobs" like Greg Evigan and Andy Gibb were in their 20s. We also thought mimes were cool (Shields and Yarnell, anyone?). And magicians who wore tie-dyed leotards ala Doug Henning were off the chain. *Dynamite* had a special "The Bee Gees vs. The Beatles" issue, kicking off the "battle of the bands" craze.

I was lucky, later on in life, to get to interview some TV icons of the 70s — Sid and Marty Krofft, who are the masterminds behind so many kids' shows, invited me to their office and showed me all kinds of treasures from the old days. This was when they were promoting the first-ever big screen adaptation of *Land of the Lost*.

I read a lot during the day, since we, like most 1970s folks, watched television only at night. We'd start with the evening news. If Richard Nixon came on, I'd be called into swift action to change the channel for my mom. We didn't have a remote control; they didn't come standard with sets until the 1980s. Imagine getting up from the couch and hiking over to the television every single time you wanted to change the channel. Yes kids, the channels were actually located on a dial on the set. There were 13 of them, but only three or four had anything worth watching. Also, if you went past the channel you wanted, you couldn't go backwards and you'd have to turn to the right all over again. It was brutal.

Mom was lax on rules and bedtimes, so I was allowed to stay up late to watch *Star Trek* reruns and *The Tonight Show* with Johnny Carson. Carson made the move from New York to Los Angeles — or, more accurately, "Beautiful downtown Burbank" — in 1972. We loved all his jokes about the Santa Ana winds (sorry if you didn't get it, Middle America).

I was absolutely allowed to watch horror movies. I loved them so much! In the days of yore, their scary titles acted as warnings: *Don't Look in the Basement, Don't Answer the Phone, Don't Look Now, Don't Go in the Woods, Don't Go Near the Park, Don't Go to Sleep, Don't Open the Door,* and *Don't Be Afraid of the Dark.*

Before cable, before home video, and before streaming — also known as The Dark Ages — young movie geeks were forced to rely on late shows and weekend afternoon creature features to get their fright fix. We couldn't get enough of *Killdozer, The Night Stalker, Trilogy of Terror, The Norliss Tapes, Satan's School for Girls, Bad Ronald,* and *Salem's Lot* — every few weeks there was a new one to look forward to.

Don't Be Afraid of the Dark was the most traumatizing of the lot. Kim Darby and Jim Hutton star as newlyweds who inherit a crumbling mansion. Despite dire warnings from the obligatory superstitious handyman, the wife unlocks a mysterious room and opens the bricked-up fireplace. Not a good idea. She unwittingly unleashes a horde of hideous, whispering, murderous mini-demons that only she can see and hear. Or maybe not *only* her: I saw and heard them in my nightmares for weeks!

The first horror movie I distinctly remember is *The Pit and the Pendulum* starring Vincent Price. I watched it with my dad at his house. Years later, when I got into the profession of covering and reviewing horror movies, I became a bona fide Roger Corman fan — he directed not only *The Pit and the Pendulum,* but one of my all-time favorites, *Edgar Allan Poe's The Masque of the Red Death* — and I got to interview him a number of times. One of the highlights of my professional life was when I showed Roger my first short film, which was based on the poem

Annabel Lee, and he said I really "captured the spirit of Poe."

I watched all kinds of movies — I loved *The Thin Man* series, and Bob Hope and Bing Crosby's *Road* pictures. I never thought of movies as being too old, or substandard if they were in black and white. Movies were either good or bad. I learned to enjoy sweeping epics like *Gone with the Wind*, *Giant*, and *The Godfather* by watching them with my mom.

Some of my favorite childhood movie memories are parked at the drive-in. Mom took me to see *The Exorcist*, which scared the bejesus out of me. For days after, she teased me by imitating the devil's voice before I went to sleep. Come to think of it, no wonder I never wanted to go to bed.

I was at the premiere of *Blazing Saddles* at The Pickwick in Burbank. That was a huge deal for me, because I loved horses and *horses were there!* The palomino pictured on the poster was the main attraction, and later in life, I would get to know him as a rescue case (yes, even equine stars hit the skids sometimes).

At the zenith of their popularity, eight drive-in movie theaters operated in the Valley. Screenings began at dusk at the Pickwick, the Victory, the San Val and the Laurel in the east Valley, and the Reseda and the Canoga in the west. Not a single drive-in screen survived the video craze, but the Pickwick lives on as the backdrop in movies like *Grease* — in fact, young me swung on the very same swings as John Travolta.

Records made even more money than movies, and comedy albums were extremely popular. I loved listening to my dad's copy of *The Button-Down Mind of Bob Newhart*, but I also got into broader comedy when I went next door to the Florence residence and listened to Richard

Pryor and Cheech and Chong records with their sons. I was too young to be smoking pot then, but I knew all about it — and I probably still have a contact high from my mom's parties. (Funny aside: when Mom was in her 70s, she got a medical marijuana prescription. She said, "I'm about 40 years ahead of you, Doc!")

Gayle and Mal Florence's sons Jon and Matt were teenagers, and they hung out with my mom a lot. Maybe a little too much... well, I'm sure the statute of limitations for corrupting minors has run out by now. As I've said, my mom was irresistible — the Fountains of Wayne guys even wrote a hit song about it decades later, called *Stacy's Mom*. They spelled my name wrong though. (Yes, I'm kidding about the song's inspiration — but in an alternate dimension, it's totally true.)

Mom — a montage of Joy perfume, Virginia Slims, black coffee, caftans, cats, hot rollers, Aqua Net — was a magnet for male admirers from eight to 80. One evening when she was over at Gayle and Mal's place for a small BBQ party by the pool, she was holding court with her groovy stories and flirting with everyone. Mom was quite the flirt. Men, boys, women, girls, gays — no one was exempt. It was all in fun, and half the time she didn't even realize she was doing it. It was second nature. Along with our hosts, one of Mal's fellow L.A. Times sport writers, Harley "Ace" Tinkham, and his wife Ena were there. Everyone was sitting at the patio table, having Sanka and dessert. Ace and Ena were sloshed from imbibing earlier. Ace passed out, forehead-first in cake and whipped cream. Suddenly, Ena accused Mom of making a play for her husband.

Mom just laughed it off and said, "I don't need your stupid, fuddy-duddy drunk old man — are you kidding me?" Ena's response was a coffee mug full force to my mom's jaw. Next thing we knew, there were shards of teeth on the table and blood was gushing everywhere. The ambulance came, and so did the cops. I believe Ena got a free set of bracelets and an all-expense paid stay at a minimalist-inspired pad with 24/7 security. But it wasn't much justice for my mom. She went through lots of oral surgeries, on top of her cancer surgeries.

It was a painful year for me, too. I broke my right leg in three places when I foolishly forced Smokey jump over a hedge that was too high for him. He slipped upon landing and wasn't hurt, but he fell squarely on me. Pony payback! I was becoming quite the daredevil and would often come home with bumps, scrapes, cuts and bruises. I simply got back on and rode him home, but my leg really hurt. I told my mom and she said it was probably just sprained and told me to stop whining. It swelled up, and I started limping around like Shakespeare's Richard III. My mom thought I was trying to get out of doing my chores. (That wouldn't have been an unfair assessment.) Almost a week later, she took me to the doctor. My broken leg was in a cast for three months.

The cast was cool. But in those days, wearing any kind of protective gear was not. Whether you were riding a bike, roller skating, or on horseback, one thing was for certain: you were not wearing shin guards or elbow pads. Nerd alert! And helmets? Those were for Poindexters or retards who rode the short bus. (Sad but true: politically incorrect words like retard, spaz, and moron flowed from our tongues as easily as groovy, dig, and funky.)

If someone asked you to close your eyes and picture the landscape in Hollywood, you'd probably see palm trees. But in spite of their proliferation, most of the shady sentinels are not native to Southern California. The tall, skinny Mexican fan palms and the feather-topped Canary Island date palms that line so many of our boulevards were imported to beautify the place in prep for the 1932 Olympic Games. The city put 400 unemployed men to work planting trees alongside 150 miles of city boulevards. Los Angeles' forestry division planted more than 25,000 palm trees, and they still sway above the city's boulevards to this day. When they were newly installed, *The Los Angeles Times* printed puff pieces, praising the palms as "plumed knights" with "magical" restorative powers.

But not everyone loves the L.A. palms. In the mid-70s, there was a serial arsonist going around lighting them on fire. I remember one night while I was sleeping, it suddenly got really light in my bedroom. I could see the cracking bonfire outside, so I woke my mom up. (I guess Daisy the smoke-sensing feline was off-duty that night.) She hadn't noticed the brightness because her bedroom windows were covered with tinfoil (the poor-stoner's equivalent to black-out curtains).

We called the Fire Department, and crisis was quickly averted.

Shortly after that, we moved. Whether it was to stay ahead of kited checks and angry landlords, jealous wives or palm tree arsonists, it doesn't matter. It was time to go. Not onward and upward to Beverly Hills, or even Hollywood, but to another humble abode in the San Fernando Valley.

So L.A. is available in paperback and electronic versions

CPSIA information can be obtained
at www.ICGtesting.com
Printed in the USA
LVOW11s1836130817

544854LV00004B/367/P